MAKING SENSE
OF OUR
NON-LINEAR WORLD

STRAIGHT LINES:

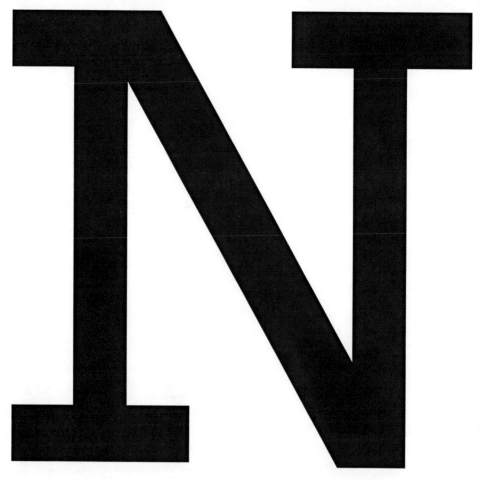

'Economic transactions and markets have warped perceptions
to such a degree that most people fail to see what is important
in life, even when it's right in front of them. Alan Moore's
No Straight Lines offers a vision that is at once more humane,
more forward-thinking, and more realistic.'

HOWARD RHEINGOLD

BY
ALAN MOORE

First published 2011
by Bloodstone Books, Cambridge, England
www.BloodstoneBooks.com

1 3 5 7 9 8 6 4 2

Text © 2011 Alan Moore
Cover design: Alan Moore

This book has been typeset in FFQuadraat.

Printed and bound in Great Britain by Lightning Source UK Ltd.

British Library Cataloguing in Publication Data:
a catalogue record for this book is available from the British Library.

ISBN: 978-0-9567662-4-3

Contents

Acknowledgements

This project could not have been made without the wisdom, guidance and enthusiasm of many people. But my most special thanks must go to Henry Jenkins, Provost Professor of Communication, Journalism, and Cinematic Arts, USC Annenberg School for Communication, who, outside of his immense knowledge on participatory cultures, media and education, has encouraged and guided me from the get-go. Special thanks must also be extended to Arjan Postma and Jorgen van der Sloot and their team at the FreedomLab Thinktank in Amsterdam, who have helped enormously in the shaping of the work. I would also like to offer a special thank you to Howard Rheingold for endorsing my project. Thanks to all of you who at various stages and in those dark moments gave me the sense that this journey was worth the effort. In particular eternal thanks to Dave and Claire Hieatt, founders of the Do Lectures, for lending me their house in Wales where I could write undistracted, and for also being a constant source of encouragement in pirate endeavour. I am most deeply grateful to Jane Young (resonanceblog.com) who unselfishly has given her time and knowledge.

I would also like to thank John 'Jay' Burton Rogers of Local Motors, who has happily engaged in conversations about Local Motors, sharing his time in a very demanding schedule, and Ariel Ferreria, Community Manager at Local Motors. Gerd Leonhard has been a great sparring partner. Tomi Ahonen, Philip Sugai, Marco Koeder, Ludovico Ciferri, Kazi Islam, then CEO of Grameenphone, Lars Cosh-Ishii of WirelessWatch Japan and Nathan Eagle have been invaluable in helping with the mobile part of the project, with Robert Rice providing wisdom on augmented reality. David Doherty and Dr Mohammad Al-Ubaydli have both been prepared to share and discuss the politics and the business of healthcare both in the UK and the US, and have shown me how doing things better does not need to cost the earth. Thanks to Tim Mead, MD and owner of Yeo Valley farm, for sharing his time and views on how systems thinking in organic farming has wider implications for us all.

Thanks must also go to Nicco Mele of the Harvard Kennedy School of Political Science for sharing his knowledge and views on the challenges of running big government, and how it could be done better, and to Dominic Campbell of FutureGov, who has shared his knowledge. I would like to acknowledge Lee Bryant of Headshift as someone whose views have deeply resonated with me on how and why the socialness of the world is key to our future. Thanks also to Sandra Harrild, clinical psychologist at Addenbrooke's in

Cambridge, who has shared her professional experience of how identity construction built out of personal and collective narrative is such a challenge in a fast moving world, with its subsequent worrisome implications. Tim Merry from the Art of Hosting taught me about participatory leadership, and Jon Bradford of Springboard invited me to participate in his programme of peer-to-peer entrepreneurial learning, which enabled me to gain insight into how one unleashes intellectual capital for entrepreneurs and accelerates innovation.

Thank you to everyone at Hyper Island, for inviting me to share my knowledge and views with their students, and other organisations, and for giving me the space to explore my work with a wider international group of people. Special mentions to Alex Bedoya, for first inviting me; Åsa Siverberg and Christina Andersson for being my champions. And thanks to Lauren Puglia, Thomas Reibke, Jakob Widerberg, Jonathan Briggs, Micke Ahlstrom – it would not have been the same without you.

I would like to thank Susan and Tim Bratton for their generosity and kindness, and Susan for her doses of pragmatic advice.

Thanks also to Ruth Reed, President of the Royal Institute of British Architects, for helping me understand how good design in our built environment can be a true civilising force, helping shape our societies for the better; to Gabriel Branby of Gränsfors Bruks for teaching me about whole systems design and the axeness of an axe; and to Gregor MacLennon of Amazon Watch for teaching me about the Achuar tribe living in the Amazon rainforest and how participatory culture, networked mobile-web communications technology combined with some pens and paper really can be used as a political tool, so that the powerful can truly feel the pinch of the powerless.

To Laura Maliszewski, Ph.D., Senior Officer for Science and Innovation, and Chris Ilsley, Head of Science and Innovation of the British Consul in Boston – my sincere thanks for connecting me with so many wonderful people in Boston who helped me on my learning journey in understanding how ecosystems connecting academia to the commercial world enable innovation to thrive. Thank you to Jaideep Prabhu for showing me some of the wonderful innovation that is going on in India, and also to Joerg Geier for pointing me to the work of people and organisations that subsequently became a part of this project – both from the University of Cambridge, Judge Business School.

I would like to thank Per Håkansson for all his help, connecting me and the NSL project to some truly great people.

Richard and Cissy Ross always travel in my heart, and I thank them for their ever-constant warm-hearted generosity – Santa Barbara is warm because they live there.

Jouko Ahvenainen, Valto Loikkanen and Markus Lampinen enable me to practise what I preach, and that same acknowledgement must also go to John Roberts, Agustin Calvo, Fernando Sánchez-Teran and Marco for allowing me to influence the ground truth of innovation in mobile communications – fortune favours the brave and the visionary.

Susie Hinchliffe of Little Nomad for web design wonderfulness, Dale Tomlinson for great book design and production, Linda Randall for eagle eyed copyediting, Matt Hilbert of Bloodstone Books for networked publishing brilliance, and Janek Priiman, Rait Ojasaar and Marius Arras of Publification for e-publishing genius – I thank you all.

And finally to Tricia my partner of 20+ years, thank you for your trust, and your enduring love.

The challenge: be realistic, imagine the impossible

WHAT DO THESE HAVE IN COMMON? A car company built around a global community as an organisation, enabled by combining flex manufacturing techniques, open source platforms, open legal frameworks and social communication technologies premised upon cooperation, fuelled by the desire to be a great company and green; that can build cars 5 times faster at 100 times less the capital costs. A crisis management platform and organisation born out of the Kenyan post-election crisis of 2008 that can record critical information of events unfolding on the ground via a blend of location-based data, eyewitness accounts and mobile telephony, from often hard to reach places which visualises those unfolding events so that others can act and direct action at internet speeds. And now utilised for free in many parts of the world. Or, the largest organic diary farm in Britain, that has evolved a methodology that allows it to remain autonomous, profitable and sustainable in a market that is acutely volatile, because large-scale agricultural farming is mostly run on an oil-based economy, plus diary farmers are at the calculating mercy of the marketing needs and whimsies of large chain supermarkets.

They are collectively representative of a new reality of living, working and organising. These organisations or companies have quested to find a means to serve humanity better, to search for meaning in the work that they and others do, and offer up new viable alternatives for the ways that, in the past, these things were done. They seek an outcome that is more distributive of wealth, ideas and resources. In fact, one might argue an outcome that is more humane and community centric. Rather than premised upon the extraction of wealth, and resources, whether they be physical, mineral or otherwise, these very different initiatives represent both moral courage and a collective purpose, if you will. And why is that important? Because it does not matter if you are an employer, a worker, VC fund, an NGO, an organisation, a local council or a government, you will miss out on the energies and capabilities of your people who will increasingly seek those new realities to discover a better way of living, working and being, when better and viable alternatives are on offer. And the fact is we now have the possibility to truly transform our world, to be more lightweight, sustainable and humane, through the tools, capabilities, language and processes at our fingertips. As Tony Judt argued: 'Why do we experience such difficulty even imaging a different sort of society? Why is it beyond us to conceive a different set of arrangements to our common advantage?' [1]

Which brings me on to the title and the challenge of this project. Be realistic, imagine the impossible is taken from a poster from the 1968 Paris riots. In making sense of its meaning for our time, I would argue that what we face at the tail end of our industrial society is a design problem. The reason is that we are witness to a systemic failure of many of the institutions that have brought us so much prosperity and it is this convergence of failures that requires us to understand the challenge from a whole systems approach.

Many of the institutions, organisations and systems that we still use were designed and built for a less complex world, the increase in the complexity of our world is placing an unsustainable load upon those institutions, organisations and systems. One could argue the our industrial world has reached the nadir of its adaptive range. Consequently, fault lines are running through our society which present a trilemma based around interlocking social, economic and organisational

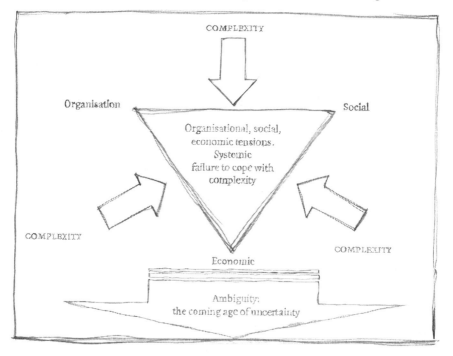

---

1. Tony Judt, *Ill Fares the Land*, Allen Lane, 2010.

tensions and questions. The design challenge involved in resolving these questions comes because the non-linearity is causing a comprehensive restructuring of society at large, breaking old models of organisation, and the trilemma heralds the coming of the age of uncertainty. All three tensions are in flux, and cannot be addressed without considering the other two. So each and every part of this story reflects upon and relates to this trilemma: the relationship of the individual to companies and other organisations and forms of power, economically, socially, politically.

Now is the time when we need a way of evaluating of what comes next, when we face a world that has gone in a very short period of time from seemingly linear (simple) to complex and non-linear (chaotic). When we move into a world that is inherently more complex, the result is concussive, its disorientating effects surround us, and our responses either individually or at an organisational level result in reflexes and perspectives that can be dangerously corrosive or inappropriate. And yet, this chaos seems to be, if anything, accelerating. At this very moment, great debates are raging. The spanners are in the works, defined by 9/11 (we now talk about asymmetrical warfare) and the near collapse of the world banking system (and its asymmetrical impact on every single one of us). And, as the global centre of economic gravity moves east, this has set off a series of events that are having significant asymmetric economic effects on societies around the world. These are but three examples of fault lines creating battles, ideological or otherwise, that are exploding and imploding at the same time. They all surfaced in a single decade. Though it is important to add that their gestation period has been much longer and is indeed multidimensional. These challenges are highly interlinked and interdependent, so a one-size-fits-all response just won't do. There are no longer simple problems; what we face is the trilemma of a complex world. This book does its best to face them, because we are in more than just an economic crisis; it is equally political, educational, spiritual and moral.

The biggest challenge we face is cultural. How we contextualise (make sense of) the world around us determines how we engage and what action we take. Those actions then determine the outcomes we must live with and this requires a change from our industrial mindset and behaviour to one that is more cognisant of what is now seen as a non-linear world. This is where I want to return to the idea that what we face is a design problem, where answers exist not at an unattainable theoretical level but on the floors of our factories, in the streets of our towns and cities, the classes of our schools, the waiting rooms of our hospitals. These answers will manifest themselves as true acts of creation, originating new ways of getting stuff done, informed by the decisions we collectively take. So in re-designing the world, we need human creativity in the sense of the capacity to 'make', we need visionary leadership in the sense of making a difference. And we seek the craftsman's critical eye, steady hand and creative mind. It is this process of seeing – realising new pathways to success, by bringing two 'unlikes' (new information, tools, processes etc.) together in close adjacency – that we create, and make new things. Then we can meaningfully apply that capability.

Why is the idea of craftsmanship significant at this epochal moment in time? Because it is about shaping our future and the 'engaged' craftsman brings the full power of humanity to bear upon his work. His hand is guided by his eye, informed by his creative mind; his productivity the act of unique creation. Indeed, the master craftsman is adept in using a philosophical framework, as well as tools and materials, to deliver useful things to the world. But more than that, the craftsman must be open constantly to new ideas; he is essentially always in beta. Therefore, we cannot engage with our uncertain non-linear world with the linear and inflexible orthodoxy of logic alone. The craftsman's critical eye and creative mind is vital to evaluating new possibilities; he must be open to new ideas, information, tools and materials to make things that enable humanity to flourish. This approach is inherently more creative in that it synthesises all aspects of what make us truly human. But the 21st century craftsman does not only exist in the dusty workshop of a forgotten age; a games designer is a craftsman, a Linux programmer is a craftsman, innovative organisations like Local Motors and Ushahidi, which are discussed in more detail in Chapters 3 and 8, embed craftsmanship into everything they do. These are well designed responses to what real life previously perceived as intractable as the plot line in *Catch-22*.

And so I come to this project with a strongly held belief, that there is an opportunity to bring a way of thinking to many of the seemingly intractable problems that confront us today. But this requires us to think and act as craftsmen and women and apply our critical thinking to understanding our non-linear world, which is in part shaped by participatory cultures, open, complex and seemingly ambiguous systems that are highly interdependent of each other. We need to be inspired to be epic, to seek epic wins, to make informed choices and co-author innovative new possibilities that can enable humanity to lead a life not constrained by the crushing reality of industrial-age thinking but one designed around the primary needs of humanity. We need to explore our non-linear world, not exploit it.

I believe there is much evidence demonstrating the possibility of this society. It exists in philosophical frameworks, language and literacy, legal frameworks, tools and technologies, and real stories of how others have been motivated by a real desire to create new and better answers to what others would call unsolvable, wicked problems. And it has been my mission to bring together these separate component parts to offer to you a vision of the world which is both realistic and eminently possible. But to create this regenerative society requires us to take a voyage of discovery and to look upon the world as Proust would say with fresh eyes. This is the world of no straight lines and this project is how we make sense of this non-linear world, and then act in it.

ALAN MOORE, *Cambridge* 2011

travels in
Darwin's topbox:
my story,
my narrative,
my song-cycle,
my fable,
my folk culture,
my truth

THIS PROJECT WAS GOING TO BE CALLED 'Travels in Darwin's topbox' because I have been on an incredible journey, and it was Darwin who said that it's not the strongest or most intelligent that survive but the most adaptive to change. A topbox is a little storage that sits on the back of a motorcycle, and my preferred mode of transport is a large sportsbike that has taken me many hundreds of thousands of miles. My journey has not only been 'an intellectual journey', it has been a real journey, a visceral journey that has shaped and defined me.

As a young man I was trained as a typographer by Derek Birdsall. Mastering my craft under the tutelage of a formidable teacher, I desperately wanted to be the best typographer I could be, so a belief in craftsmanship and design as a larger idea was something I was weaned on. But I came to realise that there was much more to this desire. My fierce motivation was fuelled over many years by my search for a coherent identity. Having had a sporting career cut short by injury, and then seen my ambition to study music unfulfilled, I was unmoored in a modern world, often feeling anxious and somewhat fearful.

Amidst this sense of dislocation was also the 'gift' of dyslexia or dyscalculia or probably both. Simply put, I engaged in and interpreted the world in my own particular way. I can't count, I struggle with linear verbal instructions (thank God for Google maps) and I am unable to read instruction manuals. My grammar is non-existent, and I was told in a school report just before my 'O' level exams that I wrote in 'convoluted prose' – I had to ask what that meant. Not the most encouraging news for a 16-year-old majoring in English, English Literature and History.

At 21, I met my partner Tricia and her young son Richard, who was also dyslexic, though we didn't know that at the time. His primary school teachers kept complaining that he craved too much attention in the class, and struggled to sit still. This was because he wanted more help to understand, and his restlessness was borne out of frustration. Richard struggled to keep up, and then gave up. In his view, reinforced by the teaching system – he was simply stupid. By the time he went to up to senior school his motto was: 'If you don't try, you can't fail.' What a life sentence at 12.

After that, my daughter Emma was never going into the state system but she had to board away from home. Not one fee-paying school in Cambridge would take her, as her admission of dyslexia made her an undesirable pariah in the world of school league tables. My son Josef has had exactly the same experience.

What to make of all this – were I and my children the problem? Increasingly, I realised that the answer was no. It is the system; a linear, inflexible matrix that schools us in a very unique way. And it doesn't stop there, for education is a window into and onto an entire framework of society, business and politics; all of which appeared to me to be out of date and redundant.

I graduated from book design and graphics to advertising, working in the UK, Austria, Finland and Sweden and travelling the world. I never thought I would be doing a photo shoot in Red Square at 5am, filming at the Bauhaus at night or directing a film in the mountains in Spain and this journey profoundly changed me. But as I embarked on it, a small revolution happened. I had been trained to code manuscripts, marking them up so that a trained typesetter could turn my code into the raw material for book production. In 1988 I sat down to my first Apple Macintosh and experienced the epiphany that, unless I embraced a journey of lifelong learning, I could find myself without the necessary skills to survive.

With this realisation, I constantly strived to be the best I could be and to learn. A decade later, I was creative director of an advertising agency, working on global business and getting on and off aeroplanes 150 days a year and was asking myself what the communication company of the 21st century should look like. Having evolved into a creative director with no formal training and enabled by my dyslexia, I approached solving communication problems holistically, being comfortable with the creative skills I had developed in typography, design, photography and film directing.

However, I could also see that few clients were able to buy integrated communications and that big ideas had to be expressed in a singular format: the big one being the 60-second TV spot, which to my mind was extremely linear. I asked whether traditional advertising and marketing would remain as effective and efficient as it once was and the answer, after some research and reflection, was a firm 'no'. So what was the answer? If the 20th century was about interruptive mass media communications, I mused, then the 21st century has to be about engagement. Then I had to define what engagement was.

In 2002 I was exploring that concept in depth, looking at architecture, mobile communications, digital online services, TV formats and the physical world. Engagement was about the principle of inviting in a participatory audience, it was about creating memorable experiences and enabling brands and people to better engage with each other – the benefit being that companies were more sustainable and more profitable. This resulted in the publication of *Communities Dominate Brands: Business and Marketing Challenges for the 21st Century*.

My questioning and conclusions continued to develop, and in 2006 I made a presentation to a chief executive of the Johnston Press, Britain's largest regional news group. Since the business model of display advertising was all but dead, I argued, his company had to work out how it could attract and engage readers and create more value for its advertisers via a service-based model that was all about commercial information being offered in a timely, relevant and contextual manner. We had a chat, Tim shook my hand, thanked me for coming and we never spoke again. Subsequently, Johnston Press sold its controlling stake in the business to a Malaysian businessman and continued to struggle. And the tragedy was not that I did not get the business but the human cost of lost jobs, and livelihoods. That filled me with anger and frustration. Why could I not help these people see what was coming down the road towards them like a freight train?

I could tell this story again and again with different company names but, as a friend once told me, sometimes being right is not necessarily the right thing to be. My company SMLXL won some clients, and I was evangelical about the promise of engagement marketing. SMLXL created FantaLife, an advanced living course for young people to get more out of life, for Coca-Cola; 'This is Modern Britain', a project designed to get the UK talking about what it means to be British, for Vodafone; and the Quentin Tarantino Film School for Nokia to launch the N-Series phones. But all these projects faltered as I was unable to help these companies see the true and enduring commercial benefit of engagement.

SMLXL also created a drink for Coca-Cola called Ipsei. With Ed Barber of Barber Osgerby, we designed and produced the first asymmetric bottle in the Coca-Cola system. When you think about how many bottles Coca-Cola produces daily, that's quite a big deal but again Coke's research and development people said it could not be done. Our thinking challenged the straight lines approach to innovation. We persevered but it was an interesting lesson in innovation inside closed systems – fear of risk, perceived risk and risk of failure.

As I continued to research the evolution of the media and the commercial communication environment, I had a dawning realisation that what I was witnessing was something deeper, more profound and epochal. It was in fact a communications revolution with deep social undercurrents that are having and will have a profound effect on every touch point of our society and our daily lives. And there is no doubt that technology, particularly communications technology, can be wielded as a powerful agent of social and political change. But we seem to have arrived at a crossroads, and this makes me fearful that too few commentators truly understand the underlying reasons for what's happening now or the implications of what happens next. Too many companies are locked into a linear system, a framework and model that only allows them to look at and engage with the world in a particular fashion. And this communications revolution is not about just companies and organisations; it is about us – you, I and society per se.

My journey has led me into the worlds of media, communications theory, communication technologies, technology, manufacturing, data, the law, psychology, anthropology, theology, philosophy, education, science, business, politics and history. I have studied all these phenomena and reflected on the deeper causes of what's currently under way. This project has been created to help and inspire you and those around you to become better stewards and guardians of your own futures. I hope you feel it to be a comprehensive framework that makes sense and provides you with the necessary insight to possess the clarity of thought and deed to remake this world afresh, with new hope and vigour. We must become the change we want to see in the world, and as Howard Rheingold wrote – 'What we make is up to us'. This is my story, my narrative, my song-cycle, my fable, my folk culture and my truth. Because without it, I don't exist.

I dedicate this book and project to
my mother and father,
KATHLEEN and PETER MOORE,
as it was their own natural sense
of humanity and dignity
that has ultimately had a direct
impact on this project.

No Straight Lines:
a navigational guide

THE PURPOSE OF THIS BOOK IS to highlight the corrosive effect that an industrial mindset and free market economy has ultimately inflicted upon humanity. My hypothesis is that we have got to the point where our industrial economy, projected onto society, can no longer support humanity. As a consequence, we need to explore what makes us human and to give this insight context by examining new ways of recreating our world.

The title encompasses my central argument. The industrial society was the endgame in reconstructing humanity in a linear fashion devoid of sense, emotion and spirituality and structured instead to be highly efficient and productive, like a machine. As post-industrial society in Britain, and, indeed, throughout the developed western world, has arguably increasingly become neither, we need to examine what we are left with and whether there is a better way. I believe that better way has been revealing itself with, for example, the evolution of digital communication tools, organisational capabilities, legal frameworks and flex manufacturing techniques over the past ten years. But utilising them will require us to interpret humanity and society in different ways. A clue is found in nature, where straight lines are very rarely found. So what would a no straight lines society and economy look like, what are the constituent parts and how should we piece them together?

Without falling into the trap of being too linear in its own structure, this book aims to set out such a journey. Chapter One demonstrates why we are at the end of the industrial society and why we have a 'system breakdown' in industry, healthcare, education, banking, finance and politics and capitalism itself. It dissects the breakdown of trust and the quest for identity and concludes that answers have to be found in renegotiating the power relationships between individuals, communities, organisations and governance. The challenge, I argue, is how we can engage differently as human beings, companies, governments and as society at large.

Having demonstrated why we are at the end of the industrial society, Chapter Two goes on to look at the social context of identity and the human need for connection and interaction. What's emerging to fill the vacuum in post-industrial society is essentially a modern version of a participatory culture, where communities can connect, organise and get stuff done enabled by communications technology. But it will happen best in natural, non-linear ways that reflect the shapes of humanity and of life itself. What are these ways, in which we can again start to define ourselves by our connection to communities, not by our lack of them?

Some of the answers, I believe, are already evident in the innovative ways that leaders of the new networked society are introducing new modes of interaction, whether these are to do with transacting business, connecting with friends or solving some of the inequalities of nature's distribution of resources. The rest of the book seeks to explore these ideas, sector by sector, whilst not being restricted by their boundaries. As navigating the new non-linear world begins with the networked society, Chapter Three explains its rise and discusses what it really means, arguing that what mankind now needs is a new human operating system to organise it. Chapters Four, Five, Six, Seven and Eight go on to envisage what such an operating system might look like and what needs to change to bring it about. As truly mobile communications underpin this new society, this is examined first in Chapter Four. But getting to this new infrastructure will also require change in political mindsets and structures (Chapter Five), the relationship between work and play (Chapter Six) and knowledge and participatory cultures (Chapters Seven and Eight). Finally, Chapter Nine offers six principles to guide your journey into the non-linear, networked society that I believe is necessary to solve the problems of the system breakdown with which I begin the book. This seems a logical order to address all the changes that will be required but this is a no straight lines philosophy so I make no apology for diving in and out of these sectoral boundaries, led by the shapes of the new economy and society that is emerging.

A constant theme throughout is the way that the language we use shapes our thinking and how we ultimately engage with the world. While new collaborative ways of working brought about by the digital revolution are the answer to the trilemma we face, the ways that we currently describe and understand these technologies and cultures lack proper understanding in many cases. I believe there are fundamental problems with inaccurate and unhelpful terms like 'digital', 'social media' and 'online', so we also need a new language to aid our navigation of the new possibilities that technology brings.

By illuminating this philosophy and language with practical examples and case histories, I seek to explore how we as individuals and organisations can play a meaningful role in shaping our future. This book investigates the deep interrelationships between sustainable economic models, how we work and create individual and collective meaning and identity and how we think about healthcare, education, regional development and civic engagement. It is not a book about technology but rather about what society can do with the new modes of connection and communication that technology now enables. Because what we are faced with is not, as Paul Hawken argues, a management problem, but a design problem, a flaw he says that runs through all businesses,[2] and indeed all the institutions of society.

Many people, both as individuals and professionals, are at a loss to truly understand the epochal changes that they are living through. This project not only explains these properly but offers up a pathway for evolution and adoption, so that those individuals can understand why the extraordinary rise of communication technologies is framed around the fundamental needs of human beings.
By applying the thinking and the language of No Straight Lines to daily life and to the strategic needs and goals of organisations, we can liberate ourselves from the cultural, ideological and economic cul-de-sac in which we now find ourselves.

My advice: read this book like a road movie.

---

2. Paul Hawken, The Ecology of Commerce: A Declaration of Sustainability, Collins, 1993, p. xiii.

Chapter One

System breakdown: the trilemma of our current age

'You look up the highway and it is straight for miles. Coming at you, with the black line down the centre coming at you, black and slick and tarry-shining against the white of the slab, and the heat dazzles up from the white slab so that only the black line is clear, coming at you with the whine of tires, and if you don't quit staring at that line and don't take a few deep breaths and slap yourself hard on the back of the neck you'll hypnotise yourself and you'll come to just at the moment when the right wheel hooks over the black dirt shoulder off the slab, and you'll come to jerk her back on but you can't because the slab is high like a curb, and maybe you'll try to reach to turn off the ignition just as she starts to dive. But you won't make it of course.'[3]

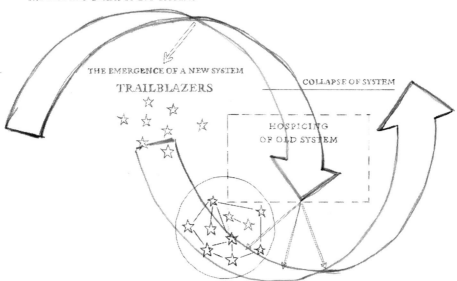

THE LIFE AND DEATH OF ECO-SYSTEMS

THE EMERGENCE OF A NEW SYSTEM

TRAILBLAZERS

COLLAPSE OF SYSTEM

HOSPICING OF OLD SYSTEM

---

3. Robert Penn Warren, *All the King's Men*, Harcourt, 1946.

Why has it all gone a bit Pete Tong? I want to make a series of propositions that challenge our thinking and perspectives of the world we live in. You may or may not agree with them but I hope that by setting up the challenges we face in today's world, the suggestions I make philosophically and practically can enable you to see the world from a different perspective.

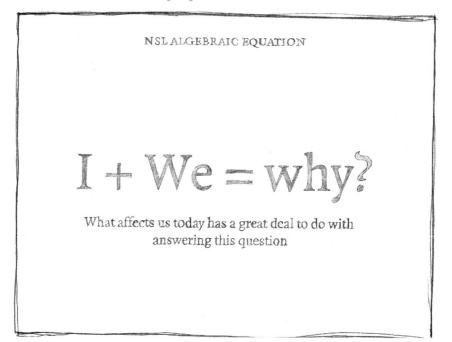

We as a species are on a quest to rediscover our role as humanity. As individuals who are part of, and belong to a bigger whole, we wonder how and why everything fits together. An algebraic equation for this might read: I + We = Why?

As I have explained, we are witnesses to a structural and transformational change in society, from an industrial age to something we are currently defining. The tragic legacy of the last 150 years is that humanity has been thin-sliced and deconstructed almost to the point of destruction. For example, human beings have become little more than individual units of capitalism: cogs secured in place and time whilst serving the feudal needs of the company. There's a threat to humanity, which is unsustainable in its current condition. We fret about intelligent machines but the machine has already taken us over. It is linear and industrial and forces us to act and behave in a lifeless, compartmentalised fashion without joy, without meaning and without a soul. All these things are against our fundamental human nature.

The machine is us/ing us

At the beginning of the industrial revolution, we created machines to perform specific functions. There was no flexibility but they were all-powerful. These machines can be said to have liberated humanity from being strapped to the earth but they were unfeeling, unseeing, non-sentient and linear. I like to argue that every person, company, region and country has its own DNA; its own unique code. And the industrial mass consumer society had its own version too. Through major social engineering in the industrial age, communities were deconstructed, and we ultimately came to celebrate the nuclear family, which does all the things the industrial society needs it to do. The nuclear family can work, it can reproduce, it pays taxes, it is subservient to organisations and to the state and it shops, but it has no collective voice. That deconstruction continued; with the odd break-out of permitted national communal activity like the Queen's Silver Jubilee in 1977, which ironically arrived when punk rock was at its zenith, attacking the monoculture and stratified establishment thinking through its music, clothes, literature and DIY culture. I remember the Jubilee street party when I was 13 and how powerful and special it felt. But I didn't know why I had that feeling or why afterwards we felt somehow more bonded as a local community. There were extra smiles, willing hands to jump-start cars, more families invited over for Christmas drinks. Yet eventually we went back to the old ways, the kids grew up and moved away and new families slotted in. We went back to shutting the front door in the evening consuming our soma, broadcast TV. No one mourned the loss of a participatory culture. We didn't know what we had lost.

The consequence is that humanity now ekes out its existence under the industrial tyrannical twins of obsession with numbers and measurement of efficiency in every walk of life, whilst ignoring its fundamental needs. In addition, an unfettered pursuit of material wealth over any other value has come at a terrible cost for society. Witness the 2008 financial crisis: the near collapse of the global banking system, a poster child for the decades of institutionalised abuse that has deeply damaged us spiritually and, ironically for many, materially.

Meaning, passions, interests and socialising are now things for free time, not work time. Worse, we are cut adrift from a personal and collective sense of belonging, identity and community. The atomisation of society has left people trapped as individual atoms in a no-man's land. Without a life satnav or a Google map for humanity, this loss of identity incubates fundamentalism and manifests itself in myriad forms. The increasing articulation of more fundamentalist worldviews culturally, politically and economically should not surprise us as we attempt to find and save ourselves in more extreme perspectives of this world.

And we're all component parts of a complex system so if we're sick, the system becomes sick: a patient in intensive care. This is not a recent phenomenon, as Henry Canby wrote in 1926:

> What we are encountering is a panicky, an almost hysterical attempt to escape from the deadly anonymity of modern life ... and the prime cause is not vanity ... but the craving of people who feel their personality sinking lower and lower in the whirl of indistinguishable atoms to be lost in a mass civilisation.[4]

Most of us are still groping for answers about what makes life worth living, or what confers meaning on individual lives, argues Charles Taylor in *Sources of the Self.* Taylor says this is an essentially modern predicament,[5] but why is that?

The answer is that we have without doubt been through some extraordinary times.

System breakdown: industry

In the west, the linear economics of industrial supply and demand have been found wanting, with the rise of an increasingly complex world. Whilst the control of information distribution systems are being fought over daily. Big media belatedly erects the edifices of subscription walls to 'protect revenues' as digital communication technologies dissolve its control over news and information and the industry haemorrhages cash, then staff, then trust. The film and the music industry thrashes around like a wounded grizzly, slapping court orders on people for illegal file-sharing but failing to adapt to the new digital reality. Car manufacturing is collapsing with jobs lost forever, as companies migrate their businesses to economies that are prepared to work for lower wages. Large supermarkets stomp on anything that closely resembles 'local', whilst inappropriately hijacking the name for their small-store formats. And industrial globalisation and rising oil prices place so much strain on society that the spectre of food security eloquently expressed by Soil Association director general Patrick Holden[6] spells the death knell to what so many have taken for granted: not only what we eat, but how we farm our land.[7]

---

4. Henry Siedel Canby, Yale Professor (1926) about life on an assembly line, in a modern metropolis, quoted in Michael Wesch, The Machine is (Changing) Us: YouTube Culture and the Politics of Authenticity – http://www.youtube.com/watch?v=X6eMdMZezAQ.
5. Charles Taylor, *Sources of the Self: The Making of the Modern Identity*, Cambridge University Press, 1989.
6. Patrick Holden, speaking at the Do Lectures, 2009, Wales.
7. Spencer Wells, *Pandora's Seed: The Unforeseen Cost of Civilization*, Random House, 2010.

System breakdown: healthcare

The divisive debate on healthcare in the US is about vested commercial interests, pitted against the interests of the entire US population. US healthcare is procedure-driven, and not framed around preventative medicine. It is oriented around providers, not patients, with much the same results as the privatisation of prisons. Prisons run on such a basis, must operate at a profit therefore they need customers, the implications of which are significant to contemplate. Under a 'fee for service' framework, the more a patient is tested, scanned and has procedures done to them, whether they need them or not, the more the hospital or clinic gets paid. Consequently, the waste is astronomical, unnecessary, avoidable, un-coordinated care, combined with hospital and administrative inefficiencies, fraud and abuse amounts to between $600 and $850bn annually. Of course the people that suffer are us, both physically, and financially. And of course it is of no surprise that there is vociferous resistance to advance reform.[8]

In the UK, hospitals run from Whitehall are increasingly driven by targets and markets, not human need. The *Lancet* has argued that although the NHS has benefited from very large sums of money being introduced in recent years, the translation of that cash into real benefits for patients has been difficult to ascertain. And due to the way government wants the NHS to operate, the sheer scale of paperwork and red tape that is integral to the running of the NHS stifles innovation, to such an extent that it is virtually impossible to design the services that local populations so desperately need.[9] The NHS it seems is being sucked of its own vitality and dynamism. Essentially one might argue that this has been organised to put the state between healthcare and its patients – a rather large, damaging and unnecessary auditing exercise.

To demonstrate the design challenge the NHS faces, in January 2008, Birmingham health officials drew up a strategy to terminate the contracts of 76 existing GP practices and award them to private sector companies with no experience in community healthcare. In Northumberland, government considered terminating GP contracts, risking hundreds of thousands of patients being left without access to a GP. Department of Health officials meanwhile had been in talks with Virgin Healthcare, Boots and other companies no doubt seeing the possibility of large profits in elements of service provision to the NHS.

Today, in a planned restructuring of the NHS, far from removing GPs, it is proposed to offer them significant budgets to buy patient care. It is interesting to note that in Britain's 2010 General Election, the Conservatives promised to protect

8. 'Quality, not quantity', *Economist*, 18 June 2011.
9. *Lancet*, 377, 9763 (January 2011), p. 353.

the NHS. The party did not reveal its plans for GPs, or indeed the future of the NHS, but the actions of the coalition Government of which it is part have been swift and so far ranging that they are the biggest changes to the NHS since it was founded in 1948. The Conservatives pledged that, were they to be elected, they would scrap 'politically motivated targets that have no clinical justification' and called themselves the 'party of the NHS'. There is a feeling within the profession of medicine that once again market economics justify the means. The *Lancet* argues that as a consequence, the emphasis will move from clinical need (GPs' forte) back to cost (not what GPs were trained to evaluate). The ethos will become that of the individual providers, and will differ accordingly throughout England, replacing the philosophy of a genuinely national health service. Moreover if this is to come to fruition GPs will become the whipping boys in the political blame game when it all goes wrong.

In Norway, meanwhile, a report[10] by Stein O. Petersen and Asmund Myrbostad of the Scandinavian research organisation Sintef indicates that if hospitals are used in their current fashion then by 2030 the nation's health service will need to employ every second young person in the country. In a linear pursuit for efficiency, damage is done to the long-term well-being of people. The market, by definition, can only be interested in profit, yet all the indications are that we need to build around the fundamental needs of humans.

It's the chronically ill that suck up the vast costs of healthcare in the US. According to Jane Sarasohn-Kahn,[11] that's $2.2 trillion, yet many people don't get the care they need, and a significant proportion of the population has no healthcare cover whatsoever.[12] Where coverage does exist, insurance companies squirm to avoid payouts, whilst maximising returns for shareholders. And it's a problem that's set to continue.

In Britain, hospitals are facing the rise of superbugs that kill people. Why? Because healthcare has become politicised with waiting lists, waiting times and conveyor-belt patients moved from all over. The free market has become the accepted model for the public sector. Politicians compete to spread the gospel, proclaiming massive investment in public sector 'improvements', wider 'customer choice' and more stringent targets, but governments have invested in the wrong things. Through

10. http://www.sintef.no/Home/Press-Room/Research-News/Dramatic-pressure-on-Norwegian-hospitals/.
11. http://www.chcf.org/publications/2009/09/participatory-health-online-and-mobile-tools-help-chronically-ill-manage-their-care.
12. Remote Area Medical, http://www.ramusa.org/ a voluntary organisation initially designed to bring free healthcare to people in far-flung corners of the globe are now working extensively in the United States of America. 'The brutal truth about America's healthcare', *Independent*, 15 August 2009. http://www.independent.co.uk/news/world/americas/the-brutal-truth-about-americarsquos-healthcare-1772580.html.

their belief in targets, incentives and inspection, their obsessions with economies of scale combined with a compulsive attention to 'deliverology', governments' obsessions with efficiency are killing healthcare with a tyranny of numbers.

Emergency medicine is a case in point. Although official statistics show that 98% of UK patients are now seen in less than the target of four hours, academics have used queuing theory – a mathematical analysis of waiting time statistics – to show this can have been achieved only by 'the employment of dubious management tactics'. Well-documented examples, confirmed in surveys by the British Medical Association, include moving patients to clinical decision units, making patients wait in ambulances, admitting patients unnecessarily, discharging people too early and miscoding data. All are detrimental to patient care, yet politically charged league tables show only those hospitals and health trusts that don't meet targets.

Critics will cite badly designed targets, or say audits should have been more effective. Indeed, studies have shown targets inducing change and delivering against their narrowly defined goals. Waiting times have fallen for inpatients, outpatients, in accident and emergency and across the referral to treatment pathway. Increases in staff numbers and facilities typically exceeded targets set out in the NHS Plan; and rates of methicillin-resistant Staphylococcus aureus (MRSA) and Clostridium difficile infection are falling.

However, it is the wider impact we should be concerned with. What you can't see and measure doesn't exist. The target is met and taken as evidence of good performance but its true impact is concealed. After targets were introduced for inpatient and outpatient waiting times, median waits increased, waiting time was shifted to diagnostics, and bed occupancy rose to levels associated with excessive risk of infection. Yet the government's solution was to search for the right target and introduce further targets for 18-week referral to treatment and infection rates for MRSA and C. difficile, rather than understand the extent of the problems they cause.

John Seddon, an authority on systems thinking in organisations, argues that a failure to think of the whole system or pathway of help leads instead to focusing on parts of the system.[13] The result, he says, is that, although each part may be doing its bit, the parts clash with each other and performance is poor. This dynamic is endemic in Britain's public sector, leading to valueless activity, meaningless measurement and poorer service at ever greater cost. Business and management writer Simon Caulkin even goes as far to say that the Labour governments of 1997–2010 betrayed their party's entire history because they 'not only encouraged ethics-free market-led management principles in the private sector but imposed

13. John Seddon, *Systems Thinking in the Public Sector: The Failure of the Reform Regime and a Manifesto for a Better Way*, Triarchy Press, 2008.

them wholesale on the public sector'. He adds:

> The credit crunch is man(agement)-made – management, not market, failure.
> So is the Soviet-style targets and inspection regime, locked in place by lucrative
> IT contracts with private suppliers, that has made the public sector systemically
> less capable than it was 12 years ago, despite the billions spent. The emails of
> rage and despair from public-sector workers at what has been done to their
> profession have to be read to be believed. And still ministers don't get it.[14]

The dynamics of not trusting staff or believing their reports and working to
meet targets, rather than need, eat at the foundations of life's social fabric. But the
mindset of management is that there is not a problem because they are asked to
look at the world in a particular way. They are misdirected from the start, so
services get poorer even as all the targets are met.

Seddon's thinking makes a powerful case that most of the people in the public
sector involved in regulation, management, specification of roles and contracts are
actually wasting their time. Worse, they get in the way of front line staff trying to do
their jobs.

System breakdown: education

Ivan Illich in Deschooling Society[15] argues that a pupil is 'schooled' to confuse teaching
with learning, grade advancement with education, a diploma with competence and
fluency with the ability to say something new. He adds:

> His imagination is 'schooled' to accept service in place of value. Medical
> treatment is mistaken for healthcare, social work for the improvement of
> community life, police protection for safety, military poise for national
> security, the rat race for productive work. Health, learning, dignity,
> independence, and creative endeavour are defined as little more than
> the performance of the institutions which claim to serve these ends, and
> their improvement is made to depend on allocating more resources to the
> management of hospitals, schools, and other agencies in question.

Sir Ken Robinson famously said: 'We educate our children from the waist up,
then we focus on their heads, and then we only educate one side of their brain.
The whole purpose of education is to produce university professors who live in

---

14. Simon Caulkin, 'Farewell, with a last word on the blunder years'. http://www.guardian.co.uk/
business/2009/jun/14/final-management-column
15. Ivan Illich, Deschooling Society, Calder and Boyers, 1971.

their heads, their bodies are only there to transport their heads to meetings.'[16]
He recalls that, when he went to watch his young son at a school nativity play,
in the part where the three wise kings meet baby Jesus, the wise king bringing
Frankincense, forgot his lines and said: 'Frank sent me.'

Yes, the young boy forgot his lines, but Sir Ken's point is that children make
creative leaps of the imagination because at a young age they have not had the
creativity educated out of them. Education was created at a time when the need was
to fuel the explosion of industrialisation, yet in its present form, it is becoming a
devalued commodity. The current education system educates creativity out of us.
We need to educate children holistically. Children have extraordinary capacities for
innovation and creativity. And, just as Picasso argued that we are all born artists,
social philosopher Richard Sennett says we are all born craftsmen and craftswomen.[17]
The true struggle is to hang on to that creativity as we grow up. The world is engulfed
in a revolution, which requires us to think deeply how we prepare our children for
the future.

Pretty much every education system around the world has the same hierarchy
of education. Is this right? Yet, intelligence is diverse and dynamic. Intelligence
engages us totally and collectively. Creativity can be defined as original ideas that
have value, and it will be combinations of interdisciplinary capabilities that allow
us to reframe the world in a new way. Sir Ken argues that creativity is as important
in education as literacy. It will be our ability to imagine and create the previously
thought impossible that will build tomorrow's companies and economies. Our only
hope for the future is to redefine and rethink how we educate our children. Stephen
Heppell considers the 21st century to herald the 'learning age'. In the 20th century,
he argues, we built major infrastructure like railways and universities but the focus
for the next century is 'helping people to help each other'.[18] Our education system
should reflect this, rather than the 20th century model which was designed to deliver
a specific type of workforce, from a different age. Heppell argues that universities
present the biggest barrier to innovation. They confuse quality assurance with
quality control, standards with standardisation and creativity with productivity.
What should a 1,500-word-equivalent assignment look like in the 21st century?
How does managing an online discussion, editing a 10-second video, making a
podcast or critiquing 10 websites equate with 1,500 words? When at least two-thirds
of the population ought to be eligible for higher education, why do we have such a
high drop-out rate in the first year of university?

---

16. Sir Ken Robinson, Schools kill creativity, Ted Talk – June 2006. http://www.ted.com/index.php/
talks/ken_robinson_says_schools_kill_creativity.html.

17. Richard Sennett, The Craftsman, Allen Lane, 2008.

18. Stephen Heppell, RSA, Edward Boyle Memorial Lecture, 26 April 2006. http://www.teachers.tv/
videos/4957.

Government edicts describe in several educational courses not just the scope of the learning but minute-by-minute, blow-by-blow instructions as to exactly how lessons should be run. If anyone is good at their job, are they going to want to work like that? You can feel Seddon seethe as he details five types of waste associated with our current way of operating.

- The costs of people spending time writing specifications: 800,000 people have been added to the public sector since 1997, all busy writing specifications based upon opinions and ideology.
- The costs of inspection: with its tick boxes and flip charts, inspecting against specification is a costly business.
- The time and effort of preparing for inspection. Organisations learn how to 'window dress' the organisation, with expert advisors and consultancies specialising in advising how to perform on inspection day.
- The costs of the inspection going wrong. The greatest cost is the cost of compliance, which will actually result in a poor performance.
- The costs of demoralisation: perhaps the greatest cost of all. Says Seddon: 'Talk to people who have been through an inspection and you will be struck by their sense of emptiness. They have been through all that preparation, worry, unhelpful bureaucracy and stress, only to be met by someone for a brief time who sat over them in apparently arbitrary judgement. Purpose is replaced by compliance. How can it be other than demoralising?' [19]

With the current policy emphasis on standardisation, creativity is chopped out of the learning process. And if a child falls outside of 'standard' there is a fair chance their experience of education will be a solitary frustrating journey, in which their joy of learning will be slowly eroded. Compare that to a country like Finland that consistently tops education league tables yet is able to offer greater freedom and flexibility in how it teaches.

System breakdown: capitalism

George Soros worried that unfettered capitalism is creating a closed society in which material success is the only outcome that counts. He argued for an open society; a new type of operating system that was not built upon market fundamentalism, dogma and avarice.[20] Since then, the wholesale pursuit of material wealth has come at a terrible cost for society. We have refocused our lives not on the common good

19. Seddon, *Systems Thinking in the Public Sector*, pp. 194–5.
20. George Soros, 'Towards a global open society', *Atlantic* (January 1998). http://www.theatlantic.com/ past/docs/issues/98jan/opensoc.htm.

of man but of shareholders and stock markets. We have allowed the appropriation of public life by private interests. Inner city regeneration, healthcare, biotechnology, the food chain and even the funding of science are increasingly being exploited by corporations keen to expand into new markets in the never-ending quest for profit. You could argue that through worshipping at the altar of unfettered markets we have taken ourselves out of the very quality that makes us who we are – nature. This is a wholescale tragedy for human nature both collectively and individually.

This is what many have described as the tragedy of total competition or what Robert Reich calls 'supercapitalism'.[21] Reich argues that the widening inequalities of what we earn and who gets wealthy, exacerbated by the tenuousness of work, are the logical outcomes of supercapitalism. Companies which do their unmerciless best to maintain market position consequently become engaged politically. One example is petroleum giant Shell's reported behaviour in Nigeria, placing staff into all the key ministries of the Nigerian government, giving it access to politicians' every move in the oil-rich Niger Delta.[22] These companies increasingly finger all aspects of our society with all the accompanying corrosive fallout that entails; indeed as we run on a market economy literally fuelled by oil, it is important to note that this industry is unable of comprehending how to run a business that does not exploit precious and limited resources. Reich points to the weakening of trade unions, poor financing of education and an unfair taxation system. Eventually we are forced as individuals to take and make decisions motivated by the financial gains of the stock market and investments; this erodes our own sense of morality. People then find themselves prepared to look the other way, if it means personal financial gain.

It's what Naomi Klein calls 'disaster capitalism', arguing that the tenet that free markets thrive on freedom is a lie. As an example, she points to what ensued in the aftermath of the devastation wrought on New Orleans by Hurricane Katrina in 2005. 'In sharp contrast to the glacial pace with which the levees were repaired and the electricity grid brought back online, the auctioning-off of New Orleans' school system took place with military speed and precision', she writes. Within 19 months, with most of the city's poor residents still in exile, New Orleans' public school system had been almost completely replaced by privately run charter schools.'[23]

21. Robert B. Reich, Supercapitalism: The Transformation of Business, Democracy, and Everyday Life, Alfred A. Knopf, 2007.
22. WikiLeaks: US Embassy Cable ABUJA 001907, 08LAGOS368.
23. Naomi Klein, The Shock Doctrine: The Rise of Disaster Capitalism, Penguin/Allen Lane, 2007, p. 5. Dave Eggers in his acclaimed book Zeitoun (McSweeny, 2009), which tells story of the Syrian American Abdulrahman Zeitoun, who tried his very best to save those he could in the aftermath of Katrina but was arrested by security forces fearful he was a terrorist, locked in a cage, then a prison, without being charged and not allowed to phone his wife, is as the New York Times states: 'a more powerful indictment of America's dystopia in the Bush era than any number of well-written polemics'. 'After the deluge', New York Times, 13 August 2009. http://www.nytimes.com/2009/08/16/books/review/Egan-t.html?_r=1&pagewanted=2.

Will Hutton says something similar happened in the way that ideological zealotry, stupidity and greed informed the reconstruction of Iraq, after the invasion of 2003. 'The ambition to have low taxes, minimal regulation, no state, free markets, low tariffs and maximum corporate involvement because they conformed to the free-market blueprint distorted economic priorities and generated huge opportunities for waste and racketeering', he writes. 'Worse, they involved a scorched-earth policy towards Iraqi institutions that created the vacuum occupied by the sectarian, murderous militias. It was the true denouement of disaster capitalism.'[24] Of course economic ideology used as a political weapon can be traced back to the destabilisation of Chile by the CIA, Argentina and even Russia post-Gorbachev as the US waged its ideological war.

Former US Defence Secretary Donald Rumsfeld, got a $37m payout when he left Halliburton to join the George W. Bush in the Whitehouse. It frightens me that you can't have a war without Blackwater or reconstruction without Halliburton. It frightens me that Médecins Sans Frontières fights for money and that the United Nations struggles for universal support for a great deal of what it does. There are people out there that seem to have scant regard for society or community, but a deep attraction to power. And then you have to ask what type of world is that? What's left for us?

Thomas Frank talks about 'extreme capitalism',[25] which Rob Walker précised as 'the obsessive, uncritical penetration of commerce into every aspect of public life, and the attempt to devalue every other institution, including law, art, culture, public education, social security, unions, community'.[26] It's depressing stuff, if you only believe half of it. Frank like Reich sees that the ascendance of the marketplace as an arbiter of all things brings with it an endgame that ultimately hurts us all, by diminishing us all. As a consequence, he argues, the only way many people can fund old age, a university education or healthcare is to throw in their lot and speculatively play the market. Frank's perspective is drawn from an analysis of the US, but I think that it's fair to say we can broaden that to a worldview.

'Capitalists are capitalism's worst enemy', writes John Kay[27] – 'and particularly the market fundamentalist tendency which has been in the ascendant for the last 20 years.' Kay adds:

Once we appreciate the historical anomaly of the post-war moment, we might see the capitalism of our own day in a proper light. With its imperious bosses,

24. Will Hutton, *Observer*, Sunday, 23 September 2007.
25. Thomas Frank, *One Market under God: Extreme Capitalism, Market Populism and the End of Economic Democracy*, Secker & Warburg, 2001.
26. Rob Walker, *New York Times* book review, 19 November 2000.
27. John Kay, *The Truth about Markets: Their Genius, Their Limits, Their Follies*, Penguin, Allen Lane, 2003.

its overworked employees, and its benediction of uncomplaining servility to the prerogatives of money and power, the 'new capitalism' emerges as the same old monster it always was, just larger, faster, and colder at heart than ever.

It's a thought eloquently expressed by Paul Hawken, Amory and L. Hunter Lovins:

> Capitalism, as practised is a financially profitable, non-sustainable aberration in human development. What might be called 'industrial capitalism' does not fully conform to its own accounting principals. It liquidates its capital and calls it income. It neglects to assign any value to the largest stocks of capital it employs – the natural resources and living systems, as well as the social and cultural systems that are the basis of human capital.[28]

All these observations and arguments come to life in a novella called *The Reluctant Fundamentalist*, in which one comes to realise that the real fundamentalism we are concerned with is that extreme strain of market capitalist ideology pursued by an American company, and specifically that practised by the central character's former employer, Underwood Samson, whose mantra is 'focus on the fundamentals'. The clever subversion of what we are led to perceive as fundamentalism reveals itself and in so doing forces a recalibration about such words and their meanings; indeed, it becomes a debate about what type of society we want to live in.

Compare that with the lives of people that live in poverty, 'a life sentence without parole', writes Polly Toynbee in *Unjust Rewards*. 'Birth is now destiny', she says. 'Parental income predicts who will run the investment banks and who will clean their floors.'[29] Indeed, the poor have few true defenders. Inequality has become an unbridgeable chasm. Toynbee interviews City bankers and lawyers in the top 0.1% earnings' bracket who are shocked to discover that 90% of British people live on less than £40,000 a year. Asked what they think constitutes poverty, they suggest £22,000 a year, which would place most British people in poverty. 'I have no idea how they survive on the incomes they have', one banker says. But when it is suggested they pay higher taxes to start putting this right, the bankers dismiss the proposals.

System breakdown: banking, finance and politics

If we reflect on the banking crisis that nearly was a global catastrophe of even more epic proportions, we understand the dysfunctional nature of banks and banking. In the light of some of the greatest austerity cuts in the UK it is clear that 'too big to

---

28. Paul Hawken, Amory Lovins and L. Hunter Lovins, *Natural Capitalism: Creating the Next Industrial Revolution*, Little Brown, 1999, p. 5.
29. Polly Toynbee and David Walker, *Unjust Rewards: Exposing Greed and Inequality in Britain Today*, Granta, 2008.

fail' has failed. People's livelihoods, retirement funds have been wiped out –
yet the finance and banking industries are still consumed by their own mythology
– a form of myopia which prevents it from comprehending its own excess.

A friend interviewed the number four executive at a high street bank in autumn
2008 as the financial markets were in meltdown. His view was that 'governments
need banks' and so circumstances wouldn't change much. That number four
worked for Barclays Bank which busily employed lawyers in March 2009 to try to
prevent the *Guardian* publishing allegations of tax abuse. Lord Oakeshott of
Seagrove Bay said in the House of Commons:

> Barclays has developed tax avoidance into a massive profit centre in its own
> right, with vast sums of the bank's money touring tax havens on what in one
> case amounts almost to a three-day super saver return ticket from Canary
> Wharf, saving Barclays, not the taxpayer, mountains of tax ... Barclays had a
> whole department, the structured capital markets division, inside Barclays
> Capital, dedicated to dodging the taxman.[30]

Oakeshott detailed that £330m had been added to Barclays' bottom line by six
'projects' that involved tax benefits. Project Knight, set up in 2007, with capital of
more than $16bn, involved making loans to American banks which now need
federal funding and allowed Barclays to benefit from 'double-dip' tax credits,
making the bank £100m or more. Project Faber, also in 2007, involved capital of
£1.5bn and made Barclays £29m in tax profits through using tax havens in the Isle
of Man and the Cayman Islands for subsidiaries to channel loans to Luxembourg
banks. Project Brontos in 2007 made Barclays £15m profit. Then there was Project
Valiha, involving an elaborate trade with interest rate swaps, Project Brazil, which
made Barclays £30m in tax profits from currency trades, and Project Berry, which
saw a Barclays subsidiary buy index-linked gilts and lend them back to Barclays so
that it could collect tax relief worth £134m.' A commentator to the *Financial Times*
who read some of the Barclays documents, wrote:

> It was absolutely breathtaking, extraordinary. The depth of deceit, connivance
> and deliberate, artificial avoidance stunned me. The intricacy and artificiality of
> the scheme deeply was absolutely evident, as was the fact that they knew exactly
> what they were doing and why: to get money from one point in London to
> another without paying tax, via about 10 offshore companies.[31]

---

30. Hansard, 26 March 2009, col. 772. http://www.publications.parliament.uk/pa/ld200809/ldhansrd/text/90326–0003.htm.
31. Hansard, 26 March 2009, col. 774. http://www.publications.parliament.uk/pa/ld200809/ldhansrd/text/90326–0003.htm.

But whilst all that is going on, there are other issues with our financial system. The worst kept secret is that the pension funds that should be paying out for people who work hard all their lives can no longer deliver, and at the other end of the scale the venture fund industry that should be fuelling entrepreneurship and innovation – which creates wealth and new jobs – is not delivering the quantity of deal flow that is required. So at either end of people's lives, the creation of jobs and then a happy retirement, the system which should support that has failed. So where do the new entrepreneurial companies that create the new jobs come from? How will we finance our retirement? We desperately need novel ways to make this all happen.

In 2008 I was in a government ministry discussing how policy consultation could be more participatory and was fascinated to hear how policy is drafted – bright young things from university being asked to knock something up for a senior minister overnight is far from unheard of. I was also bemused that the Communications Bill, an extremely controversial piece of legislation, was put out for public consultation not because the drafters of the legislation wanted to listen to what people had to say, but to buy time to introduce it into Parliament at an appropriate time. A political cynic might sneer at such naïvety and point to the reality of how things really get done. But such wanton abuse of democracy means we abandon the public realm and its people, governments and the civil service then just pay lip service to the words 'public', 'policy' and 'consultation', and consequently there's no public, no policy and no consultation. Tony Blair's WMD Dossier is perhaps the most telling of the levels of abuse (in the UK at least) that a government will go to get what it wants in complete contradiction to what its people wanted.

We seem exhausted by our current democratic institutions, distrusting politicians and the political process. The World Economic Forum says trust in governments is at its lowest since its tracking began in 2001. The question is whether democracy as we know it has had its day.

So where are we now? In *The Life and Death of Democracy*, John Keane points out that when democracy takes hold of people's lives, it gives them a glimpse of the contingency of things. They are, he says: 'injected with the feeling that the world can be other than it is – that situations can be countered, outcomes altered, people's lives changed through individual and collective action.' Do people feel this today? Democracy, says Keane, 'thrives on humility and a shared sense of equality among citizens needs to be visceral'.[32]

These co-joined unhappy triplets of recent history speak truth to the notion that free market capitalism enabled people to become socially mobile; that banking and financial institutions served the needs of local communities and

---

32. John Keane, *The Life and Death of Democracy*, Simon and Schuster, 2009, pp. 853 and 863.

business and that Parliament was a paragon of virtue, dedicated to ensuring the well-being of all citizens. What strikes me most of all is the absence of the idea of the 'morality of enough'. Although Dick Fuld, CEO of Lehman Brothers, knew his company was in financial crisis, he refused six times to sell Lehman Brothers because the price was never high enough. Thus precipitating global financial crisis that has brought levels of suffering and instability to entire countries; Greece, Ireland, Spain, Portugal and indeed the UK. The investigation into the fall of Lehman also revealed the extent to which the firm tried to hide its debt via a financial mechanism called Repo 105, aided and abetted by the British law firm Linklaters and Ernst and Young.

System breakdown: work and consumerism

We work to shop; we're educated via the mass media to demonstrate our wealth through material gain. We even go to war and get sent shopping. After 9/11, America was a nation traumatised, consumed by grief and fear, President George W. Bush had the opportunity to show true statesmanship and unite his people. Yet, all he asked of his people was to go shopping.[33] Pure consumerism according to Tibor Scitovsky[34] is in The Joyless Economy,[35] which has become recognised as a study of people's happiness in relation to consumption. Sociologist C. Wright Mills observed in 1951 that working Americans found themselves trapped in corridors and offices, unable to envisage, let alone take charge of, the entirety of their work or their lives.[36] We built citadels to consumerism and when we fall into recession or war or both, the only escape exit according to our political leaders is to shop till we drop. As J. G. Ballard so eloquently put it: 'to be a consumer is to be a citizen; where ownership of a loyalty card represents membership of humanity itself; and where spiritual experience takes the form of retail epiphany'.[37] Lizabeth Cohen argues that mass consumption is deeply embedded into economic systems, in our political culture, in people's relationships to government, in the dynamics of power in the family. 'I think it's unrealistic to think that we will disentangle citizenship and consumerism any time soon', she adds.[38] Chindogu is a Japanese word for all the useless things we might be tempted to buy, but as Charles Handy

---

33. http://blogs.suntimes.com/sweet/2006/12/bush_on_iraq_still_the_right_d.html.
34. Tibor Scitovsky, Professor of Economics at Stanford University from 1946 through 1958 and Eberle Professor of Economics from 1970 until his retirement in 1976.
35. Tibor Scitovsky, The Joyless Economy: The Psychology of Human Satisfaction, Oxford University Press, 1992.
36. C. Wright Mills, White Collar: The American Middle Classes, Oxford University Press, 1951, p. 226.
37. J. G. Ballard, Kingdom Come, Fourth Estate, 2006, pp. 86, 102, 145.
38. Lizabeth Cohen, A Consumer's Republic: The Politics of Mass Consumption in Postwar America, Vintage, 2003.

wrote: 'If buoyant consumer demand means a world full of junk, it's hard to see why we would want to work so hard for it?'[39]

Defenders of market capitalism say it's an essential contributor to liberty and democracy because it's the engine of material prosperity and underpins freedom of choice. Benjamin Barber, for example, argued that capitalism and democracy delivered on this promise when capitalism was about producing goods that met human needs.[40] Yet that time has evaporated. Companies now work very hard to engineer 'needs' and marketeers convince those with money to buy them. So Viagra and Botox are readily available while, in developing countries, drugs to combat life-threatening malaria and diarrhoea are not.

In an epic effort to ensure that consumption remains the centrepiece of every person's material existence, marketeers have succeeded in infantilising adults, says Barber. This is a radical and provocative perspective that we instinctively flinch from but, having come from the world of airbrushed adland, I'm afraid that Barber is not wrong. Like Pavlov's dogs, we have been trained to 'desire' goods, products and the latest bling. It's why consumer debt and personal bankruptcy now haunt the western world. 'I' rules over 'We', and 'now' can't wait for 'later'. Barber presses the point, arguing that entitlement now dominates responsibility, individualism conquers community, and private overshadows public. And for two generations, consumerism and citizenship have been slugging it out, ropa-doping each other in the ring, without time limit.

It is Barber's contention that capitalism was once allied with virtues that also contributed at least marginally to democracy, responsibility and citizenship. Today it's linked with vices which, though they serve consumerism, undermine democracy, responsibility and citizenship. In the modern era, it's not so much a case of democracy and capitalism as it is democracy or capitalism. Or, as he puts it:

When you have religion everywhere it's Theocracy
When you have politics everywhere it's Totalitarianism
When you have commerce everywhere it's Freedom.[41]

---

39. Charles Handy,The Hungry Spirit, Arrow, 1997, p. 46.
40. Benjamin R. Barber, Consumed: How Markets Corrupt Children, Infantalize Adults and Swallow Citizens Whole, W. W. Norton & Company, 2007.
41. Benjamin Barber interview, Freedom Lab, Amsterdam, 2 October 2007. Transcript, 'When religion is everywhere – when it dominates politics, when it dominates the market place, when it dominates the education – what do we call it? Theocracy. When the state is everywhere, when politics is everywhere, when the party is everywhere, we have a name for it: Totalitarianism. But today we live more and more in a world where the market is everywhere, shopping is everywhere, 24 hours a day, seven days a week. Advertising is everywhere. And what do we call that? Freedom. Sorry, you can't do it. You can't call religion everywhere theocracy, politics everywhere totalitarianism, but commerce everywhere that's freedom. It's not.'

Yet the paradox is that such is our dysfunctional relationship with businesses and organisations that there is no freedom. As Shosana Zuboff describes in *The Support Economy*:

> People want something that modern organisations can't give them: tangible support in leading the lives they choose. They want to be freed from the time-consuming stress, rage, injustice, and personal defeat that accompany so many commercial exchanges. Despite the centrality of consumption for an advanced economy and the fact that everyone is a consumer, people have come to accept that their consumption experiences will be largely adversarial.[42]

The spiritual bankruptcy of the mass consumer society

The greatest modes of cultural expression in the Middle Ages were directed towards the service of religion, whilst the Renaissance was largely engaged with the recreation of cities in the service of an emergent monarchy. By the Enlightenment, that emphasis switched to the development of knowledge to improve citizenry and society. Thus grew the 19th-century cultural institutions of museum, galleries, public libraries and symphony halls: all aimed at democratising knowledge to uplift and improve people to suit the emerging conditions of the industrial era and nation state. A century later, that cultural world was plundered and ravished by right-wing market economists who argued that the consumer is always right and that the effectiveness of the arts or culture had to be measured in quantitative factors. The tyranny of numbers was at work again, although it's interesting to note that when civilisations fail, the only thing left that endures is its art.

What price are we going to pay when we strip ourselves of the qualities that make us what we are? The constant pressure to consume has come at a very high price for humanity. And we are paying for it with our very existence.

The future is not bright and it's not orange

On 11 September 2009, a Frenchwoman who worked for France Telecom sent an email to her father; she wrote: 'I can't take the new reorganisation. I prefer to die.' Then she threw herself out of a fourth-storey office window. She had worked at France Telecom for nine years. Her story is, that after constant re-organisations, her suicide was a welcome relief from the stress of her daily working life. Her suicide was the 23rd at France Telecom in 18 months. It caused a national outcry in France, but the story went worldwide because it touched a raw nerve and a very real

---

42. Shoshana Zuboff, *The Support Economy: Why Corporations Are Failing Individuals and the Next Episode of Capitalism*, Viking Adult, 2002.

modern-day issue: the demoralising nature of the modern office/work environment: workers broken not by hard manual labour but by the relentless demands of their employers and the crucifying effects of management and office culture. Claire Wolfe describes 'job culture' thus, 'Job culture isn't just jobs, work, and business institutions', she says.

> It's a comprehensive way of life in which millions of people place institutional paid employment at the center of their world. The daily act of surrendering individual sovereignty – an act we have been conditioned to accept and call a part of 'capitalism' and 'free enterprise' when it's not – is the key reason why the present job culture is a disaster for freedom.[43]

Another France Telecom staffer killed himself on July 14 – Bastille Day. According to the *Guardian*,[44] he left a note stating that work was the 'only reason' for his suicide. Describing a living hell of 'management by terror', and constant stress, he wrote: 'I have become a wreck.' Imagine, workers on call centre floors having to ask permission to go to the toilet or file a written explanation because they were 60 seconds late from lunch and senior staff being bullied and being repeatedly forced to move job.

Simon Caulkin, writing his last post for the *Observer* newspaper (a casualty of cost-cutting himself), issued a stunning indictment of the development of modern 'management'.

> The talk was empowerment, shared destiny, pulling together: the walk was increasing work intensity, tight performance management, risk offloaded on to the individual. The talk was flat organisations: the reality, centralisation and a yawning divide between other ranks, required to minimise their demands for the greater good, and a remote officer class whose rewards had to soar to motivate them to do their job. Employees were the most valuable asset – until costs had to be cut. Repeated mis-selling and other scandals demonstrated it certainly wasn't the customer who was king. Somewhere along the line, the edifice of management had been turned upside down – it was shareholders who had become monarch, their courtiers lavishly rewarded managers whose MBA courses had taught them to manage deals and numbers, not things or people. Management had suffered a reverse takeover. Finance annexed reality, cost ousted value; the means became the end.

---

43. Claire Wolfe, 'Insanity, the job culture and freedom', Loompanics Unlimited, Winter supplement, 2005. http://www.loompanics.com/Articles/insanityjobculture.html.
44. 'France: stress and worker suicides mean the future's not bright at Orange', *Guardian*, 18 September 2009.

Our industrial society can brutalise its workforce. For example, stress is the second most commonly reported work-related illness, with more than half a million people in Britain claiming to suffer from stress, depression or anxiety caused or made worse by their employment. Stress-related absenteeism according to the Labour Force Survey in 2004/5 led to the loss of 13.4 million working days (more than twice as much as in 1995). One in three people on salaries of more than £60,000 wish they had put happiness ahead of earning money. The National Institute for Health and Clinical Excellence estimates the cost of work-related mental illness was £28bn – a quarter of the UK's total sick bill. From 1993 to 2002, Department of Health statistics show that the number of antidepressants prescribed rose from 10.8m to 26.6m. A report into the scale of occupational stress in 2000 found that the groups in the UK reporting high stress were teaching, nursing, management, professionals, other education and welfare, road transport and security. In all these groups, at least one in five reported high stress. For teachers it was two in five. Each day, 270,000 working days are lost to sickness absence. People are literally paying with their lives or, as David Brent eloquently expresses in the television black comedy The Office: 'Put the key of despair into the lock of apathy. Turn the knob of mediocrity slowly and open the gates of despondency – welcome to a day in the average office.'[45]

And this is what this means in practice, a woman working for a regional newspaper group in the UK as an editor was informed because of cost cuts that she would become editor of three newspapers, and later heard that she had to manage five papers. Feeling overwhelmed she visited her GP, who said she should take at least four weeks' sick leave. On learning of this advice, her boss warned her that any time taken off would be a career-changing decision. Nice. She had the nervous breakdown anyway.

Modern life is rubbish: the deconstruction of character

Christophe Dejours, professor at the Conservatoire National des Arts et Métiers and author of a book on suicide at work, says that workplace suicides were largely limited to the agricultural sector until the 1990s.[46] Today, he adds, they occur across social sectors spanning hospitals to schools and construction to the electronics industry and banking. In, The Corrosion of Character: The Personal Consequences of Work in the New Capitalism, Richard Sennett describes how the sense of hopelessness, and isolation, deconstructs our character in the workplace. For Sennett, 'character' is defined as 'the capacity to construct and keep commitments'[47] in marriage, through

---

45. David Brent was a character in the acclaimed TV series The Office, written by Ricky Gervais and Stephen Merchant, and has been shown internationally.
46. 'Workplace suicides spark French outcry', Financial Times, 18 September 2009.
47. Richard Sennett, The Corrosion of Character: The Personal Consequences of Work in the New Capitalism, new edn, W. W. Norton & Co., 1999.

friendships, in situated communities and the workplace, and this enables us to construct 'continuous, coherent narratives of personal experience'. He adds that the 'unfettered capitalism' that describes our recent history has made it impossible for us to create coherent 'character' with its deadly consequences. Whether we call it 'Extreme Capitalism' or 'Supercapitalism', as Mallory Knox in *Natural Born Killers* said to one of her victims: 'There's no escaping here.' We have effectively deconstructed many of the social and cultural foundations of what makes us who we are.

As a consequence we become psychologically dislocated from a collective sense of belonging. Jettisoned into an existential no-man's land, isolated people become extremely fragile. No wonder antidepressants are the world's most prescribed drugs.[48] The modern workplace does not create the necessary bonds and narratives of 'character', instead creating a void into which we fall defined by indifference and apathy, argues social philosopher Richard Sennett, who asks whether a baker is still a baker when his work requires him to merely push a button? Even the baker asks himself the same question. The consequences for individuals when work becomes meaningless is all too obvious. Sennett believes that there's been a sustained and an unprecedented assault on the dignity of humanity; a true descent into the heart of darkness.

To seek an explanation as to why this becomes central to where we are and what comes next, let's turn to Carl Jung, who argued that 'I needs We to truly be I',[49] while Paul Ricoeur argued that our ability to be reliable and accountable to ourselves and to others requires us to feel needed, understood and included. This implicit bonding of I and We is so fundamental to our existence that it simply cannot be ignored. It must be embraced, and embedded into a way of doing things that enables us all to exist as fully formed individuals, coherent as a collective entity.

In *The Truth about Markets: Their Genius, Their Limits, Their Follies*, John Kay believes there are four central myths behind what he calls the American business model. Two are relevant here. The first is that greed is overwhelmingly the most important motivation in economic affairs, when in fact it is just one motivation. 'Generally, people work because they want to do a good job, and be recognised for doing that job well', he writes.[50] Through good work, he argues, people enjoy the respect of their friends, gaining social capital. If you ignore these other motivations, you

48. National Institute for Clinical Excellence, 2004 – UK, Marie N. Stagnitti, MPA, 'Antidepressant use in the U.S. civilian noninstitutionalized population', 2005.
49. It was Handy, in *The Hungry Spirit*, p. 130, who credited Jung with this observation. This is further explained by Douglas Griffin: 'selves are formed in social interaction at the same time as they form this interaction. This paradox of "forming and being formed by" is thus at the heart of the emergence of self and society ... Both the self and the social are the same process', quoted in Dr Josie Gregory (ed.), 'Living spirit – new dimensions in work and learning', University of Surrey, 2003, p. 56.
50. Kay, *The Truth about Markets*, pp. 308, 315.

undermine the relationships that make corporations effective. I'm sure Sennett would agree.

Kay's second folly is market fundamentalism: the belief that you should impose as few restrictions and limitations as possible in the operation of markets because it is unfettered markets that drive successful economies. 'This doesn't recognise that markets actually operate – and can only operate – through an elaborate social, political and cultural context', he observes. 'While some of that may be government regulation, a lot of it is self-regulation; the ways people expect to behave.' To suggest that unregulated markets are more efficient is wrong. Markets rely on rules and signals, without which we descend into chaos.

Eric Beinhocker in *The Origin of Wealth: Evolution, Complexity, and the Radical Remaking of Economics* points to the failure of neoclassical economics. Although we've become enslaved to its ideology, and consequent outcomes, he argues that economists left out one very important element in their development of economic theory: people, with their messy lives and inconsistencies. He says that since the late 19th century, the organising philosophy and framework has been that the economy is an equilibrium system: in other words a system at rest, whose primary source of inspiration was not biology but physics. 'For over a hundred years', he writes, 'economics has made do with a model of human behaviour that most economists now recognise as overly simplistic and fundamentally at odds with an enormous body of evidence.'[51] Beinhocker points to the comments of Joseph Stiglitz on current economic thinking. 'Anybody looking at these models', mused the former World Bank chief economist, 'would say that they can't provide a good description of the modern world.'[52]

Beinhocker claims neoclassical theory is in the process of being supplanted by what he calls 'complexity economics' – the view that the economy is a complex adaptive system made up of realistically rational people who dynamically interact with each other in an evolutionary system.

The 21st-century captive state: culture lockdown and the enclosing of the commons of the mind

'We make culture and you buy it' is how big media likes to do things and it is representative of the industrial logic that proscribes ownership and control in very specific terms. So, as transnational media groups seek to exercise their full control

---

51. Eric D. Beinhocker, *The Origin of Wealth: Evolution, Complexity, and the Radical Remaking of Economics*, Harvard Business School Press, 2006, pp. 17, 70–5, 138.

52. Beinhocker quotes Stiglitz from an article by John Cassidy, 'The decline of economics', *New Yorker* (1996), and widely distributed at the American Economics Association, 2006, p. 22.

over media, culture and the distribution of culture and information, we are caught in what many describe as a culture lockdown. One could argue that we have existed for the last 100 years in a mass media feudal system in which society at large are the serfs to media barons, who serve us up with what they think we want to buy so they can make their money selling advertising that implores us, seduces us and scares us into being good consumers. But why is this important? Because as Frantz Fanon, perhaps the pre-eminent 20th-century thinker on decolonisation, said: 'A people will only be free when they control their own communications.'[53] So, in a time when we are using communications technology to redefine our world, control of culture becomes our Tolkienesque epic battle of Helms Deep. And as we take back the control of cultural production, and repurpose it, once again to become part of our participatory and to a degree our folkloric heritage, big media has been keen to tourniquet such endeavours.

The problem with the media

Robert McChesney, author of The Problem of the Media, says the first myth is that media merely reflects, rather than shapes, reality. McChesney's view is that media are a social force in their own right, and not just a reflection of the world around us. These are complex relationships, which are often difficult to disentangle, because media are interwoven into the fabric of our lives. McChesney argues that big business is standing firmly in the path of ordinary folk to retard their growing awareness among citizens that they can create a media system superior to the one that currently serves the needs of a handful of media corporations.

McChesney takes a US-centric perspective, but the symptoms of the crisis of the US media – a decline in 'hard news', proliferation of info-tainment and commercial messaging, reduction in staffing, concentration of ownership, narrowing of viewpoints and suppression of genuine debate – is far from a uniquely American dilemma.[54] Moreover, he argues that, outside of the over-zealous desire of corporations to maximise profits, no matter the consequences, at the heart of all this is the means by which public policy was formulated, enabling the development of the media system we have today: made corruptly, behind closed doors, with minimal or non-existent public awareness or participation. And of course in the

---

53. Frantz Omar Fanon (20 July 1925 – 6 December 1961) was a psychiatrist, philosopher, revolutionary and author from Martinique. His work remains influential in the fields of post-colonial studies and critical theory. Fanon is perhaps the pre-eminent thinker of the 20th century on the issue of decolonisation and the psychopathology of colonisation.

54. Robert McChesney, The Problem of the Media: U.S. Communication Politics in the 21st Century, Monthly Review Press, 2004.

UK, the sad and sorry tale of the extent to which *The News of the World* went in order to gain competitive advantage over its rivals, by hacking into the voicemails of many thousands of people to sell newspapers with, it appears, collusion of the Metropolitan Police is clear evidence of the legitimacy of McChesney's argument. Indeed, Rupert Murdoch's News Corp was all set to get its highly contested (highly contested for all the reasons above) merger with BSkyB through Parliament, until information was released that the newspaper he owned, *The News of the World* had indeed not only listened in on countless private conversations and messages but had also done so in the case of two young girls who had been murdered.

Then and only then, when the public reacted with horror, were politicians able to feel they could stand up to Murdoch and his all powerful media empire and say no.

The truth: a slightly twisted comedy

Of course media likes to profess its adherence to the highest ideals, the sacred search for and presentation of the truth. But McChesney's research belies that claim. Over 10 months in the early 2000s, the Center for Media and Democracy (CMD) documented television newsrooms' use of 36 video news releases (VNRs) – a small sample of the thousands produced each year. CMD identified 77 television stations, from those in the largest to the smallest markets, that aired these VNRs or related satellite media tours (SMTs) in 98 instances, without disclosure to viewers. Collectively, these 77 stations reach more than half of the US population. The VNRs and SMTs whose broadcasts CMD documented were produced by three broadcast PR firms for 49 different clients, including General Motors, Intel, Pfizer and Capital One. In each case, these 77 television stations actively disguised the sponsored content to make it appear to be their own reporting. In almost all cases, stations failed to balance the clients' messages with independently gathered footage or basic journalistic research. More than one third of the time, stations aired the pre-packaged VNR in its entirety.

'There never was a time when news media were perfect', writes Nick Davies. Journalists, he says, 'have always worked with too little time and too little certainty; with the added interference from owners and governments; and with laws that intimidate and inhibit the search for truth'. But in his book *Flat Earth News*, Davies commissioned research from Cardiff University specialists who surveyed more than 2,000 UK news stories in the *Times*, the *Daily Telegraph*, the *Guardian*, the *Independent* and the *Daily Mail*.

There were two important discoveries. First, only 12% of the stories were wholly composed of material researched by reporters. With 8% of the stories, they just couldn't be sure. The remaining 80%, they found, were wholly, mainly or partially constructed from second-hand material, provided by news agencies and the public relations industry. Second, when they looked for evidence that these 'facts' had been thoroughly checked, they found this was happening in only 12% of the stories. Davies concludes there's a problem with the media, with news presented as fact actually being poorly researched news from secondary sources, and, more likely, stories originated by PR companies that is not news at all but serves an ulterior motive, the commercial or political agenda of others. He adds: 'These are corporations that think greatly about commerce and casually about journalism. This is the heart of modern journalism, much of it designed to service the political or commercial interests of those that provide it.'[55]

The issue of who controls 'our' media plays a critically important role in society and one could go so far as to say that current media owners have been found wanting. In *Community Media, People, Places and Communication Technologies*, Kevin Howley demonstrates the importance between identity, community and media communications, especially when that world becomes more increasingly more complex.[56] He turns to Raymond Williams for a better articulation of what he means, noting that in an essay on the 19th-century English country novel, Williams coined the phrase 'knowable communities' to describe the distinctive approach of the novel, as a cultural form, in dramatically and forcefully revealing the character and quality of people and their relationships. Tracing the historical development of the novel, Williams observed the increasing difficulty of this task – a challenge confronting not only the novelist but also the whole of society – in the wake of the profound social, economic and political transformations associated with the industrial revolution.[57]

Williams said that 'the significance of relations between people and their shared environment must be forced into consciousness'. And he was prescient when he viewed modern communication as an important and necessary cultural response to the increasing complexity of how we connect and relate to each other, especially when co-joined to the eternally intertwined issues of individual and collective identity. 'Identity and community became more problematic, as a matter of perception and as a matter of valuation, as the scale and complexity of the characteristic social organisation increased', he wrote. 'The growth of towns and especially cities and a metropolis: the increasing division and complexity of labour; the altered and critical relations between and within social classes: in changes like these any assumption of a knowable community – a whole community, wholly knowable – became harder and harder to sustain.'[58]

55. Nick Davies, *Flat Earth News*, Chatto & Windus, 2008, p. 61.
56. Kevin Howley, *Community Media: People, Places and Communication Technologies*, Cambridge University Press, 2005.
57. Howley, *Community Media*, pp. 264–5.
58. Raymond Williams, *The Country and the City*, Hogarth Press, 1973, p. 165.

Writing some 20 years before Robert McChesney wrote *The Problem with the Media*, Williams found the content of modern mass media communication to be a 'poor substitute for direct engagement and social interaction'. For both Howley and Williams, this shortfall in the quality of mass media communication comes down to a central defining issue, the minority ownership and control of a mass media which results in the perversion of how we truly communicate with each other. It encourages exclusive access to the instruments of mass communication, and the one-way transmission of information – information that promotes a shared, though limited and uneven, consciousness in the support of systems of domination. The final consequence is the further erosion of a means to identity, and the corruption of 'a vital resource for a vibrant culture and a democratic society'.[59]

The problem with all this is that we create meaning by building cultural narratives of our lives:[60] what is described as context. Therefore, without context there can be no meaning. Meaning is a crucial part of human experience, the key component of belonging, sharing, understanding, perceiving, associating, finding relevance, feeling included, seeing value, engagement, belief, acceptance, receptiveness, expectation and often attraction and desire.

The media content manufacturing model that is, say, Hollywood but in fact extends to all mass media, meanwhile, has its chips invested in a top-down model of information, culture and entertainment manufacture and distribution. Minority owners don't like the idea that you can create stuff on your own. This is the war between the read-only versus the read-and-write culture, well documented by Stanford University and now Harvard law professor Lawrence Lessig.[61] The reality is people need to do both, but big media and business wants us to do only one, because that is how they maintain power and make their money.

James Boyle says that underlying all property law is the question of how wealth is created. Where does original creation come from, he asks, saying it is 'built from the resources of the public domain, from language, culture, genre and the scientific community'.[62] Those creators must be rewarded critically and financially but what we find are corporations relentlessly lobbying, legislating and prosecuting in the name of legal ownership. Tight control of media and 'culture' in all its forms clearly comes at a high price for society as a whole. As Lessig writes: 'Never in our history

59. Howley, *Community Media*, p. 265.
60. Taylor, *Sources of the Self*; John T. Cacioppo and William Patrick, *Loneliness: Human Nature and the Need for Social Connection*, Norton, 2008; Jerrold Seigel, *The Idea of the Self: Thought and Experience in Western Europe since the Seventeenth Century*, Cambridge University Press, 2005.
61. Lawrence Lessig, in *Remix: Making Art and Commerce Thrive in the Hybrid Economy*, Bloomsbury, 2008, argues that we now live in a Read Write culture, which fundamentally challenges the legal system of copyright and how we today make culture; art, literature, music, film, books, etc.
62. Boyle, James, *The Public Domain: Enclosing the Commons of the Mind*, Yale University Press, 2008.

have fewer had a legal right to control more of the development of our culture than now.' He fears that eventually what we call the digital realm will be locked down so tight it will be little more than a closed circuit surveillance system, a breathing chamber where there is no air to breath.

The quest for identity in the post-modern world

I was in Cambridge doing a spot of shopping, when I came across a man holding a sign that said 'FREE HUGS'. I stood and watched with great interest as men and women came up to him for a hug. Is this humanity's response to understanding that being alone is a lonely place to be; that society is very unwell? In fact, who is helping whom here? Later, I searched 'free hugs'. It seems people the world over are offering them. Flickr is deluged with pictures from Amsterdam, Russia, Japan and South America of people offering in their own small way a brief respite from the acute loneliness and spiritual disembodiment that so many perceive and experience on a daily basis.

The underlying reason we are driving communication technologies, legal frameworks, business models, organisational structures, innovation and enterprise so hard towards tools, frameworks and capabilities that amplify human talents for cooperation is because on the one hand we desperately seek meaning and identity in a world that forces us to quest for identity and meaning, and secondly we as a species are designed to work in aggregates. Social isolation effectively dismantles us as individuals. A large part of this effect is driven by the subjective sense of social isolation called loneliness. Research shows that human beings are simply far more intertwined and interdependent physiologically as well as psychologically than our cultural preconceptions have allowed us to acknowledge. Again: 'I needs We to truly be I.'

In Loneliness, Human Nature and the Need for Social Connection, Cacioppo and Patrick observe that human beings do not thrive as the 'existential cowboys that so much modern thought celebrates'.[63] It may be true, they observe, that we enter this world alone and exit the same way, but social connection not only defines who we are in evolutionary terms, it also determines who we become as individuals. Human connection, psychological health and emotional well-being are all inextricably linked. One of the most terrible things we can do to people is to exclude them from society. And there's a reason why the ultimate punishment in prison is solitary confinement.

---

63. Cacioppo and Patrick, Loneliness, p. 131.

I am, and you are perfect strangers

Clinical psychologist Sandra Harrild of Addenbrooke's Hospital in Cambridge says that until post-modern times, people dealt with problems that had their origins in relation to the other or the outside in a concrete way, and imagination problems tended to come from people with psychosis or personality disorders. We are still getting those problems, she says, but what's changed for some people are the triggers to illness, in so much as people who do not have a strong inner sense of self tend to feel fragmented more easily and the idea of self-construction is very threatening to these types of people. They seem to need more direct human contact to help them to define themselves and years ago would have been defined and lived within the confines of their families, villages, social classes or friends, with daily personal interaction reinforcing that.

What does this mean? Ralph Borsodi in *This Ugly Civilization* sheds some light on this by describing the day-to-day activities of Thomas B. Hazard in the 1780s. His diary, writes Borsodi, included the following:

> Making bridle bits, worked a garden, dug a woodchuck out of a hole, made stone wall for cousin, planted corn, cleaned cellar, made hoe handle of bass wood, sold a kettle, brought Sister Tanner in a fish boat, made hay, went for coal, made nails at night, went huckleberrying, raked oats, plowed turnip lot, went to monthly meeting and carried Sister Tanner behind me, bought a goose, went to see town, put on new shoes, made a shingle nail tool, helped George mend a spindle for the mill, went to harbor mouth gunning, killed a Rover, hooped tubs, caught a weasel, made nails, made a shovel, went swimming, staid at home, made rudder irons, went eeling.[64]

Try applying the local ethos of that age to your own life. I live in Over, an old agricultural village north of Cambridge. Some 250 years ago, I would have been born in Over. I would have worked and gone to church there, married my wife from the village, gone to market there, socialised mainly with people from the village, ice skated on the fens in winter and died and been buried in the place I lived my entire life. I would have never gone the few short miles to Cambridge. My entire world perspective and identity would have been defined by the external forces, both physical and social, that surrounded me.

In contrast, nowadays, a great many phobias and depressions are linked to fearfulness of how to be in the world and whether one is acceptable or not. The symptoms include not knowing how to operate in the world, poor problem-solving

---

64. Ralph Borsodi, *This Ugly Civilization*, Porcupine Press, 1929, pp. 138–9.

skills, fearfulness of even mild risk-taking and an inability to form healthy relation-ships due to suspicion. People suffering with these issues often don't have the skills to take advantage of the opportunities presented in our society and so become a population that's difficult to motivate and engage. They often end up living vicariously through media-constructed images in imagination and become very depressed when the reality fails to match. Since most people get their reality from edited news or programmes and operate in a very small segment of real time, standards are becoming lower and people are often confused between what they have actually experienced for themselves and what has been constructed for them to experience.

Another outcome is an overdeveloped sense of entitlement, far beyond a person's natural skill and ability. People who have the social and intellectual skills to truly define themselves are in a good position, the rest become what Harrild calls 'a ghost army, noisy ghosts in the machine called life'. Harrild observes that one of the biggest problems she can see is the slow destruction of people's general mental health.

Into the wild

After graduating from America's Emory University, Christopher McCandless abandoned his possessions, gave his $24,000 savings to Oxfam and hitchhiked to Alaska to live in the wilderness. Unhinged by constant parental pressure to be a high achiever, where achievement equalled more money, more material possessions and deconstructed by the aggressive and dysfunctional nature of his parents' relationship to each other, Christopher's story unfolds in a film called *Into the Wild*. It was a personal journey into extremity for Christopher to find his identity and discover the true meaning of his life. Christopher died in Alaska, in an old bus after accidentally eating poisonous mushrooms. When he was found, a notebook was discovered, in which he had written his unfolding thoughts about his personal sense of himself in the world; it was in this self-imposed isolation, when overwhelmed by the beauty of the place and his experience that he wrote: 'Happiness is only real when it is shared.'[65]

The one thing he could not do. Christopher's story is a fable of our modern times. It is this complex journey from 'I needs We to truly be I' to 'I needs I to truly be I' and back again that underpins so much of our modern predicament. Over the last two centuries, we have migrated from our identities being framed and formed by belonging to tight-knit social communities to becoming self-absorbed in the new phenomenon of personality with an obsession with validating the self. The problem that we discovered, however, was that there was nothing to validate

---

65. *Into the Wild*, directed by Sean Penn, 2007.

without the 'we'. In some ways, the vacuity of celebrity magazines is testament to that. Yet we cannot ignore the ulterior needs of an industrialised society that required us to become singular, and malleable units of production. And outside of the mantra of progress, there was a greater meme that urbanisation, mobility and an industrialised society introduced into the world – the celebration of the individual to coerce a harder-to-govern community into a form that was essentially easier to manage and control, even to the point where it was decided a woman's eight-hour labour shift was worth less than a man's.

The glorifying of the isolated personality at the expense of a public life and the suppression of communal rituals and festivities are entangled in intricate ways. From 1600 the rise of depression as a recognised disease and individual malaise manifests itself. Barbara Ehrenreich writing in *Dancing in the Streets: A History of Collective Joy* tells us about the dismantling of communal festivities from around the 1600s, communal festivities which we enjoyed about 115 times a year at least in northern Europe. So although we lived a limited feudal existence, our identities were forged in a continual round of participatory culture. But in the late 16th and early 17th centuries, Ehrenreich believes a mutation of human nature took place. This change, says Ehrenreich, has been called the rise of subjectivity or the discovery of the inner self.

> Since it can be assumed that people in all historical periods had some sense of selfhood and capacity for subjective reflection, we're really talking about a drastic intensification of the universal human capacity to face the world as an autonomous 'I', separate from, and largely distrustful of, 'we'.[66]

It is at this time that mirrors became popular with the urban upper middle class, the autobiography began its early journey to becoming one of the staples of the vain and the curious and houses became not communal living spaces but buildings divided into public and private realms, where the public persona could retire behind closed doors to become truly 'oneself', whilst our engagement in the public consumption of culture required us increasingly to be passive observers at such public events like the ballet, the play or the opera.

So the quest for the self begins

'So highly is the "inner self" revered within our own culture that its acquisition seems to be an unquestionable mark of progress', writes Ehrenreich.[67] Though, as we have discovered, there was a price to be paid for the buoyant individualism we

---

66. Barbara Ehrenreich, *Dancing in the Streets: A History of Collective Joy*, Granta, 2007, p. 137.
67. Ehrenreich, *Dancing in the Streets*, p. 139.

associate with the more upbeat aspects of the early modern period, the Renaissance and Enlightenment.

As the 19th-century French sociologist Emile Durkheim observed, 'Originally society is everything, the individual nothing ... but gradually things change. As societies become greater in volume and density, individual differences multiply, and the moment approaches when the only remaining bond among the members of a single human group will be that they are all [human]'.[68] Indeed, if we reflect on Harrild's direct professional experience, we can see that is how swathes of humanity, the 'ghost army', now tenuously live. Heroic autonomy, wrote Ehrenreich 'is said to represent one of the great achievements of the early modern and modern eras'.[69] Sadly, what we have achieved in so doing is to essentially deconstruct what makes us as human beings.

Compare that to the observations of Patrick Skinner, a Ph.D. in anthropology at Cambridge University. He argues that the idea of identity as a networked phenomenon runs in parallel to much of the social theory being used within archaeological theory today. Many archaeologists are now beginning to realise that the behaviour of people about 20,000 years ago when creating and using mobile art, figurines and parietal – cave – art had much to do with building and maintaining networks, not just with people but also with other elements of the world. Of particular interest is that some archaeologists are now discussing the role of possessing and interacting with mobile (e.g. animal) figurines as a means of creating and maintaining human identity. Much of the ethnographic data suggests that these people actually thought of these objects, and other things in the world, as actually being part of them in a very real way. Thus, when objects such as these are exchanged, it is not simply that they represent the identity of a person (e.g. relative); they actually are part of the person. Archaeologists are also beginning to employ social theories such as Actor-Network Theory to explore such concepts.

Patrick believes that the way that people engage with objects and media in the western world today is not so different to 20,000 years ago. He's not saying that people thought about the world in the same way. But what seems to be apparent, especially with the enormous rise of social networking today, is that human identity is embodied within the very objects (real and virtual) that people use, and when people communicate with each other it is not simply a matter of communication, but it is in a very real way part of themselves that is being sent/communicated. This is very interesting, because human identity then becomes something which is not confined to the immediacy of the person and the immediate surrounding world, but is distributed throughout the world in the form of pictures, emails, etc.

---

68. Emilie Durkheim, quoted in Ehrenreich, *Dancing in the Streets*, p. 140.
69. Ehrenreich, *Dancing in the Streets*, p. 140.

Interaction with these things (both real and virtual) then becomes a matter of necessity, as it did during the Palaeolithic, as people's identity or personhood is embodied within these things. No longer can people be socially secure (i.e. interact with important elements of the known world on a regular basis) through normal modes of communication; in order to maintain a sense of social cohesion people must now continually interact with elements of their identity that are distributed throughout the globe via objects (e.g. phones). Today, social cohesion becomes a matter of blending remote and direct interaction.

Richard Sennett in The Fall of Public Man says there are other consequences, which have wrenched humanity from its foundations; politically, power is seen in terms of personality not community, public life is abandoned as illusory and formal, not capable of bringing us 'self-fulfilment'. And ironically, this privatisation of the modern individual is a crucial factor in the pervasiveness and strength of social control in all our constituencies of life. In the lives of everyone, both in public and in private, intimacy is the new god, says Sennett. Anxiety about individual feeling is joined with the narcissistic search for self, which brings no satisfaction.[70]

Humanity's wheels are coming off in such spectacular fashion for we live not only in the shadow of the fall of public man but in a time of secular immanence; spiritually we are bankrupt. Our modern times leave us bereft of ritual, of transcendent myths and symbols, like waves crashing onto rocks in a mighty storm we're repeatedly thrown back upon ourselves. In Britain, majoratively, our individual and collective transcendence is drug and alcohol fuelled. Sennett argues that the modern world has burdened us with a peculiar form of self-consciousness that precludes the direct creation of a sacred, ritualistic context for social life. As Edward J. Curtin Jr observed: 'Our gods are too small, we are suffocating to death.'[71]

System breakdown: religion and fundamentalism

Peter Herriot, writing in Religious Fundamentalism and Social Identity,[72] says the attacks on the World Trade Centre and the Pentagon on 11 September 2001 brought into sharp focus the reality of religious fundamentalism and the world took notice. Sociological research, he says, has clearly demonstrated that fundamentalists are primarily reacting against modernity, and believe that they are fighting for the very survival of their faith against the secular enemy. Moreover, the increasing interest in more fundamental views of the world is a response to the increasing uncertainty of the post-modern world.

---

70. Richard Sennett, The Fall of Public Man, Cambridge University Press, 1977; Penguin 2002.
71. Book review: The Fall of Public Man, Edward J. Curtin, Jr, 1 June 1977, Worldview Magazine, vol. 20. http://worldview.cceia.org/archive/worldview/1977/06/2883.html.
72. Peter Herriot, Religious Fundamentalism and Social Identity, 1st edn, Routledge, 2007.

Indeed, in *The Man Who Mistook His Wife For A Hat*, Oliver Sacks describes patients with various neurological problems struggling to construct or remember an identity.[73] It is only the remembrance of how we have developed that gives a sense of continuity and that it is extremely fragile. This fragility is meat and drink to fundamentalism as the fear is if you do not get everyone agreeing with your worldview, then you will shatter internally and all the external cues that validate your perspective will be swept away and all will have been for nothing.

There are not more fundamentalists in the world, simply, that for many people a retreat into fundamental worldviews salves the agony of inner turmoil. As Sandra Harrild pointed out, isolation, and how to be in the world, creates great anxiety as the worst thing that can happen to any person is to be ostracised from one's social grouping. This provokes anxiety beyond coping and most people would do almost anything to avoid such punishment. The only way to fail in managing this is to achieve the last chance saloon of the holy state of victimhood. Once one is an acknowledged victim, it doesn't matter how useless a person is because nothing is ever their fault again. And the word that keeps coming back to me like a boomerang is the word – fragile.

Humanity please check the engine

In *Loneliness: Human Nature and the Need for Social Connection*, John T. Cacioppo and William Patrick delve into what they call the invisible forces that link one human being to another and see something profound. Their research tells us that our brains and bodies are designed to function in a collective and networked fashion, not in isolation. That is, they say, the essence of a social species. So our attempt to function as autonomous individuals, as 'I' in denial of our need to be 'We', violates our design specifications. The warning light for humanity is on, 'Social connection is not just a lubricant that like motor oil, prevents overheating and wear, social connection is a fundamental part of the human operating and organising system itself.'[74]

This has significant implications for society. Then as leader of the Opposition, and now British Prime Minister David Cameron famously said we should all 'hug a hoodie' in response to a vigorous debate about how society should respond to the anti-social and perceived anti-social behaviour of young people. But such perceived outcasts often have bravado in one hand and abject fear of the world around them in the other. For many of us, living in a world where our identities are not constructed and defined by tradition, customs and geography, as in the immediate external forces around us, we undertake, a tricky quest for self-identity.

---

73. Oliver Sacks, *The Man Who Mistook His Wife For A Hat, and other Clinical Tales*, Summit Books, 1985.
74. Cacioppo and Patrick, *Loneliness*, p. 127.

This is described as psychological self-determination, the ability to exert control over the most important aspects of our life, especially personal identity, which becomes the source of meaning and purpose in a life no longer dictated by geography or tradition. This quest in fact dominates our lives, because without an identity we do not exist.

This then is the stage backdrop; the loss of, and quest for, identity, the need for belonging and cohesive community that in part shapes the trilemma of our age.

The hungry spirit

In The Hungry Spirit, Charles Handy introduces us to the African idea of the lesser and greater hunger. The lesser hunger is for the things that sustain life; the goods and the services, and the money to pay for them, which we all need. The greater hunger is for an answer to the question 'why?', for some understanding of what that life is for. 'It has been mightily convenient', he continues,

> to think that better bread, and a bit of cake to go with it, would make us all content, because governments and business together might be able to deliver on that contract. The consequence of that thinking is that money ultimately becomes the measure of all things. We can measure our lives in pound notes, deutschmarks or dollar bills and then compare our scores.[75]

We have all become Hungry Spirits.

The market that ate itself and everyone else

Sygmunt Bauman wrote: 'You judge a modern society, not by what it consumes, but by what it throws away';[76] so my friend Dave Hieatt asked me: will landfill say more about us than our obituary? At the root of this is a systemic way of thinking that has shaped us for the last 150 years, and that has passed its sell-by-date. The market is voracious: we have long worshipped at its feet. Yet what happens when market fundamentalism fails to work, when consumerism leaves us feeling unfulfilled, when work destroys our sense of ourselves; after we've been processed by the education system from birth to business school? What happens when we die in hospitals due to the politicisation of healthcare; when media locks us down culturally to ensure we buy the right stuff and when our only north stars of certainty are increasing fundamentalist views of the world? This is where we have netted out:

---

75. Handy, The Hungry Spirit, p. 13.
76. Sygmunt Bauman, Consuming Life, Polity Press, 2007, pp. 21, 31, 38, 86, 114, 140.

the erosion of personal identity, the erosion of community, the erosion of trust, the erosion of respect, the erosion of the public realm, the systemic corrosion of society.

Some questions spring to mind. Any fundamentalist religion leaves us with what? Unfettered capitalism leaves us with what? The human taken out of nature leaves us with what? Consumerism as a form of identity leaves us with what? Culture lockdown leaves us with what? Avarice leaves us with what? Neoclassical economics leaves us with what? Opaque politics leaves us with what? The inability to participate in cultural production leaves us with what?

In asking these questions, we can illuminate how the economic, social and organisational trilemma touches our daily lives in big and small ways. The complexity and inherent tensions in how we currently organise ourselves means it is not business as usual. I believe the answers are to be found in understanding what makes us as people and how that defines new ways in which we will design and build new ways of living, working and organising ourselves.

Chapter Two
Solution: Me We – Jung rewired for the 21st century

So, WHO ARE WE NOW IN THIS CHANGED and rapidly changing society? This question would be recognised by Erik Erikson, who writes that 'the concept of identity is inextricably connected to its social context'.[77] Erikson goes on to explain that 'self' and 'identity' can be taken as collective names for answers to the question 'who am I?', while Barbara Ehrenreich holds that 'the human capacity for collective joy is encoded in our DNA almost as deeply as the ability to enjoy erotic love'.[78]

This investigation leads on to technology because technology does not come out of nowhere; it's a human invention in the first place that succeeds or fails to the extent that it meets fundamental human needs.[79] That is why we're reprogramming our communications, as a tool to reshape society. It's our collective reaction to living in an unsustainable atomised world.

I believe that the implications of living in today's networked world are truly significant because its evolution allows us to reconnect and understand the core nature of what makes us human. After all, 'communication' comes from the word 'communion' – the ability to share and transcend together.[80]

Dancing in the streets

'Carnival is a festival that is not really given to the people, but that one people give to themselves', observed Goethe.[81] The point being, we are much happier when we exist in participatory cultures. As an example, Barbara Ehrenreich tells of happening

77. Erik Erikson, *Identity: Youth and Crisis*, Norton, 1968.
78. Ehrenreich, *Dancing in the Streets*, p. 260.
79. Carlota Perez, *Technological Revolutions and Financial Capital: The Dynamics of Bubbles and Golden Ages*, Edward Elgar, 2002, pp. 11, 52, 54, 60.
80. Late 14th century, from Old French *comunicacion* (Modern French *communication*), from Latin *communicationem* (nom. *communicatio*), noun of action from *communicare* 'to share, divide out; communicate, impart, inform; join, unite, participate in', lit. 'to make common', from *communis*.
81. Quoted in Ehrenreich, *Dancing in the Streets*, p. 79.

upon preparations for Carnival on Copacabana beach in Rio de Janeiro, chancing upon the Samba dancers in their full spectacular garb, whose ages ranged from toddlers to octogenarians, she observed:

> The samba school danced down to the sand in perfect dignity, wrapped in their own rhythm, their faces both exhausted and shining with a religious kind of exaltation. One thin latte-coloured young man dancing just behind the musicians set the pace. What was he in real life, a bank clerk, a busboy? But here, in his brilliant feathered costume, he was a prince, a mythological figure, maybe even a god. Here for a moment, there were no divisions among people except for the playful ones created by carnival itself.[82]

Ehrenreich's insight is not that humans are social animals, this is a given. It is our rituals, ecstatic or otherwise, that are an expression of this fundamental need, a means by which we revitalise and strengthen the hidden ties that hold community together.[83] Victor Turner who made a study of 'the ritual process' drew the conclusion that collective ecstasy was a universal capacity, arguing that its expression was defined as 'communitas', meaning the spontaneous love and solidarity that can arise within a community of equals.[84]

The word ecstasy comes from the Greek – 'to stand outside of oneself'. To lose oneself in ecstasy is to let go of the physical and temporal boundaries of our earthly existence. We have our 'compensatory pleasures'. And of course we can point to a world where 'compensatory pleasures' means personal affirmation made through acquiring material possessions that confer status, identity and well-being; ergo, the more we own, the less lonely we become. 'That's the promise', argues Ehrenreich, but 'the mall may be a dreary place compared to a late medieval English fair'.

We measure our ecstasy today not by communal transcendence, as such, but by the huge quantities of the drug MDMA that we individually imbibe. But it is a poor substitute that cannot quench this human need for true connectedness. Ehrenreich concludes that

> These compensatory pleasures don't satisfy fundamental human needs at all and that anyone who can resist addiction to the consumer, entertainment and drug cultures arrives sooner or later at the conclusion that 'something's missing'. What that might be is hard to pin down and finds expression in vague formulations such as 'spirituality' or 'community'.[85]

---

82. Ehrenreich, *Dancing in the Streets*, pp. 260–1.
83. This is something that Nicholas Wade explores in *The Faith Instinct: How Religion Evolves and Why It Endures*, Penguin, 2009.
84. Ehrenreich, *Dancing in the Streets*, p. 10.
85. Ehrenreich, *Dancing in the Streets*, p. 255.

What does this mean for our media culture? In *Convergence Culture*, Professor Henry Jenkins, who at the time was the De Florez chair of the Comparative Media Studies Program at Massachusetts Institute of Technology, articulates a world in which young people have a very different relationship with media consumption. This is the migration, he points out, from consumption as an individual practice to consumption as a networked practice. Culture, Jenkins argues, is today participatory. 'We create, we share, we collaborate, we consume, we discuss',[86] he says, adding that convergence is a cultural rather than a technological process. 'We now live in a world where every story, image, sound, idea, brand, and relationship will play itself out across all possible media platforms. In a networked society, people are increasingly forming knowledge communities to pool information and work together to solve problems they could not confront individually.'[87] Jenkins' conclusion is that we're seeing the emergence of a new form of participatory culture as everyday people take media in their own hands, reworking its content to serve their personal and collective interests.

> When people consume and produce media together, pool insights and information, mobilise to promote common interests and function as grassroots intermediaries, their personal media becomes communal media or social commerce that's part of their lives in communities, whether face-to-face or over the Net.[88]

Modern folk poetry: a bit of ooh ahh Cantona

In football, the singing, chanting, face-painting and costumes are all indicative of a participatory culture where people are communing together. I haven't been to a football match since I was 11 but friends describe in euphoric terms the magnificence of the spectacle, and more significantly the power of the experience. The last Poet Laureate Andrew Motion even described the chanting as modern folk poetry. Motion describes the singing from the terraces as 'a natural upswelling of rhythmical thinking and feeling'. Football chants, he says,

> can be bracingly vulgar, but they can often be very funny, and sometimes quite ingenious. Poetry is a simple, primitive thing and, although it's unusual to find football chants being elaborated to the point at which they'll make anything that resembles a poem as we ordinarily understand it, they are an aspect of poetry.[89]

86. Henry Jenkins, *Convergence Culture: Where Old and New Media Collide*, New York University Press, 2006, pp. 183–4, 243, 244, 245, 246.
87. Jenkins, *Convergence Culture*.
88. Jenkins, *Convergence Culture*, p. 255.
89. Tom Lamont, 'Shall we sing a song for you?', *Guardian*, 3 May 2009. http://www.guardian.co.uk/football/2009/may/03/football-chants-manchester-united.

Tom Lamont describes what Motion means:

> The pack direct their attention towards current heroes: a reworked church hymn in praise of Paul Scholes, a few twisted Andrew Lloyd Webber lyrics to eulogise Dimitar Berbatov, and a long-standing song, originally about Gary Neville and brother Phil, that borrows the tune of David Bowie's Rebel Rebel, one so droll it has achieved a kind of infamy in chanting lore.
>
> Neville Neville, your future's immense,
> Nevile Neville, you play in defence,
> Neville Neville, like Jacko you're bad,
> Neville Neville, is the name of your dad.[90]

'Who on earth comes up with these chants?' asks Lamont.

> How are they taught? Do they spontaneously erupt one day, like-minded wags hitting upon something that catches? Do they develop over time, added to line-by-line, as events on the pitch dictate? Or is there some terrace elder who sits down before matches, sucking his pencil and thinking up rhymes for players like Tomasz Kuszczak, for phrases that will embalm the moment Wigan were overcome one-nil?

I find this achingly funny, but I also see the connection between the idea of collective joy, transcendence, the making of meaning and the connection of 'I' within a social context.

Writes E. O. Wilson: 'People must belong to a tribe; they yearn to have a purpose larger than themselves.'[91] Cacioppo and Williams argue that without such meaning or belonging, social isolation deprives us of both our feeling of tribal connection and our sense of purpose. On both counts, they say, the results can be devastating for individual and societies.[92] And Pico della Mirandola's 'Oration on the Dignity of Man' of 1486 was based upon the notion that as the force for custom and tradition wanes, people have to 'make experience'[93] for themselves. Humans are meaning-making creatures. That's what this is all about; our personal and collective reclamation of meaning, purpose and identity. As the first human societies were formed, people were binding themselves together, with social information such as kinship and friendship. Evolutionary biologist Martin Novak observes that perhaps the most remarkable aspect of evolution is its ability to generate cooperation in a

90. Lamont, 'Shall we sing a song for you?'. http://www.guardian.co.uk/football/2009/may/03/football-chants-manchester-united.
91. Quoted in Cacioppo and Patrick, Loneliness, p. 144.
92. Cacioppo and Patrick, Loneliness, p. 144.
93. Quoted in Richard Sennett, Respect: The Formation of Character in an Age of Inequality, Penguin, 2003, p. 28. http://www.cscs.umich.edu/fficrshalizi/Mirandola/.

competitive world.[94] I believe there's a palpable desire to rediscover some qualities that are significant to us as humans, to reconnect those inward forces that make us a living thing. We are midwives to a world that's evolving from the straight lines that were representative of an industrial era, to a world that in its networked beauty is more like nature; more like us. Nature's default setting is connection.

Embodied and knowable communities

In stark contrast to Harrild's noisy ghosts, struggling for identity in the machine called life, according to Jane Young this fear is less stark in remote, geographically bound communities. Young is from Shetland, Britain's most northerly island with a population of 22,000. There's 210km of North Sea between the island and the northernmost tip of Scotland. It's a 14-hour boat journey to reach the UK mainland and Young says the ways Shetland has responded to its communal isolation offer some important lessons to society at large.

The pursuit of material wealth in Shetland is not at all high on the priority list, despite being one of the richest islands in Europe, she reports. Millionaire fishermen are indistinguishable from crofters on the bread line. Consumerism offers identity tags, but tags are not required when everyone has your mark. Such tight-knit communities have all the binds and safety of a net. There's insufficient population for segregation by age, occupation or values. Protected by the collective, you've less need to protect yourself. Worried about losing your house? It probably won't happen so you don't really think about it. You wouldn't be homeless anyway. Once the need to self-preserve is stripped away, decorum and reputation-coveting evaporate, setting free the ability to lose yourself, an essential human need we've forfeited since feudal festivities were quashed by capitalism.

The focus on festivity is evident in folksy status criteria. In London, people might strive for status as cleverest, best-connected or richest. In Shetland, you're more likely to win acclaim as best dancer, fighter or musician or hardiest party-animal. The biggest Shetland festival is Up Helly Aa, a fire festival to welcome in the light after a long dark winter. Participants known as Guizers form themed squads and spend months rehearsing their acts. There's a super-squad, the Viking Jarl Squad, headed by the prestigious Guizer Jarl (king of the festivities), which leads a procession around the town, each man carrying a huge blazing torch. The spectacle culminates in all the Guizers throwing their torches into an ornate galley ship, built by the Jarl Squad in the debaucherous Galley Shed throughout the previous year. Once the galley has burned to the ground, each squad jumps on their

---

94. Quoted in Cacioppo and Patrick, *Loneliness*, p. 62.

squad bus and tours the local halls, performing their act ... then on to the next hall. More soup. More whisky. More dancing. The following day, you're likely to pass burly spice girls lying on the roadside; and perhaps see the odd hairy-chested Kylie Minogue and dishevelled Viking scattered around the lanes.

'Shetland thrives on clan behaviour', says Young. 'Fancy dress is rife. People live fast and wild, then live with the consequences. Nobody can avoid or be avoided. Social consequences are a rusty control mechanism. When Young started her second job in Shetland with a quirky software company, she was given a laptop – not a tag conducive to the community's values. In fact, it was so misaligned that walking across the road with it in hand was enough to incite passing vehicles to roll their windows down and make mocking 'Ooh!' noises at her overly businessy-ness. 'God forbid I should ever possess a handbag and a suit?' she tells me, 'The default response was: "Funeral or court?"'

This is an example of the powerful levelling effect of cultural values within a geographically bound community. Nobody can get above their station. The need for self-esteem and meaning is met through the constant tension between We and I. In our discussions about identity, Young says that the search for identity is less considered, less serious, but inherent in festivities. A sense of belonging is enforced by laughing at yourself and the essence of your extreme, unique identity. This is stark in the annual Yokfest, Shetland's spoof festival to celebrate being yokels. It involves dressing up in overalls, traditional woolly jumpers, wellies and flat caps, then rampaging through town with the Yokfest mascot (a cardboard sheep), for a couple of days and nights.

The intimacy gleaned from co-existing in close, safe quarters, where doors are open is intense, but therapeutic. The physical intimacy of festivities – dancing, hugging, sharing homes – makes people feel OK with their lot. Scientific studies prove our need for intimacy: our need to be touched. Even placebo acupuncture and alternative therapies that involve stroking or any sort of physical contact make us happy. The free hugging in cities is an attempt to reach out, touch and comfort our fellow humans, who've found themselves too self-conscious to be spontaneous. This introversion has caused us to grow self-absorbed and false, because we're making up an identity we've lost. Our narrative is veiled with niceties and empty phrases.

Humans are physiologically interdependent. We depend upon one another for happiness. Those with fewer friends die younger. The mood of another in the same room affects our mood. We mimic, mirror and send signals. This pattern of connectedness is rife in humanity, technology and science. If you have two similar tuning forks, whack one and the other will sing, despite the fact they're not touching. It's the same in humans. Everything has a natural frequency of vibration. We resonate at certain frequencies, seeking and finding meaning in different experiences, clans and value-sets. Also, resonant objects usually have more than one resonant frequency. We will easily vibrate at those frequencies, and vibrate less strongly at others. We will 'pick out' our resonant frequency, in effect filtering out all frequencies.

The ideal life balance, Young believes, is a state of resonance and consonance – encompassing the intimacy, communal festivities and safety net of a geographically bound community, with the freedom, opportunity and drive of city culture. Surfers riding the wave of revolutionary change brought about by our networked society understand we can stop relying on institutions and take responsibility for change and quality of life. This responsibility breeds happiness, because it arises from feeling part of something. Knock on every door on your street and ask your neighbours if they've ever thought how crazy it is that there are 40 lawns and 40 lawnmowers, then set up a lawnmower sharing club. Start a global tribe of like-minded passionistas around something that matters. Fed up with poor council service? Crowd-source an alternative. Chip in and take it upon yourself. The technology is a given.

And her conclusion:

> The revolution will not be clad in cotton wool, to save us from our deadly expectations; our fake chase for happiness down roads to nowhere; our serious-ness and decadent independence. The revolution will embrace the real and the surreal; discard the fake and the auto-pilot. We will triangulate our identities within a frame of reference that is human, do-unto-others, bold and true.

Repossessing folk culture for the 21st century

In 1994, I was in a small restaurant in Helsinki, Finland; it was May Day, I was eating with a great friend, Jon Granström and there were six people on a nearby table. Two brothers stood up and sang *Meine Schöne Liebling* in exquisite harmony, receiving enthusiastic applause. One of the brothers then announced that he couldn't help but hear the strains of English and American accents and that in the Finnish tradition we should also sing a song. I was mortified. Jon urged me on, but my mouth was dry, my heart pounding, having not sung in public for years. But I also recognised the personal shame I would feel, days, weeks, even years afterwards if I did not contribute to this impromptu social ritual. My compatriot American stood up and sang 'Gravy for Breakfast, Gravy for Lunch and Gravy for Dinner', a story about the Great Depression. She sang beautifully and received an enthusiastic round of applause. 'What's the Englishman going to sing?' they inquired, pointing out that failure to honour the 'tradition of Vappu' would result in me buying champagne for everyone. I was feeling a little humiliated. I really don't know where the inspiration to sing 'The Black Leg Miner' came from, it's a folk song about the birth of the unions in England's coalmining industry, and I last sang it in my first year at senior school. Jon chinked his wine glass with a spoon, and as only he can, grandly announced in Finnish that his English friend had indeed a song to sing. Silence fell, I stood up, shut my eyes; then from somewhere deep inside I found the 'English soul' of this folk tune. What came out was not a song, but meaning, context, history, so powerful that I surprised myself on so many levels and I received a standing ovation.

I loved listening to the 'Gravy for Breakfast' song, and I enjoyed the speaking voice of the woman who explained why she found this song so moving. The memory of that evening in that restaurant has lived close to me for 15 years. Now why is that?

Folk culture, from my personal perspective anyway, conjures up images of a man of a certain age sitting in the back of a pub, with a beard, with a big baggy jumper singing about stuff that means nothing to me and drinking warm beer. But every society on this planet needs its folk stories. The folk culture, the culture made by everyday people, the folk we hang out with, is the way we create context and meaning for our lives, critically placing us in time and in history so we can understand and make sense of our world. The other day when I was researching military blogging around the Iraq war I typed in military and Iraq into the search engine. What I got was thousands of videos of all combatants involved telling their stories about their experiences. Some films are shoot-'em-up, fast video edits set to a thumping track, others are humorous and some give you glimpses of what it's like to be in the line of fire. I no longer need to watch *Saving Private Ryan* or *Black Hawk Down* to understand what it's like to fight in a modern war. And some video memorials to those lost in conflict are so emotionally charged, the tears roll down your cheeks.

As of writing, YouTube uploads over 36 hours of audio visual content every minute of every day of the year, or one million videos a day. It represents a folk culture of the 21st century – but on steroids. It's not surprising to learn then that 25% of all media will be created by us by 2012.[95] Raymond Williams explained that

Culture is ordinary: that's the first fact. Every human society has its own shape, its own purposes; its own meanings. Every human society expresses these, in institutions, and in arts and learning. The making of a society is the finding of common meanings and directions, and its growth is an active debate and amendment under the pressures of experience, contact, and discovery, writing themselves into the land.[96]

95. *A Glimpse of the Next Episode*, Nokia research paper, 2007.
96. Raymond Williams, 'Moving from high culture to ordinary culture', originally published in N. McKenzie (ed.), *Convictions*, 1958. http://www.wsu.edu/gened/learn-modules/top_culture/culture-definitions/raymond-williams.html.

Indeed, Norbert Weiner constructed a vision of the world built not from vertical hierarchies and top-down flows of power but out of the ebb and flow of networked communications.[97]

A defining story about power

Through all forms of collaborative media and grassroots communication tools, we have taken our culture back to make it for ourselves. As Jay Rosen states: 'In the age of mass media, the press was able to define the sphere of legitimate debate with relative ease because the people on the receiving end were atomised, connected "up" to Big Media but not across to each other, and now that authority is eroding.'[98] The endgame of that is an expectation, in fact a demand, for nothing less than a participatory engagement with the world around us. We need to have our voices heard and we now have the technology to make that happen. Henry Jenkins writes:

> The emergence of modern mass media spelled the doom for the vital folk culture traditions that thrived in 19th century America. The current moment of media change is reaffirming the right of the everyday people to actively contribute to their culture, like the older culture of quilting, bees and barn dances, creativity, and a bartering gift economy. This is what happens when consumers take media into their own hands.[99]

Jenkins mentions cultural anthropologist Grant McCracken, who believes that media producers must accommodate consumers' demands for participation or risk alienating their most passionate audience in the way that American folk culture was the victim of mass media. Why? Because, as we argued in *Communities Dominate Brands*,[100] it's the mechanism for commercial survival but perhaps not as we know it. Communities are still very much situated, which means they still live mostly cheek by jowl. Kevin Howley makes the case that it is only through local communities having the ability to use all forms of media communications, to be the producers of content, culture and information that they become properly engaged in the world around them.[101] It's part of the building of contextual narratives that makes us who we are.

Jenkins states that initially the emerging mass media saw folk culture as a talent

---

97. Fred Turner, *From Counterculture to Cyberculture: Stewart Brand, the Whole Earth Network and the Rise of Digital Utopianism*, University of Chicago Press, 2006, p. 38.
98. http://journalism.nyu.edu/pubzone/weblogs/pressthink/2009/01/12/atomization.html.
99. Jenkins, *Convergence Culture*, p. 132.
100. Tomi Ahonen and Alan Moore, *Communities Dominate Brands: Business and Marketing Challenges for the 21st Century*, Futuretext, 2005.
101. Howley, *Community Media*, pp. 34–5, 37, 258–9, 264–5.

pool, but once established, mass media had another agenda which was profit and the drive of mass consumption. To do this it needed not folk culture but mass media stars such as Bing Crosby and Frank Sinatra, or the modern-day versions, such as *Friends*, *Seinfeld* and *Frasier*: mass media products for a mass media age.[102] But where does some of the great classical music come from? From eastern Europe, Russia, Scandinavia, Spain and Britain: the music of Dvorak, Smetana, Grieg, Rimsky-Korsakov, de Falla, Wagner, Sibelius, Vaughan Williams, Delius, Bartók and many others drew upon folk melodies. Increasingly, commercial culture generated the stories and sounds that mattered most to the public, and folk practices were pushed underground. But the web, audio-visual and audio software technologies have altered that, a trend that Yochai Benkler argues is structural and will impact and direct how our economies evolve.[103]

We're migrating from a locked-down, mass media world (we produce – you consume) to a networked participatory world in which the human is deeply embedded in the system, which challenges how organisations work, how we work, how money is made and exchanged, how we govern and how we will learn, etc. In this networked world, as we embark on a quest for self-identity, we reach out to the things that mean the most to us; we are demanding a high degree of participation, because we need, to write ourselves into existence. As a species, we need to co-create, to share and commune. Jenkins argues that consumption is no longer a solitary practice but a participatory one. It's not just technology that's converging but culture, he argues. The telling point is that this participatory culture is without doubt an expression of a common will, as humanity is reprogramming communication media to reprogramme society.[104]

The technology of man

I bid you all sweet dreams of ancient evenings in hopes of creating a new dawn!

Do not adjust your set – the future of TV will be made with simple equipment, unqualified people, small budgets and bad taste.[105]

Carlota Perez in *Technological Revolutions and Financial Capital* points out that at a certain point in a technology life cycle, people take that technology and direct it towards very specific goals and purposes, like the tools of Web and the Mobile-Web

102. Jenkins, *Convergence Culture*, pp. 135–6.
103. Yochai Benkler, *The Wealth of Networks*, Yale University Press, 2006, pp. 27, 32.
104. Manuel Castells, *Communication Power*, Oxford University Press, 2009. However, this view is made explicit by a number of academics including Yochai Benkler, Henry Jenkins, Lawrence Lessig, Jay Rosen, Howard Rheingold, Jan van Dijk, Carlota Perez, Eric Beinhocker.
105. William Morris (1835–96) and Brian Eno –1991.

2.0, or legal frameworks like Creative Commons. We're reshaping society today through specific forms of technology, but we need to understand why we are creating today technologies that manifest themselves in forms that are essentially cooperative and participatory. I believe this is our collective reaction to living in an unsustainable world.

Robert Logan in *The Alphabet Effect* wrote that 'a medium of communication is not merely a passive conduit for the transmission of information but an active force in creating new social patterns and new ways of looking at and connecting with the world around us'.[106] And Marshall McLuhan argues in *The Gutenberg Galaxy* that 'technologies are not simply inventions which people employ but the means by which people are re-invented'.[107] Michael Wesch, Professor of Social Anthropology at the University of Kansas, is interested in exploring that reinvention. As a consequence, he believes we need to rethink a few things: copyright, authorship, identity, ethics, aesthetics, governance, privacy, commerce, love, family – ourselves.[108] People obsess about technology, whether it is web, mobile or business 2.0–3.0. But all 2.0 technologies are designed around social interaction of one form or another. We're creating an 'I + We communications infrastructure' for an 'I + We species'. It was humans' ability to trade and collaborate that enabled us to evolve and survive so it's no wonder when society is so sick, morally bereft, isolated and unhappy that we're ubiquitously harnessing and using technologies that enable us to cooperate.[109] Culture, according to Richard Holm and Paul Ehrlich, has grown out of man's biological evolution.[110] It's the cultural activities of politics, art, conversations and play that enable the survival of our species.

Soshana Zuboff in *The Support Economy* explains what happens after recognising the extreme folly of our current existence:

> Today's individuals have a hard time believing in the corporate institutions of managerial capitalism, even the best among them. As end consumers and as employees, they find it increasingly difficult to trust that their interests are being served. The evidence suggests that not only are the new individuals forced to absorb the consequences of corporate indifference, they are ready to blaze new trails. As their needs go unheeded, they are pioneering wholly new kinds of

106. Robert K. Logan, *The Alphabet Effect: A Media Ecology Understanding of the Making of Western Civilization*, Hampton Press, 2004, pp. 24–5.
107. Marshall McLuhan, *The Gutenberg Galaxy: The Making of Typographic Man*, University of Toronto Press, 1962
108. Michael Wesch, The Machine is Us/ing Us – 31 January 2007 – http://www.youtube.com/watch?v=NLiGopyXT_g.
109. Howard Rheingold, *Technologies of Cooperation*, Institute for the Future, January 2005, SR-897. www.rheingold.com/cooperation/Technology_of_cooperation.pdf.
110. Paul R. Ehrlich and Richard W. Holm, *The Process of Evolution*, McGraw-Hill, 1963,

consumption experiences, hoping to find what they are after. The industrial economy is no longer adequate to their demands. The service economy cannot fulfil their needs … but this depressing scenario harbours an electrifying possibility: Everything about the new individuals that is ignored today is waiting to become the focus of a new 'support economy'.

Reprogramming social, organisational and economic life

Exploration into understanding a non-linear world has been going on for some time, back to Norbert Weiner and Vannevar Bush who taught at MIT and were heavily involved in military research during the Second World War. In order to innovate at speed, the once separate disciplines of science were brought together at the Red Lab. 'Like members of linguistically distinct tribes who came together to trade goods and services, the scientists, technologists, and administrators of the Red Lab developed contact languages with which to exchange ideas and techniques', says Weiner.[111] Ironically this was the birthplace of a different way of thinking about the world that had the means to reshape it through tools, and a philosophical framework.

Weiner expanded his theory of a different type of world in *The Human Use of Human Beings: Cybernetics and Society*, arguing that society operates like an organism, and seeks self-regulation through the processing of messages.[112] And, as Fred Turner writes, 'Embedded in Weiner's theory of society as an information system was a deep longing for and even a model of an egalitarian, democratic social order.'[113]

'Emerging digital technologies present new opportunities for developing complex cooperative strategies that change the way people work together to solve problems and generate wealth', writes Howard Rheingold.[114] He believes that technologies premised upon cooperation are the means to invert forever the power relationships that define our world. Indeed, something that Martin Luther achieved by harnessing the power of Gutenberg's printing press to reform the church in the 16th century, changing the social, economic and political landscape forever. As George Orwell wrote: 'To write in plain, vigorous language, one has to think fearlessly and if one thinks fearlessly one cannot be politically orthodox.'[115]

So how can this be done? Rheingold offers us seven steps.[116]

---

111. Quoted in Turner, *From Counterculture to Cyberculture*, p. 19.
112. Norbert Weiner, *The Human Use of Human Beings: Cybernetics and Society*, Da Capo Press, 1988.
113. Turner, *From Counterculture to Cyberculture*, p. 24.
114. Rheingold, *Technologies of Cooperation*.
115. George Orwell, *The Prevention of Literature*, 1946. http://en.wikipedia.org/wiki/The_Prevention_of_Literature.
116. Rheingold, *Technologies of Cooperation*.

- Shift focus from designing systems to providing platforms (though I argue that we must think about whole systems).
- Engage the community in designing rules to match their culture, objectives and tools; encourage peer contracts in place of coercive sanctions by distant authority when possible.
- Learn how to recognise untapped or invisible resources.
- Identify key thresholds for achieving 'phase shifts' in behaviour or performance.
- Track and foster diverse and emergent feedback loops.
- Look for ways to convert present knowledge into deep memory.
- Support participatory identity.

There is a view that there's a psychological reformation going on that suggests, interesting parallels to the religious reformation of the 16th century. It seems we are forcing into consciousness an alternative view of society and using communication technologies to enforce that view. Henry Jenkins writing in Jean Burgess and Joshua Green's book YouTube[117] makes the point that a primary reason that YouTube is so hugely successful is because so many people were 'ready for something like YouTube'.

Ronald Inglehart and Christian Welzel in Modernization, Cultural Change, and Democracy argue that the values that shape our society are in transition, eroding, they say, key institutions of industrial society. They describe what they call 'self-expression values', which are 'inherently emancipative and people centred, giving rise to a new type of humanistic society that promotes human autonomy on numerous fronts'.[118]

Inglehart and Welzel describe a post-industrial world that is substantially different from the industrial one. The desire for people to feel autonomous, and yet also to work together on projects that confer meaning, is valued highly. But this is made as a clear choice, whereas we reject traditional organisational structures. Therefore one can see how communication technologies that enable us to achieve these goals will be heavily used. Inglehart and Welzel also highlight the desire for young people to want to collaborate to effect change. And this networked humanistic generation show strong preference for leadership 'that emphasises the collective participation of many individuals over the strong leadership of the few'.[119] One might argue this is the evolution from a world defined by coordination to one built upon cooperation.

117. Jean Burgess and Joshua Green, YouTube, Polity Press, 2009, p. 110.
118. Ronald Inglehart and Christian Welzel, Modernization, Cultural Change and Democracy: The Human Development Sequence, Cambridge University Press, 2006, p. 43.
119. Inglehart and Welzel, Modernization, Cultural Change and Democracy, p. 44.

The quest for an authentic life

Emergent is an articulate but growing minority of the people who are rejecting the idea that the unstoppable march of progress means a fake, second-rate world and are demanding something authentic – real human contact, real experience, real connection. Their desire is to embrace the world authentically, and as a consequence increasingly reject a world defined by material things as the panacea for everything. Interestingly, Inglehart and Welzel also point out that the world we now inhabit, described as 'the knowledge economy', depends 'less on material constraints than on ideas and imagination'.[120] This creates a climate of intellectual curiosity and creativity. And although we live in a more secular society, we have increasingly come to ponder about the spiritual meaning of life.

In the UK, a new generation of people are living as much as they can off the land and, as described by Louise France,[121] are 'swapping inner city gardens for smallholdings, a daily commute for early morning goat milking, domestic cats for pedigree pigs and blackberries for home-made compost'. There's a shift in ambition away from consumerism and city life. For the first time in generations, more people are moving to rural areas than are moving out of them. Exhausted by consumerism and a wage-slave life, people are beginning to ask what more means, realising that it doesn't exist at the bottom of a shopping bag.

David Boyle in *Authenticity, Brands, Fakes, Spin and the Lust for Real Life* has observed a significant trend in the UK which he believes has engaged nearly half the population. People that define themselves through anything and everything that they recognise as authentic. Boyle believes 'the rise of local brands, real ale, reading groups, organic vegetables, slow food, poetry recitals, unmixed music, materiality in art and unbranded vintage fashions, are all symptoms of the same thing – a demand for human-scale, face-to-face institutions and real experience'.[122] For Boyle it also means:

- That this desire for the authentic life is not a conservative force – though there are elements of that – but a forward-looking movement that looks to adapt traditional wisdom for modern life.
- It is a progressive revolution: cosmopolitan foods from all over the world on our supermarket shelves were able to satisfy people's demands for authenticity a generation ago, but now people are increasingly demanding what's local, healthy and real.

---

120. Inglehart and Welzel, *Modernization, Cultural Change and Democracy*, p. 31.
121. Louise France, 'Meet the greenshifters', *Guardian*, Sunday, 7 September 2008. http://www.guardian.co.uk/environment/2008/sep/07/ethicalliving.family.
122. David Boyle, *Authenticity: Brands, Fakes, Spin and the Lust for Real Life*, Harper Perennial, 2004.

- The idea of authenticity has been hi-jacked by the advertisers, who claim brands are the source of authenticity in people's lives but the exact opposite is true: brands disappoint. (Peugeot, for example, claims that driving its cars gives the 'ride of your life'. I got the ride of my life once but it was not in a car).
- What enough people demand, they will get. We seek a different way to work, one that provides greater meaning. This quest is driving a revolution in the structure and methods of business.

This part of the story is, I would argue, a meme with a view, as well as inconvenient truth for some. As I have researched this project, it has become increasingly obvious to me that there is a defining inevitability to a world defined by networks, networked thinking and participatory cultures which must challenge us all to reconsider our preconceptions, either at an individual or organisational level. Comprehending the possibilities of what we might do, what we could do and what we should do is for me imperative. This is not some pie in the sky, futuristic, some day in the future thing. We have defined the participatory tools, frameworks, legal or otherwise, literacies, processes skills we now use, to achieve specific purposes, all of which at some level re-engages ourselves with our humanity.

The greater opportunity is this: that participatory tools allow us to re-design and create realistic but different forms of social and economic organisational capabilities – capabilities that may truly help resolve some of the seemingly intractable dilemmas confronting our world. There are a wide range of different types of need and application, social and economic, all of which can be enhanced by cooperative technologies. We can now think about how we design for cooperation vs. coordination, understand key principles that help us think about different ways of getting stuff done, as Howard Rheingold argues and, 'as tools people can use to tune organisations, projects, processes, and markets for increased cooperation. Specifically, each can be used in distinctive ways to alter the key dimensions of cooperative systems: structure, rules, resources, thresholds, feedback, memory, and identity.'[123]

Participatory cultures and technologies of cooperation are part of what has been up until now the quiet revolution of a networked and non-linear world.

From cold war to hot media

The networked and interactive nature of our digital world enabled us to get back to what makes us what we are: a collaborative and networking species. Exemplified by the invention of Web 2.0 technologies, these low-cost tools at their very core

---

123. Rheingold, *Technologies of Cooperation*.

support the fundamental need for human connection. The blogs, Wikis, mashups, open APIs, open source software and Creative Commons legal frameworks are enabling us to reimagine and create this world afresh. And as Henry Jenkins and Kevin Kelly assert, we are witnessing an important shift from individualised and personalised media consumption and creation towards consumption and co-creation as a networked practice. This structurally changes the relationship between media content creation and media content consumption, but it equally transforms the nature of work and of commerce. The industrialised world and mass media have conveniently forgotten that we're a 'meaning making collaborative species', and they don't like being reminded that we want to be part of creation, of storytelling and of communities. And that connection is a fundamental need of every society on this planet, no matter whether we live in forests or cities. Narrative, it seems, and co-creation of that narrative, matters.

The internet, in providing low-cost production tools and unprecedented connectivity, demonstrates that an audience can and will directly participate. Indeed, it demands the possibility for direct participation in media creation and consumption. We can think of the first five mass media as 'cold' mass media, consumed passively. By contrast, the internet was the first 'hot', conversational communication mass media, which allowed users to create, rate, participate in and propagate information and content through their own free will, and with shared common goals. In its June 2006 cover story, Business Week called this: 'the biggest change to business since the Industrial Revolution'.[124]

The wealth of networks in the networked world

Yochai Benkler in The Wealth of Networks[125] argues that in a world where we're all connected and all possess or have access to low-cost tools to make and create, then we all have the ability to become traders, creating and participating in commercial activity. The mass market does not go away, but 'It does mean that whenever someone, somewhere, among the billion connected human beings and ultimately among all those who will be connected, wants to make something that requires human creativity, a computer, and a network connection, he or she can do so alone, or in cooperation with others.' This means that what we value and are attracted to is more about us as human beings who interact with each other socially, rather than being units of production or consumption in the ecosystem of supercapitalism, disaster capitalism and extreme capitalism. Benkler points to the obvious

---

124. 'The power of us', Business Week, June 2006. http://www.businessweek.com/magazine/content/05_25/b3938601.htm.

125. Benkler, Wealth of Networks, pp. 22, 52–6, 99. http://www.worldchanging.com/archives/004691.html.

conclusion that Inglehart and Welzel draw, that when people collaborating towards common goals, they do so of their own free will, and are motivated to do their very best. Equally these lightweight flexible tools bring an altogether different frictionless capability, enabling people to work together in ways that redefine the notion of efficiency in a way that the heaviness of the industrial world simply cannot deliver. Or, a shorthand version could be articulated as – friction is fiction.

It was Bernard Baruch who said that 'the highest form of efficiency was the spontaneous cooperation of free people'.[126] As a consequence we witness an extraordinary explosion of information, knowledge and cultural production that thrives in this networked environment, and is then applied to anything that the many individuals connected to it can imagine. Importantly, Benkler points out that, increasingly, whatever it is we make either collectively or individually, we permit others to extend, evolve and develop into something else. Ownership is not seen as proprietary, but shared.[127] What we see in the networked information economy is a dramatic increase in the importance and the centrality of information produced in this way. Benkler goes on to describe a world where in fact the ability to share and co-create, information, culture and knowledge are all key components in realising the welfare of the human species, whether that's applied to agriculture, science, health, literacy or education, etc. Indeed, and the welfare of the human species is something we need to focus on now.

Of course, this has economic implications that must be considered. It is in the intersection of where innovation and information meet that spurs economic growth. But the question is who has the information, has the rights to the information and regulates access to information?

Access to information and how that information is utilised, shared and distributed has been a defining and recurring chapter in the story of civil society. Who has knowledge, who can access knowledge and how that knowledge can be deployed has once again become central to the discussions of those that decide our laws and regulate our media. It's important for industry in all sectors to come to terms with some inexorable realities; new gatekeepers will arise in the information distribution wars. Grassroots collaborations will compete with conventional hierarchies. For example, socially based innovation is already challenging corporate research and development models.[128]

126. Bernard Baruch, Presidential Adviser to Woodrow Wilson: First World War. A quote often attributed to Woodrow Wilson.

127. Benkler, *Wealth of Networks*, ch. 3: 'Peer production and sharing', pp. 59–90, ch. 4: 'The economics of social production', pp. 91–132.

128. Jeff Howe, *Crowdsourcing: How the Power of the Crowd Is Driving the Future of Business*, Random House, 2008; open source: http://en.wikipedia.org/wiki/Open_source. Social innovation: http://en. wikipedia.org/wiki/Social_innovation.

It is this fundamental human desire for change coupled with digital communication technologies that holds the promise to transform this society in the same way that Gutenberg's 42-line Bible liberated information from the controlling authority of the church and redistributed it to a wider society, which subsequently delivered the Reformation, and the possibility that man and woman for the first time could make their own way in the world. The invention of printing in the 15th century had a profound impact on society with between 8 million and 24 million books, representing 30,000 titles, printed and published within 40 years of the first Gutenberg bible. Further ahead, Gutenberg's technology, used so effectively by Martin Lurther, undermined the authority of the Catholic church, fuelled the Reformation, aided the development of science and created new social classes.

Liberation day: humanity's new deal

New tools and technologies of cooperation are empowering individuals as never before. They're transformational, challenging the centralised institutions of the 20th century to be more responsive and transparent. So much so that many believe that the future of our society lies not with institutions but with individuals. This is a people-led revolution. As low-cost technologies proliferate, we are increasingly using them to be more creative and more collaborative. At some point the technology itself will recede into the background. As Bruce Sterling observed: 'If you're under 21, you likely don't care much about any supposed difference between virtual and actual, online and off. That's because the two realms are penetrating each other; Google Earth mingles with Google Maps, and daily life shows up on Flickr.'[129] They're enabling value to be generated more efficiently, with broader participation and new types of collaboration. They're empowering individuals and self-organised communities in ways that many institutions prefer to ignore. So what's the hold up?

John Thackara's view on the limitation of an industrial mindset in a networked economy is that that 'It's like grit in the wheel.'[130] These wrenching changes have placed great financial, organisational as well as cultural stress upon industrial systems, forcing them into deep crisis as they struggle to adapt to a non-linear world. But the truth is that industrial systems were never designed around the needs of people. In a sense people were as expendable as other forms of raw material, yet that orthodoxy is clearly being dismantled; human need can be placed at the centre of new forms of social and economic enterprise and those that cannot learn this lesson will become irrevocably stuck in the trauma of transition.

---

129. Bruce Sterling, 'My final prediction', *Wired Magazine*, December 2006. http://www.wired.com/wired/archive/14.12/posts.html?pg=6

130. John Thackara, *In the Bubble: Designing in a Complex World*, MIT Press, 2006, p. 216.

Underlining the significance of what this all means, Manuell Castells, author of Communication Power and the Networked Society, points out: 'We must emphasise the role of technology in the process of human transformation, particularly when we consider the central technology of our time, communication technology, which relates to the heart of the specificity of the human species: conscious, meaningful communication.'[131] These are the types of issues we must grapple with frankly and intelligently. We need to explore how learning and education can be made more effective and cost-efficient in a world of universal information access. How can the 'sharing economy' that exists outside of the marketplace be fortified to perform its valuable work? How might digital technologies of cooperation improve the efficiency and responsiveness of healthcare?

Let's explore new participatory, open structures for learning, journalism, arts and culture, community and civic endeavours, voluntarism and more. Let's challenge government to re-imagine its services to make them more citizen-friendly and accountable. Let's seek to make the public sector information controlled by museums, universities, archives and other public institutions more accessible to all. The defining challenge of the 21st century, says Jeffrey Sachs in Commonwealth: Economics for a Crowded Planet, 'will be to face the reality that humanity shares a common fate on a crowded planet'.[132] He emphasises that our common fate will require new forms of global cooperation – a fundamental point of blinding simplicity that many world leaders have yet to understand or embrace. Our global society will flourish or perish according to our ability to find common ground across the world on a set of shared objectives and on the practical means to achieve them. Never has there been a greater imperative to take a different view of our world and how we exist in it. And were we to take a lesson on the true reason for the collapse of Athenian culture, or other civilisations throughout history that Jared Diamond describes in his book Collapse[133] we cannot afford to entertain hubristic thinking.

System reboot

'With the emergence of the next technological revolution, society is still strongly wedded to the old ways of doing things and its institutional framework. The old habits and regulations become obstacles, the old services and infrastructures are found wanting, the old organisations and institutions inadequate', writes Carlota Perez, in Technological Revolutions and Financial Capital.[134] Hubris, and an unwillingness

131. Castells, Communication Power, p. 24.
132. Jeffrey Sachs, Common Wealth: Economics for a Crowded Planet, Allen Lane, 2008, p. 3.
133. Jared M. Diamond, Collapse: How Societies Choose to Fail or Survive, Penguin, 2006.
134. Perez, Technological Revolutions, p. 42.

to perceive fundamental cultural shifts that have ushered in this non-linear world with a different operating system, has resulted in industry as well as governmental institutions all suffering financially or in organisational capability, or both. They say, days die like people do, gasping for every last ray of light, and you might say the same for our linear world.

It seems many people in all walks of life are trying to solve difficult problems in a new paradigm with threadbare thinking. The demise of the media industry is as much to do with the fact that it is 10 years too late in trying to deal with the simple truth that the old model of mass media economics is not failing – it has failed. Yet, for many in all walks of life, they are all too often unable to think the unthinkable. Failure to act results in lost jobs and livelihoods, coupled with a fundamental systemic breakdown that affects everyone on this planet. So we must be prepared to embrace a change in the full knowledge of the world we live in today. Joshua Cooper Ramo writes:

> It wasn't just Werner Heisenberg injecting uncertainty into quantum physics. It was Alfred Tarski bringing unpredictability to mathematics, Kurt Göbel bringing incompleteness to logic, Benoit Mandelbrot doing the same for fluid dynamics and Gregory Chaitin for information theory. They all proved that once you made the leap to a new model – if it was the right model – then accepting uncertainty and indeterminacy allowed you to make sense of the parts of the world you had never understood before.[135]

Companies and institutions are locked, from top to bottom, from young to old, and in every level of their bureaucratic life, in a vision of the world that's out of date and inflexible. This presents itself as a creative leadership challenge, as a design challenge, where we seek a different set of competencies to help us navigate this world which is essentially in transition. We all need to be able to imagine and visualise how to act in a more capricious world, and the reality is that the division between business and government needs to be rethought as no one can afford to go it alone.

The point is this, that today we do have the tools to effect change and challenge an ideology that's proven to now be inappropriate for its time. Aristotle mused that 'wealth obviously is not the good we seek, for the sole purpose it serves is to provide the means of getting something else. Pleasure, virtue and honour would have a better title to be considered 'the good', for they are to be desired for their own account'.[136] What Aristotle is saying is that we raise our eyes and creative minds

---

135. Joshua Cooper Ramo, *The Age of the Unthinkable: Why the New World Disorder Constantly Surprises Us and What We Can Do about It*, Little Brown, 2009, p. 46.
136. Quoted in Handy, *The Hungry Spirit*, p. 15. http://plato.stanford.edu/entries/aristotle-ethics/.

upwards and yearn for the vast endless sea of possibility of what our society could be beyond the confines of straight lines thinking. We desperately need a new language to create a new philosophical framework that enables us to make a transition, and succeed as a society and put commerce in its rightful place. We need a system reboot into a new paradigm; an Enlightenment for the 21st century. Says Richard Sennett: 'We want to recover something of the spirit of the Enlightenment on terms appropriate to our time. We want the shared ability for work to teach us how to govern ourselves and to connect to other citizens on common ground.'[137]
Of course the Enlightenment represented an extraordinary surge of human endeavour and creativity, an unleashing of the human mind to imagine, visualise, give form to science, culture, society, economics, architecture, every touch point you might say that makes civilisation.

It is imperative we have a more informed sense of our future. We must have a more honest reckoning with the transformative power of a new way of doing things, plus the need to be agile and responsive, to not work in silos, but in networks, to use open platforms that provide and support community cohesion, co-creation, sharing, cooperation, innovation and economic growth. That allow us to express ourselves creatively, that enable people and organisations to experiment with alternative answers without fear of living in a culture that seeks to punish failure.

The elegant universe

Comedian Bill Bailey observes on Stephen Hawking's *A Brief History of Time* that the universe can be three possible shapes: long and thin like tagliatelle, round like a marble or saddle-shaped. He says Hawking should come clean and admit that the universe is in fact a saddle strapped to a giant donkey being led and down an intergalactic beach by God. Similarly, we understand the shape of a straight lines world, but we don't know the shape of our no straight lines universe. We need to explore its shape and feel it physically, intellectually and emotionally. We need to embrace and comprehend it, because what comes next is down to us.

We need a new language and philosophy, an idea of a different type of society, by unfolding and exploring ideas of language and creativity that brings us new ways of describing and comprehending our world. You might call it a new common sense. This human operating system looks beyond materialism to something greater to liberate us from closed systems. In this way, we can become meaningfully re-engaged with the world, understand how we make our way in it, be truly accountable to each other and enjoy the full richness of life.

---

137. Sennett, *The Craftsman*, p. 269.

Chapter Three

System upgrade: geography is becoming history, analogue is becoming digital, individuals are becoming the crowd, niche is becoming mainstream, local is becoming global – all change please

In a mass media society, the basic units are the large collective 'masses'. In contrast, a network society is based on individuals who form voluntary connections with other individuals regardless of location. In a network society, the network becomes a basic unit of organisation at all levels (individuals, groups and organisations). Online social networks, media networks and technology networks act as the catalysts for a networked society.[138]

Steve Watts is a wealthy Californian businessman. He decided he would take his family on holiday to Europe, travelling by train, and his children implored him to take the opportunity to read the Harry Potter books that they had enjoyed. Watts decided that he would leap into the digital age by buying the latest iPod, and uploading Harry Potter books as audio files.

Donning the iconic white headphones as the 16.16 from Rome to Turin moved out of the station, Watts looked out of the train window and began to take in the scenery and the stories. At the end of the week, sitting down to breakfast, he announced to the horror of his children that Harry Potter was severely overrated. In fact, it was just plain rubbish. His kids looked perplexed. Obviously they disagreed, so Steve explained that there was no structure, no plot line and the characters constantly came and went in random order.

Steve's kids picked up his iPod, looked at it and then laughed until they were in tears, to the consternation of their father. Why? Because Watts had been listening to Harry Potter all week on Shuffle. He did not get Shuffle and this simple everyday story sits at the very heart of *No Straight Lines*. Because for many of us, we have only ever experienced a linear life and a linear culture, Watts' inability to comprehend even the possibility of Shuffle is a simple but telling example of that fact.

A linear approach to what we make, how we make it, who we make it with and how we share and communicate is a framework or lens that sets us to look upon

138. Jan van Dijk, *The Network Society*, 2nd edn, Sage, 2006.

our world and act in a very particular fashion. Shuffle is an example of a non-linear approach, a means by which we can access, curate and interpret the world in a different way. But for some, it's very hard to grasp.

Think about it like this – the only straight lines made in nature are made by man, and similarly our industrial world has been built with the same straight lines logic and philosophy. Yet nature has no straight lines. Nature flows, nature is more connected, grassroots and interdependent. Nature is interested in populations of individuals, not individuals per se. Nature is evolutionary and it is an organism. 'Living organisms are consummate problem solvers', says John Holland. 'They exhibit a versatility that puts the best computer program to shame.'[139] It suggests a different type of process and logic at play that's not centralised, bureaucratic or inflexible. This is the world of no straight lines.

For straight lines thinkers the no straight lines world is akin to living in a foreign land: the customs, language and symbols are dislocatingly alien. They're outsiders, unable to fully participate, as they don't have the comprehension, insight or the necessary capability to fully engage. They become concussed observers to the vital world around them. The visceral shock, however, is that this is not in some foreign land but in their own backyards. As one commentator on my blog wrote: 'I have no idea what particular combination of software, ethos and policies these networks have implemented that attracts people to exhibit these female qualities online, but it's basically changing people's behaviour, and that behaviour is female in nature.'

This has deep implications as to how culture is created, how business is made and how organisations are structured. Our world of business, media and communications is evolving from the straight lines of an industrial era to the more complex and networked world that mimics nature. As I have already argued, this interactive networked world isn't about vertical silos, traditional notions of product and service creation, mass production and mass media and marketing. It's about the massive flows of people who are connecting, collaborating, organising and creating in a manner that has nothing to do with a linear approach. This is truly an engaged and participatory culture. For more than 150 years our economies, culture and society have been shaped by a straight lines logic producing considerable economic success. However, in the dawn of the networked society, a straight lines logic of getting stuff done becomes a barrier to progress. Why? Because as many argue, the change wrought by the networked society is structural.[140]

---

139. John Holland, *Adaptation in Natural and Artificial Systems*, University of Michigan Press, 1975.
140. Benkler, *Wealth of Networks*. Benkler generally explores this idea in the first part of his book, the networked information economy, also more specifically in ch. 4: 'The economics of social production', also pp. 23, 30, 32, 126–7. Perez says that when a set of powerful and dynamic new industries connect, they unleash a powerful transformation in the way of doing things (Perez, *Technological Revolutions*, p. 15), and as a consequence transforms the institutions of governance, society and even culture (p. 24).

Deschooling ourselves: an appropriate language for the networked society

When you put words together, they become a philosophical window to the world, shaping and informing our actions. To we return to cybernetics and systems theory, that came about to facilitate interdisciplinary collaboration at MIT during the Second World War. Norbert Weiner put together a group of words that not only embodied but actively facilitated networking and entrepreneurship, explains Fred Turner.[141] Weiner appropriated the word *homeostasis* from physiology and applied it to social systems; he picked up the word *feedback* from control engineering; and from the study of human behaviour, he drew the concepts of *learning, memory, flexibility* and *purpose*. These words became a universal language that begat a universal discipline. Scientists working in multidisciplinary teams, says Turner, 'justify leaps across disciplinary boundaries by drawing on the language of cybernetics'.[142]

Our real illiteracy, said the artist Hundertwasser, is our inability to create.[143] And there are precedents for political change. Tony Judt argues that it was the language used by pamphleteers and journalists as the rhetoric of public action in 18th-century France that enabled the construction of a functioning and different sort of society after the French Revolution.[144] Our imperative now is to deschool ourselves in the literacy and defining philosophy that has driven us into a cultural, ideological and economic cul-de-sac. We must release this century from its current captive state. As Ivan Illich wrote, de-institutionalisation constitutes the challenge for learning our way out of the current malaise.[145] We need to liberate ourselves from the ways we were taught to think and live our lives stemming from an era of industrialisation and the mass consumer society. In 1611 the King James Bible was published. It was the first bible written in English for everyman in everyday language, and crucially its language carried within it ideas, radical ideas that have, some argue, played a defining role in many social revolutions, for example the English Civil War, the American Civil War, right up to Martin Luther King who used it to raise the hopes and aspirations of black American people and forge them into a force for social revolution and change. My observation is that what we say, and how we say it, the language we choose to use as part of our daily vernacular, therefore, has everything to do with what comes next.

And to do that we need a new language. Take these two examples: 'the production of shared software is communism', so said Steve Ballmer of Microsoft, whereas Alan Rusbridger, the Editor of the *Guardian*, said, 'mutuality is our business strategy'.

---

141. Turner, *From Counterculture to Cyberculture*, p. 24.
142. Turner, *From Counterculture to Cyberculture*, p. 25.
143. Friedensreich Hundertwasser – artist, 15 December 1928 – 19 February 2000.
144. Judt, *Ill Fares the Land*.
145. Illich, *Deschooling Society*.

These two short sentences are framed by a worldview that ultimately informs actions and consequences, in this instance for the success or failure of a company. So what is in and what is most definitely out? As straight line thinking stops here.

Out: hierarchy, silos, unsustainable value, shackled culture, market fundamentalism, dogma, creative apartheid, opacity, the war on everything, information distribution control, top-down structures and thinking, neoclassical economic theory, fundamentalist ideologies, human units of consumption, human units of production, education as battery farming,

Or if we revert to the versus model it's:

Human operating systems vs. industrial age thinking
Creative culture vs. management culture
People vs. the tyranny of numbers
Networks vs. silos
Transparency vs. opacity
Trusted authorities vs. non-trusted 'authorities'
Authenticity vs. fake
Hot media vs. cold media
Communication networks vs. broadcast communications
Co-creation of knowledge vs. closed knowledge systems
Effectiveness vs. efficiency
Flows of information vs. controlled distribution
Open platforms vs. walled gardens
Mutuality vs. 'It's all mine'
Cooperation vs. coordination
Engagement vs. interruption
Elective affinities vs. communities of necessity
Creative Commons vs. copyright
Bottom-up vs. top-down
Belief and values vs. positioning
Ecology vs. silos
Customer community vs. customer base

And as Gary Hamel explained in a book called The Future of Management:[146] Everyone has a voice – The tools of creativity are widely distributed – It's easy and cheap to experiment – Capability counts for more than credentials and titles – Commitment is voluntary – Power is granted from below – Authority is fluid and contingent on value-added – The only hierarchies are 'natural' hierarchies – Communities are self defining – Individuals are richly empowered with information

---

146. Gary Hamel, with Bill Breen, The Future of Management, Harvard Business School Press, 2007, p. 119.

– Just about everything is decentralised – Ideas compete on an equal footing –
It's easy for buyers and sellers to find each other – Resources are free to follow
opportunities – Decisions are peer-based. And, as many have argued over the last
decade, the network is mightier than the node.

As the reader will see further into this journey this language becomes extremely
important in framing what and how things get made. But let's take the idea of
blended reality and explore what it means.

There is no online or offline, there is only blended reality. This was the view of
William Gibson, the author and science fiction writer and inventor of the word
'cyberspace'. He wrote:

> One of the things our grandchildren will find quaintest about us is that we
> distinguish the digital from the real, the virtual from the real. In the future, that
> will become literally impossible. The distinction between cyberspace and that
> which isn't cyberspace is going to be unimaginable. When I wrote *Neuromancer*
> in 1984, cyberspace already existed for some people, but they didn't spend all
> their time there. So cyberspace was there, and we were here. Now cyberspace is
> here for a lot of us, and there has become any state of relative non-connectivity.
> There is where they don't have Wi-Fi.[147]

Having been fascinated by communication, culture, commerce, technology
and media for the best part of a decade, partly by watching my three children
adroitly navigate life through the virtual and the real so that it's an everyday
occurrence, I find Gibson's observation blindingly obvious. When I was a child,
living in a world of scarcity, I devoured any content I could get my hands on.
Media was structured, inflexible and non-portable, defined by its production and
distribution processes. Books were books, TV was TV and cinema was cinema,
but they didn't blend. I grew up in a linear world and one of scarcity, yes Captain
Scarlett, Joe 90 and Space 1999 were on the TV on Sunday afternoons for two
hours, but then it was back to the Lego or the Meccano or drawing.

My son Josef, however, was born into in a world of abundance. As a young child,
he would get me to bring his massive box of dinosaurs and put them in the lounge.
Then he would ask me to play the video *Jurassic Park*. After sitting with me for about
10 minutes, Josef would get his dinosaurs out, *Jurassic Park* became the contextual,
audio and emotional backdrop to his game play and this went on for hours. Then,
monsters from a Japanese TV programme, a medieval castle, fighter planes and a
superhero toy that we bought in a car boot sale for a dollar in California were introduced. I would watch, fascinated by this blended reality game play. Josef instinctively
knew how to bring different media together to enhance and augment his play.

---

147. William Gibson, *Rolling Stone* interview, 2007.

So we have multiple experiences in reality and virtuality and we will combine these two realms to augment and enhance our experiences. If we return to Josef, this could be a normal day for him: he wakes up in the morning, goes downstairs and turns on the television. He might watch CBeebies, or he might have a go on his Xbox 360. Then his mate Tom calls on the house phone, they are both playing the same MMORPG.[148] Much to my frustration, Josef turns on the speakerphone and I can hear the conversation throughout the house. Then the doorbell goes. More of Josef's mates arrive, they decide to play Call of Duty, Modern Warfare and – of course – there is a big group discussion around the multiplayer game; strategy and tactics. They then go and play a game of 'it' in our back garden. I look out of the window and see they are climbing up trees and all over the pergola – and diving through the laurel hedge. I run into the garden, tick them off and, sulking, they go off to the skate park. Later, I call Josef on his mobile, asking him to come home; he moans and groans and eventually he arrives with cuts and bruises. He watches some Simpsons on TV and we might play a game of basketball then he moves onto his computer to watch some more YouTube clips. Before bedtime, he gives me a big cuddle. Why is this story relevant? Because Josef's world is not one defined by an artificial sense of separation between real and virtual. In Josef's networked blended reality world, it is when there is no connectivity that he struggles. It is when he cannot simultaneously toggle between the arterial life-giving connection to information, content and experience, some of which he co-creates, that he becomes frustrated: 'Who turned the internet off?', he booms, or: 'I've run out of credit', or: 'No one wants to play with me!'

So perhaps when thinking about language the first port of call is the word 'digital'. The idea that digital is different to analogue is important as it creates a mental model thereafter as to how we frame the world. Russell Davies wrote on his blog Meet the New Schtick: 'There are a lot of people around now who have thoroughly integrated "digitalness" into their lives.'[149] To the extent that it makes as much sense to define them as digital as it does to define them as air-breathing, amen to that. However, the stuff that digital technologies have catalysed online and on screens is starting to migrate into the real world of objects. Ideas and possibilities to do with community, conversation, collaboration and creativity are turning out real things, real events, real places and real objects.

In this blended reality we can live two different but converged lives. We can connect locally – the close physical bonds are experiences that we as humans so desperately need – and we can also find fulfilment in co-creating further experiences across time and space via digital technologies. As I write this, I'm sitting in

---

Cambridge University Library, I will get lunch from the market square but I'm also connecting and collaborating with people as far away as Japan, the USA, Brazil and Finland. People read my blog all over the world, yet when I get to my house in my village, I'll kiss my partner, hug my son and water the vegetables. If I had to choose between either of these two life stories, it would be half a life. This to me is where networks and non-linearity come into their own. The ability to converge very different types of networks enhances the human condition and experience.

It's neither one nor the other. Personally I struggle with the word 'digital'. To me, it means machines that are not part of our DNA. As a consequence, we interpret 'digital' as something that strips us of our very souls, or that it is not of us and does not live in our 'real' world. And from an organisational perspective, digital becomes but another straight lines component; another silo in the silos of corporate culture, and consumer life. 'Got your digital strategy sorted?' one pro might ask another – meaning everything other than what it should be.

Another thought struck me whilst reading Kevin Kelly's book *Out of Control: The New Biology of Machines*.[150] It's that we're plugging our analogue world into the networked world, marrying engineering with evolution and adapting linear systems into something more complex. Yet at the same time, we're repurposing them, reprogramming them to perform in new simplified ways. In the same way that my son intuitively adapted his physical and virtual resources into blended play, Ben Terrett, Tom Taylor and Russell Davies decided to take stuff from the internet and print it in a newspaper format in limited editions of 1,000 copies.

I found Ben's blog post captivating, because having been trained as a typographic designer, and having even got my hands on a newspaper to think about its design at one point in my career, I have full sympathy for Ben's vertical learning journey on how to design newspapers, and I was even more fascinated with the blending of raw blogs, with all their glorious imperfections, into 500 years of printing history. 'We didn't edit any posts at all', writes Ben,

> so they're full of typos and a lot of the columns end in strange places. This is an odd phenomenon. In a real publication the sub-editor would shout for a fewer or more words to make it fit right. No sub editing here. But … the result is a tidy but raw blog-like feel that deals with presentation in a very matter-of-fact manner … We took everyone's content without asking, which we were terribly worried about. We put a big disclaimer in there … and we tried to make sure authors got copies before anyone else. But we obviously needed a way of crediting people.[151]

150. Kevin Kelly, *Out of Control: The New Biology of Machines*, Fourth Estate, 1994.
151. http://noisydecentgraphics.typepad.com/design/2009/01/things-our-friends-have-written-on-the-internet-2008-is-a-publication-thats-been-dropping-through-letter-boxes-over-the-last.html.

He need not have worried. As Siva Vaidhyanathan writes: 'In the networked world, the only thing worse than being sampled is not being sampled.'[152]

I love this idea, that ideas, information, communication flows like a torrent through communication networks, online and off. Ben points to a film that shows the printing monster that replicates his newspaper x 1,000 in a second on YouTube. And there are loads more pictures on Flickr. What should I take away from this observation? The imperative for any organisation interested in the possibilities of thriving in our non-linear world is to get to grips with some of the defining issues of our time. And I would propose that being able to be a literate and able navigator of non-linearity is the means by which we learn to adapt. We must seek comprehension and a full understanding of this non-linear world; we must not be reactive, but be proactive. To do that we must seek the knowledge as a craftsman would; we must be able to critically observe and evaluate as a craftsman would, and then act using the tools and processes as a craftsman would. This is the way to navigating non-linearity.

Ben, Tom and Russell and Josef are all fine examples of how to navigate non-linearity; they intuitively understand that they blend together the physical world and a digital one – which in its own way is a new reality. They've not got caught up with the idea of digital and analogue being separate and exclusive; they've taken the step into the networked society. If we go back to language and mental models of the world that differentiate straight lines thinking from no straight lines thinking, Euan Semple[153] brings another important perspective to this story. His view is that companies and indeed organisations will struggle to live in a non-linear world because:

- They'll think it's about technology.
- They're not prepared to deal with the friction generated from allowing their staff to connect.
- They'll assimilate it into business as usual.
- They'll try to do it in a way that 'maximises business effectiveness' without realising that it calls for a radical shift in what's seen as effective.
- They'll grind down their early adopters until they give up.
- They'll get fleeced by the IT industry for over-engineered, under-delivering solutions, think that Enterprise 2.0 failed to live up to its promise and move on to the next fad.
- They'll not be patient enough.
- It is individuals, not companies who do Enterprise 2.0.

---

152. Quoted from David Bollier, 'A Dinosaur Wades into the Tar Pit', http://onthecommons.org/content.php?id=650.
153. Euan was Director of Knowledge at the BBC for eight years.

The lesson I draw is that our emphasis should be placed upon an understanding of the fundamental needs of human beings and working from that fundamental truth, rather than attempting to force linear orthodoxies about business, business models, business process, market efficiency applied to healthcare or education and organisational structures into a world that is not premised upon that logic. Remember, networked nature is inefficient but highly effective, so we might need to design some slack back into our what we do to be a little more effective? We're decoupling from the 19th and 20th centuries philosophically, technologically, culturally and commercially. Creating a new society always demands we repurpose the old as we pull our age out of the captivity of the last one.

The power of networks

It may or may not be obvious to you that we live in what many call the networked society. Wikipedia's definition relates that the term was coined in Dutch by Jan van Dijk in his 1991 book *De Netwerkmaatschappij* and by Manuel Castells in *The Network Society*, the first part of his *The Information Age* trilogy of 1996. The Wikipedia entry states:

> Van Dijk defines the network society as a society in which a combination of social and media networks shapes its prime mode of organisation and most important structures at all levels (individual, organisational and societal). He compares this type of society to a mass society that is shaped by groups, organisations and communities ('masses') organised in physical co-presence.

I am networked through my blog, my mobile phone, the contacts on LinkedIn and my email address list, through the people I know who are physically close to me and those separated from me by vast distances. I can make video Skype calls to contacts in the US, Brazil and Australia. And this networked, wired-up world is just warming up. One billion people are today connected by the fixed internet. But already today some, five billion people will be connected to each other by a mobile device.

Everything springs from the DNA of thinking about and engaging in the world from a networked, non-linear and participatory perspective. Time can be altered, distances collapsed, the ability to share, harness, aggregate, collect connect, bundle and filter, information reconfigures everything we do, can do and will do. This networked non-linear world gives us access to information and, by delivering information faster than the speed of light, dismantles the toll roads that companies, organisations and governments have built up over centuries, leaving them equally valueless and meaningless. It is interesting to note that of the triplets that were Facebook, YouTube and Myspace, born in 2005, whilst two are doing very well thank you, one has not been quite so successful. Myspace bought by News Corp for $580m in the sale of the century was bought not because News Corp understood that the true value was in the network of networks social and otherwise that offered monetary salvation, but at the time of purchase Myspace was the biggest online audience. The straight lines purchasers then proceeded to treat the Myspace community, not as a community, but as an audience to be bought and sold as any other mainstream broadcast audience – except it wasn't. ITV's purchase of Friends Reunited is another example of commercial orthodoxies that worked once so well failing so spectacularly in a different paradigm.

How very dare you: the concussive effects of non-linearity

The output of a non-linear world is ambiguity and this generates huge problems for people and the organisations in which they work. How to act, how to be, what is acceptable are all questions that present themselves. A few years ago I was invited to magazine publisher EMAP, to talk about communities of practice, communities of passion, blogging and social communication. In my presentation I referenced a sketch by the comedian Bill Bailey about the three possible shapes of the universe (round like a ball, long and thin like a piece of tagliatelle or saddle shaped). As I told this story, I showed a picture of the Starship Enterprise next to Salvador Dali's painting of time, where watches and timepieces are slumped over braches of trees and giant rocks. I said that we had migrated from the 'comfy cardy' of our analogue world and were now existing in a universe in which we were, like the starship, navigating our way through a networked, non-linear universe. An employee then put up his hand. He said: 'How dare you come in here and tell me that my analogue world no longer exists, especially in a place that makes real magazines and real newspapers.' We exchanged points of view. But it was clear I had made him feel very uncomfortable. I might as well have stood and said, 'here be dragons'.

Later I sat with some of the employees to give them their first taste of blogging. The questions were illuminating. 'If I write something that my boss does not like, will I get fired?' was one. I could see the deep structural problems that organisations were going to face with a socially orientated networked world. The old rules simply did not apply. People comfortable in the rules by which they had worked most their adult lives were faced with ethical and commercial challenges that they seemed ill-equipped to deal with. There simply was not the literacy, to understand how to create within a new paradigm. Let's explore the idea that markets are conversations, organisations should be permeable and transparency plays a vital role when everything and everybody is connected to everything else.

This is a simple story but reflect on this, drop one of the examples I have used in

No *Straight Lines* into your organisation, and see what happens. Ask your legal department how they feel about open source (IP sharing), co-creation and Creative Commons and see what type of reaction you might get.

Socialness demands transparency

If we accept that socialness is redefining, for example, the psychology and practice of business, the running of organisations, local and big government this fact demands transparency. Transparency is the sunshine for trust to flourish and all the good things that come from that.

'My 1,000 bloggers at Sun have achieved more for this company than a billion dollar advertising campaign could ever have done', said Jonathan Schwartz, the former chief operating officer of Sun Microsystems.[154] For him, the ink devoted to the company from the developer community was more important than any other coverage. Sun experienced a sea change in its perception by that developer community via the persistent person-to-person conversations that were happening every minute of every day. That collective endeavour, that conversation, raw, authentic, visceral, dynamic is what made that sea change possible. Schwartz is not a marketing guy but he was very clear about his most important audiences and how he could get direct access to them with an authentic voice that was not in broadcast mode, was not top-down, but was premised upon a customer community that was engaged and saw a company behaving authentically.

Schwartz was talking about what I call the 'permeable organisation'. In social communication networks, one can only be open: this implies that organisations need to possess the ability to absorb dynamic flows of information, and people. This means using more transparent methods of communication from inside out and outside in. This allows networked and connected flows of learning, so that information doesn't get trapped in siloed databases, hard drives or the corner office. It also means being flexible and adaptive; more organic in thought and deed. We have to allow information to flow but we need also to think about multiple information flows of communication and ideas across borders and other boundaries and through people at speed through time and space.

'Only connect', was the dictum of E. M. Forster[155] – and this is something that socially orientated cooperative communications enable us to do in powerful ways that create deeper context and greater meaning in those rapid-fire

---

154. Jonathan Schwartz, http://redcouch.typepad.com/weblog/2005/04/interview_jonat.html.
155. E. M. Forster, *Howards End*, 1910. The full quote is: 'Only connect! That was the whole of her sermon. Only connect the prose and the passion, and both will be exalted, and human love will be seen at its height. Live in fragments no longer. Only connect, and the beast and the monk, robbed of the isolation that is life to either, will die.'

communications. That is why all employees of fashion accessory company Zappos use Twitter. Zappos believes everyone in the company is a representative of Zappos; a human face to a faceless organisation. The CEO of Zappos alone has nearly 2 million followers on Twitter. One could argue that Twitter reduces the emotional distance between businesses and their customers. I would add that it also intensifies the opportunity for context and meaning making. This one small story represents a bigger one. The rules of business are being rewritten, deconstructing the traditional notions of how one does business into a new reality: valuable human relationships where transparency rules supreme. This is also demonstrated by Best Buy, well known for its extensive and aggressive television advertising, doing a volte-face, ceasing its television assault on its customers and instead using Twitter as a means by which their customers can ask questions, and the staff in store respond to those questions.

When we only connect, we release flows of information; those flows are all about people: how they connect, and communicate; what they communicate about, how they judge the quality of that communication and how people derive and create meaning for themselves in those connections. Into this we interject, or introduce commerce, but the nature of commerce changes at certain points within this more connected and engaged universe.

The social, organisational and economic realities of a non-linear world sat uneasily with the EMAP employees. How to be, how to act and organise, how to undertake commercial enterprise were things one could see them fretting over as the erosion of their comfortable analogue world and the game-changing rules of living with networked complexity confronted them.

That complexity is manifest in so many ways for organisations; the very people that they now seek to employ represent another significant challenge, as Peter Drucker concludes in this networked world that there are no such things as conscripts there are only volunteers, he says.[156] 'Young people are coming into traditional organisations having spent the entirety of their young lives: collaborating, networking and getting stuff done in very different ways. They are confronted with an alien world of: linearity, silos, hierarchies and the ego of title.' The friction is palpable because the old organisational linear model cannot cope with, or take full advantage of, the new potential in the way we work. Unleashed is a profound transformation in the way of doing things, of getting stuff done.

Drucker's observation is supported by a massive body of evidence.
In *Modernization, Cultural Change and Democracy: The Human Development Sequence*,[157] Ronald Inglehart and Christian Welzel point out that modernisation is not linear,

156. Peter Drucker, *Economist*, November 2001.
157. Inglehart and Welzel, *Modernization, Cultural Change and Democracy*, pp. 34, 47.

and cultural change does not move in a straight line from industrialisation to the end of history. It changes direction in response to major changes in 'existential conditions', the stuff that surrounds us, and has a direct impact on our daily lives: materially, physically, culturally and spiritually. The current cultural change, they say, has generally been underestimated.

Drucker points out that the gear-change from an industrial society, to a post-industrial networked one erodes many key institutions of industrial society and in the political realm these values bring a declining respect for top-down authority, while Ingelhart and Welzel point to a growing emphasis on participation and self-expression. So we have to put things in their right context – we as a species are co-opting communication technologies and using them as agents of change. Our humanity demands to be released from the oppression of living a one dimensional life, or as one oppressed by a political regime that has scant regard for much above their vice like grip on power. That is the oxygen that fuels this extraordinary surge for change.

The turbulent end of the 20th century

In *Technological Revolution and Financial Capital: The Dynamics of Bubbles and Golden Ages*,[158] Carlota Perez points to the fact that as a new economy takes hold, as a consequence of the old one faltering, 'we go through a period that's painful, violent and wasteful'. She also observes that when new separate technologies become interlocking, they unleash a powerful set of forces that 'cleave the fabric of the economy' along fault lines. These are:

- Between new industries and mature ones.
- Between modern organisations and firms that stay attached to the old ways/
- Regionally between the strongholds of old industries and the new spaces occupied or favoured by the new industries.
- In capabilities between those trained to participate in the new technologies and those whose skills become increasingly obsolete.
- In the working population, between those who work in modern firms or live in dynamic regions and those that remain in stagnant ones and are threatened with unemployment or an uncertain future.
- Structurally between thriving new industries and the old regulatory system.
- Internationally between the fortunes of those countries that ride the wave of new technology and those left behind.

---

158. Perez, *Technological Revolutions*, p. 39.

The result Perez observes is that organisations refusing to yield to a new way of doing things increasingly confront exhaustion on multiple levels. When economies are shaken by a powerful set of new opportunities with the emergence of new technological capability, wedded to a profound shift in human needs and values, extraordinary things happen. Society, says Perez, 'is still strongly wedded to the old paradigm and its institutional framework'. In contrast:

The world of computers, flexible production and the internet has a different logic and different requirements from those that facilitated the spread of the automobile, synthetic materials, mass production, and the highway network … Suddenly, 'the old habits and regulations become obstacles, the old services and infrastructures are found wanting, the old organisations and institutions are inadequate. A new context must be created; a new 'common sense' must emerge and propagate.

In ten years working with technology, media and consumer companies, I have seen Perez's observations both close-up and personal.

Transformation: new ways of living, working and organising from around the world

So what does this all mean to us? What is out there that we can point to as examples that should inspire us, direct us and enable us? What happens when people get what they want from each other – what happens when the right information gets to the right people at the right time?

In the Democratic Republic of Congo, a young boy was brought into hospital after his arm had been ripped off by a hippopotamus while fishing. The arm was gangrenous and badly infected and the prognosis was that he would die in three days without medical help. Unfortunately, the boy had very little of his arm left and required a special type of amputation – a removal of the shoulder socket and the collarbone that results in enormous blood loss. David Nott, the doctor who looked at the boy, knew what had to be done but didn't have the skills or knowledge to undertake the task and had never undertaken this specialist operation. But he did know a specialist in the UK who performs this type of amputation. He contacted Professor J Meirion Thomas at the London Marsden Hospital, who agreed to send amputation advice via SMS text messages to Dr Nott. In a basic operating theatre, with only one litre of blood to replace blood loss, Dr Nott performed the operation, under the instruction of a colleague thousands of miles away in London. The young boy survived and made a full recovery.

Networked economics in Bangladesh

Iqbal Quadir had a vision to create universal access to a telephone service in Bangladesh and increase self-employment opportunities for its rural poor. In 1993, he started a New York company named Gonofone, which later became the launch-pad for GrameenPhone. At that time, Bangladesh had one of the lowest penetrations of telephones on the planet, with only one phone for every 500 people, but the GrameenPhone project distributed 25 million phones into Bangladeshi society. Today there are 100 times as many phones, or one per five people. Just as Quadir had envisioned, this decentralised connectivity has increased productivity. Economist Jeffrey Sachs says GrameenPhone 'opened the world's eyes to expanding the use of modern telecommunications technologies in the world's poorest places'.[159] Without such connectivity, you just can't get stuff done. With mobile phone connectivity, farmers maximise their profits by getting real-time prices at distant markets; shepherds can call a vet, or order medicine. One study concluded that the total lifetime cost of an additional phone, including the cell tower and switching gear, was about $2,000 but each phone enabled $50,000 of increased productivity. And the poorer the country is, the greater the increase is in wealth from connectivity.

In Africa, women in villages club together to buy a mobile phone, with which they can check the market price of goats before they set off to market: the first time that these women have not been regularly fleeced by middlemen. In India, fishermen who exist precariously through fishing now use mobile phones to ring ashore to match supply and demand and the best market price.

Networked economics in India: the e-Choupal coming to a village near you

Once a week Sanjay would leave his rural farm early and make the two-hour journey to his local market town. Over tea and something to eat he would then relax with other farmers and discuss issues of the day in a Choupal, a place where farmers traditionally meet to share information. Today, there exists the e-Choupal,[160] which has been designed to tackle the challenges posed by the unique features of Indian agriculture: fragmented farms, weak infrastructure and the involvement of numerous middle men. The e-Choupal unshackles the potential of Indian farmers like Sanjay, who has been trapped in a six-part mephisto waltz of intractable dilemmas; they are unable to take risks, so they cannot invest, which means they cannot increase production; this puts them in a weak position to compete, their

159. Jeffrey Sachs, *The End of Poverty: Economic Possibilities for Our Time*, Penguin, 2005, p. 26.
160. [1] http://www.itcportal.com/agri_exports/e-choupal_new.htm – top. [2] http://en.wikipedia.org/wiki/E-Choupal. [3] http://www.slideshare.net/ajaypanandikar/echaupal-case-study.

margins are low, so they are unable to increase the commercial value of the business. This made him and the Indian agribusiness sector globally uncompetitive, despite available rich and abundant natural resources. It is believed that the e-Choupal model can enhance the competitiveness of Indian agriculture and be the means by which Indian farmers can begin to deliver higher productivity, higher incomes, enlarged capacity for farmer risk management, larger investments and higher quality of produce.

Today Sanjay can travel to a village internet kiosk managed by local farmers – called *sanchalak*. Here he can along with his agricultural community have access to up-to-date information in his local language on the weather, market prices and knowledge on scientific farm practices. The e-Choupal also facilitates the information that all farmers need and enables farmers to sell their produce minus middlemen. Decision-making is now information-based.

Real-time information and customised knowledge provided by 'e-Choupal' enhances the ability of farmers like Sanjay to take the right decisions and to better match their farm output with market demand. The e-Choupal also enables farmers to buy seed and fertilisers in bulk, providing them access to high-quality raw materials from established and reputed manufacturers at fair prices. As a direct marketing channel, virtually linked to the 'mandi' system for price discovery, 'e-Choupal' eliminates wasteful intermediation and multiple handling. Thereby it significantly reduces transaction costs.

Launched in June 2000, 'e-Choupal' has become the largest initiative among all internet-based interventions in rural India. 'e-Choupal' services today reach out to over 4 million farmers growing a range of crops – soya bean, coffee, wheat, rice, pulses and shrimps – in more than 40,000 villages through 6,500 kiosks across ten states. I wonder if Sanjay sees his world within the context of offline and online. Or does he just stand in the flow of information happy that his life has been transformed? It was a thousand years after the Romans had left Britain that the country's fledgling and burgeoning press and publishing industry began to invest in hard roads – why? Simply to ensure that newspapers, books and letters were dispatched with the maximum speed. The speed and distribution of information drives economies. As more capability gets built into the networks of communication networks mobile and otherwise, borders of trade become irrelevant, those toll roads in which in a previous time were used as a means of control to deliver power are now obsolete. When Ezra Pound first gazed upon on Manhattan's evening skyline lit up by Edison's networked electricity, he looked out, transfixed, 'Here is our poetry, as we have pulled down the stars to our will', he wrote.[161] Perhaps Sanjay might find

---

161. Nicholas Carr, *The Big Switch: Rewiring the World from Edison to Google*, Norton, 2008, p. 96.

words of poetry to describe the effect of living in a world transformed by networked communications that in a very similar way broke the shackles that limited his horizons and possibilities.

So what are the implications of for us all? Nicholas Carr in his book The Big Switch[162] says we need to understand:

- Greater global reach.
- Greater customisation.
- Reduced barriers to entry.
- The end of scale.
- Easier entry into adjacent markets.
- Greater specialisation.
- Greater innovation and experimentation
- Greater information transparency.
- Greater organisational complexity.
- Faster turnaround times and greater speed to market.
- Greater competitive intensity and disruption of existing markets.

Collectively these represent a disruptive capability that places great stress upon existing organisations.

Economies as complex dynamic systems

Our non-linear world leaves nothing untouched, and it is time to break some taboos that in fact have been used to justify western market economies. Why is this important? Because in understanding how markets and economies truly function, and how they relate to comprehending the dynamics of complexity, we add to the knowledge that our designers and craftsmen and women will need to deliver good things to the world

Whilst in the latter half of the 21st century, economists were still working on their equilibrium system of economic theory, physicists, chemists and biologists became, according to Eric Beinhocker in The Origin of Wealth,[163] increasingly interested in systems that were far from equilibrium, systems that were in fact dynamic and complex and that never settled in a state of rest. Beinhocker calls this complexity economics.

Complexity economics has some key characteristics that we must consider, in Out of Control: The New Biology of Machines,[164] Kevin Kelly identifies the key traits of

162. Carr, The Big Switch.
163. Beinhocker, The Origin of Wealth, p. 18.
164. Kelly, Out of Control, p. 200.

the emergent network economy. Some are relevant to the following real life stories, and begin to flesh out what Beinhocker argues are the core components of economics in a networked world. Kelly identifies some key characteristics of advanced living in the networked society. They are:

Distributed Cores: The boundaries of a company blur to obscurity; companies, from one-person to Fortune 500, become societies of work centres distributed in ownership and geography.

Adaptive Technologies: Technologies than connect and also can adapt to an evolving world will take centre stage

Flex Manufacturing: Smaller numbers of items can be produced in smaller time periods with smaller equipment. Modular equipment, no standing inventory and computer-aided design shrink product development cycles from years to weeks.

Mass Customisation: Individually customised products produced on a mass scale. All products are manufactured to personal specifications, but at mass production prices.

Industrial Ecology: Closed-loop, no-waste, zero-pollution manufacturing; products designed for disassembly; and a gradual shift to biologically compatible techniques. Increasing intolerance for transgressions against the rule of biology.

Co-evolved Customers: Customers are trained and educated by the company, and then the company is trained and educated by the customer. Products in a network culture become updatable franchises that co-evolve in continuous improvement with customer use. Think software updates and subscriptions. Companies become clubs or user groups of co-evolving customers. A company cannot be a learning company without also being a teaching company.

And what does all that mean? According to Kelly the 'dynamics of a networked economy are created by the non-linear interactions of billions of people on a daily basis', 6+ billion humans are being connected up to and across each other, evolving into vast complex webs of relationships, where people are increasingly going to each other to get what they want rather than through institutions (any flavour take your pick) – this in fact has deep political and commercial implications. All matter, big and small, says Kelly, 'will be linked into vast webs of networks at many levels. Without grand meshes there is no life, intelligence, and evolution; with networks there are all of these and more.'[165] And it seems to me that this process is now set in motion. How many companies or organisations

---

165. Kelly, *Out of Control*, p. 201.

understand or want to understand Beinhocker's complexity economic theory or Kelly's 6 point constellation which is proving to both prescient and prophetic? Academic twaddle which pragmatists can ignore, or something that already is manifest in people's everyday lives? Kelly and Beinhocker present a huge ideological and cultural challenge from companies and organisations built on assumptions and orthodoxies that have nothing to do with complexity, co-evolved customers, flex manufacturing, adaptive technologies, distributed cores and industrial ecologies.

Super-global and hyper local networked economics

In *Crossing the Chasm*,[166] Geoffrey Moore defines a market as 'a set of actual or potential customers, for a given set of products or services who have a common set of needs or wants, and, who reference each other when making a buying decision'. The story of Lauren Luke subscribes to Moore's definition and to the idea of a 21st century reformation woman learning to make her way in the world. Lauren, 27 years of age and a single mother at age 15 who lived with her own mother in Tyneside, Newcastle, wondered how she was ever going to make a living, in a city with few opportunities for a single mother with few qualifications. Yet Lauren did have a passionate interest in the applying of makeup, inspired by her love of pop stars – and she was very good at it. She set up blogsite panacea81.com and a YouTube channel. Today Lauren is a global superstar, writes a column for the *Guardian* and has cosmetic companies lining up because she has the special sauce, global reach, a worldwide audience with a common set of needs, wants and authenticity. A video posted a little over a year ago, demonstrating Leona Lewis' makeup in the video for her song 'Bleeding Love', has been watched more than 2.3 million times. As an interview in the *Guardian* reveals, 'Her appeal is explained by her unaffected amateurism and great charm. Luke doesn't edit her videos – she doesn't know how – and she is painfully open about her unhappy school years, when she was bullied mercilessly, and her crippling lack of confidence.'[167]

How did Luke do it? She simply began selling makeup on eBay, posting photos of herself wearing it. Her buyers started asking how to achieve the looks she was creating, which prompted Luke to create a YouTube makeup tutorial channel. Panacea81 has attracted 56 million views and more than 280,000 subscribers since her first upload on 22 July 2007, while Luke is a YouTube site partner.

166. Geoffrey Moore, *Crossing the Chasm: Marketing and Selling Technology Products to Mainstream Customers*, revised edn, Capstone, 1998.

167. Lauren Luke: 'Just steady your little finger and practise', *Guardian*, 30 January 2009. http://www.guardian.co.uk/lifeandstyle/2009/jan/30/lauren-luke-youtube-makeup.

Luke is representative of Kelly's, Moore's and Carr's predictions, and her life has been transformed as a result of the opportunities offered by networked connectivity and people getting what they want from each other. Moreover, her identity shines through what she does. She has written herself into a successful commercial career and into existence as a person. Today, real life does not follow the straight lines rule.

Girlswalker – a mass niche community of interest

The other aspect of non-linearity is that time becomes fluid and collapses distances. This has two consequences: it allows us to find and connect to the things that we're most interested in, giving individuals access to a universe of content and information, and entrepreneurs are able to create value by attracting mass niche communities of interest, passionate about fishing, fashion, cars because we are all joined up by communication networks, and we are all on a quest of psychological self-determination – to create our meaning making framework, reaching out to the things that mean the most to us.

In Japan, Girlswalker is a mobile fashion retailing business with more than 7 million participants. The site is treated like a magazine and gets more than 1.4 billion page views per month. Each mini-magazine links to the mobile home page and users are encouraged not only to subscribe but also to publish their own writing via a simple mobile format. Yet, in 2003 Girlswalker CEO and President, Fumitaro Ohama said: 'Two years ago, everybody laughed at us when we went looking for partners for Girlswalker. They said there was no way consumers would buy goods over the keitai (mobile).'

Xavel, the company that owns Girlswalker, has a return shopping rate of 45%, while Girlswalker is the number one Japanese mobile portal site, and it's all been done by word of mouth. Girlswalker fills stadiums of 40,000 girls and the models that walk down the catwalk are from the Girlswalker community – people embrace what they create. Girlswalker is based upon relevancy, participation and commercial application, enabled by communication networks. Interestingly when analysing its sales figures, the larger proportion of sales are made up from girls that live not in Tokyo, or Nagasaki or Kyoto, but more rural areas, where they don't have access to the types of shops that exist in large urban areas. These young women can feel they are part of the cut and thrust of fashion and belong to a vibrant and dynamic community. Markets are conversations, and markets therefore thrive when there is a rich and constant flow of communication.

So what makes this particular marketplace successful? First, one cannot ignore the participatory and networked nature of the Girlswalker business model that delivers significant financial benefits. Secondly, Girlswalker is premised upon the interlocking of four key components: commerce, culture, community and connectivity. What this means is that value is created not just in the purchase of goods, it is co-created. The ownership of Girlswalker resides in the hearts and minds of the young women that want to belong to Girlswalker. Yes, they buy stuff, but they also create a community which generates its own culture premised upon self-expression, self-esteem, fashion knowledge, peer group recognition, shopping satisfaction, and, of course, everyone is connected to everyone else, creating an intensity of social communication. Thirdly, Girlswalker illustrates my point that there is no online or offline, only blended reality. The Girlswalker community is made possible by co-joining physical and digital connectivity. The other lessons are that members of the community are able to easily interface, connect, engage with one other. The ability to purchase is made simple via the mobile device or online. Finally, Fumitaro Ohama stepped outside conventional and accepted truths of retail. He created something unique, perhaps extraordinary, however it was designed, it was innovative and it was most certainly transformational.

Christopher Billich of Infinita, an authority on the Japanese mobile industry, writes that mobile commerce is already a very big business in Japan, with the value of physical goods sold via mobile online shopping totalling JPY 258bn in 2006. Online retail giant Rakuten generates 25% of its turnover through mobile sales.[168] For carriers, there is good money to be made from the increased data traffic on their networks. And since teenagers access the internet from their phones much more than from PCs these days, for fashion retailers a mobile presence is absolutely vital to staying competitive. By far the most active group of mobile shoppers are young women, which results in fashion items being the most popular category. More than half of mobile shoppers in Japan bought clothes or accessories via their handset last year. One must conclude that the commercial challenge in today's world is to create stuff that inspires people that they want to be part of, and share with their friends. It's dead simple, but it seems there is a lot of catching up to do. Girlswalker is 7 years old, yet how many people from the fashion retail industry who are facing tough years ahead have studied Girlswalker?

The car company as a community

Vineet Nayar writes:

> In the aftermath of the financial crisis, the world's leaders are trying to create Capitalism 2.0. As companies wade through these challenging times, I see a distinct shift towards another new paradigm: Collaboration 2.0. There's

168. Alan Moore, 'The glittering allure of the mobile society', commissioned by Microsoft, November 2008, p. 16.

growing recognition everywhere of the need for corporations to collaborate with government, with customers, with NGOs, with stakeholders–and even with competition. In order to survive, business requires the cover of a collaborative ecosystem that will probably render obsolete traditional views of competition.[169]

There is no doubt we are migrating to a new economic model that no longer aspires to coordinate its workforce and supply chain, but to cooperate with all. Local Motors is perhaps one of the most comprehensive examples of a revolutionary approach to the design, engineering, manufacturing, sales and marketing of cars.

Let's look at the problem: the automotive industry struggles to match supply and demand; it only works at massive scale; and it constantly works at overcapacity in relation to demand. As a consequence, it is highly inefficient, unwieldy and sucks on massive amounts of that precious stuff: cash. In December 2008, the boss of Fiat, Sergio Marchionne, predicted that the economic crisis would finally force the world's car industry to confront profit-destroying overcapacity and change its broken business model. He also thought that by the end of 2010, consolidation would result in there being only six high-volume carmakers left in the world. The automotive industry estimates overcapacity in Europe in 2010 will be around 7 million units, or 30%. But if we look to the open source networked model, we can see a new paradigm emerging that's more efficient, kinder to the planet and even more effective.

John 'Jay' Burton Rogers, the co-founder of a company called Local Motors, comes from Flint, Michigan, which was once part of the humming engine room of America's automotive manufacturing industry. In a conversation we had, Jay tells me about the economic and resulting human tragedy that unfolded as car manufacturing cities like Detroit and Flint collapsed, unable to compete and adjust in a changing world. In fact from the outside Detroit looks like a third world country in a first world one. The Packard Plant, a 40-acre site built in 1912, where reinforced concrete was first used in the construction of any building, designed by the legendry Albert Kahn, now looks more like it belongs in a war zone. It is a sad metaphor of what happens when you build and commit to building without adaptability in mind. Now Detroit sits on the verge of bankruptcy, beset by political scandal, a declining population, troubled industry, high crime and unemployment rates and, according to who you speak to, has one of the worst school systems in the country. The city's unemployment and poverty rates are at an all-time high, the city built for 2 million people now has a population of less than 800,000.

Jay's grandfather had been the owner of the legendary Indian Motorcycle company. Jays says his grandfather gave him the disease, the love of all things on two or four wheels that had an engine in it. That passion combined with his

---

169. Vineet Nayar, 'The collaboration imperative', Harvard Business School Publishing, 24 September 2009. http://www.bloomberg.com/apps/harvardbusiness?sid=Ha8c394617e42d5dcb95f59670c5d1cc3.

profound experience in the Marine Corps compelled him to want to give something back. In a note to me, Jay writes:

> I felt the friends I lost in the Marines risked dying in vain if we could not strive for a more positive, engaged worldview on business and products. I needed to know that the America they died for was growing, evolving, and had a chance to be better than the Greatest Generation.

Jay's vision was to reinvigorate the automotive industry by taking an alternative approach to how cars were designed, made and sold. He realised that one needed to decentralise manufacturing, increase agility and reprogramme manufacturing networks to better manage supply and demand. He put himself through Harvard and then co-founded Local Motors.

At Harvard, Jay's focus on sustainability grew. After studying many car companies and principles from leading sustainability experts, he shaped Local Motors to have long-term, sustainable profit potential in addition to an eco-friendly production process and end product. Local Motors now has the world's largest community of car designers and engineers who embrace open collaboration to develop innovative cars for under-served, passionate enthusiast communities. In one year 44,000 designs were submitted to Local Motors, and 3,600 innovators have shared their knowledge and insights. The cars are built in regional micro-factories, which are a groundbreaking fusion of advanced, small-volume manufacturing and unprecedented ownership models. This open business model is significantly more capital-efficient than traditional automotive companies and participation is driven primarily through low-cost digital communication tools and platforms, some they have built, but these are plugged into both Facebook and Twitter. If you go to the company's Facebook page, follow Ariel (who runs the Local Motors community) on Twitter, read the blogs or look at the emergent community evolving around Local Motors, I think it's fair to say that Jay and his team are realising the dream. In a recent presentation, Jay said: 'We've been developing a car with our community for 1.5 years and then we're asked when are we going to start our marketing. I say: "exactly".'

Local Motors is open and collaborative with its community and customers. 'We don't guess; we ask and we collaborate', says Jay. 'I wanted to see if we could apply the Creative Commons and open source principle to our business, and we have proven that it works.' Jay adds that, through the process of co-innovation and co-creation, Local Motors get more meaningful designs and more meaningful cars. The economic benefit, he says, is that the $30bn US specialist car market could easily grow to $100bn. And he makes this point about local: 'What's cool in Boston is not cool in New York', he says, stressing that companies need to be engaged with their local community so they can be involved in a constant feedback loop.

Jay is of the view that deep context is the only way to build a sustainable, flexible business. 'This experience is engaging with our customers to feel a deep connection', he says. 'It becomes an investment in the community and car which is the product of their personal effort.'

The economic benefits are that Local Motors cars are developed five times faster than traditional cars, and with 100 times less capital. 'You can't be nimble if you have to tool big', says Jay. This is accomplished through open collaboration and development, utilising existing components, and decentralising the manufacturing process, and once again manufacturing and sales are brought together. Jay and his team have done their homework; Local Motors can reach a passionate and engaged international community via networked communications, but it's not just an online community. The regional micro-factories provide an engaged experience for customers to come together as a community to learn about cars. And in fact it is mandatory that when you buy a Local Motors car you the buyer are part of the build process, the reason being that research shows people are far less likely to default on the payments as they essentially co-created and built an emotional bond with their car. This is an agile, lightweight, flexible and adaptive business manufacturing model, enabling Local Motors to incorporate new and proven technology as it emerges; for example Tim Thomas the Local Motors CTO was telling me when we met at MIT that the company is now using 3D printers as part of its build process.

This is how the process works as Local Motors describe it:

- Vote for the designs you want. If you are a designer, you can upload your own. Either way, you help choose which designs are developed and built by the Local Motors community. Vote for competition designs, checkup critiques or portfolio designs.
- Open development, sort of like open source. Once there is enough support for any single design, Local Motors will develop it openly. That means that you not only choose which designs you want to drive, you get to help develop them – every step of the way.
- Choose the locale during the development process, help choose where the design should be made available. Local Motors is not a big car company, we are local. The community chooses car designs with local regions in mind; where will this design fit best? You tell us. We make it happen.
- Build your Local Motors vehicle. Then, once the design and engineering is fully developed you can go to the Local Motors micro-factory and build your own – with our help, of course.
- Drive your Local Motors car, the one you helped design and build, home.

For me, there are important insights we can draw from the Local Motors story. And perhaps the biggest one is that one can achieve multiple goals, by designing the business and the process in a certain type of way. Jay's understatement that building a car company is a stretch belies the true nature of the task. It is how one frames a problem, based upon certain knowledge and then by applying that knowledge into action, that the impossible becomes possible. It seems the company is forever in Beta, constantly iterating, adapting and evolving. Type in this URL (http://www.local-motors.com/rallyFighter.php?p=myRallyFighter) and you will find the Local Motors Rally Fighter car buyers community represented by a Google map and videos of those people buying the Rally Fighter, a community of passionate car enthusiasts (evangelists) being connected up to each other. Local Motors feels dynamic, authentic, driven by belief it is a child of its time.

All its CAD data is online, so Local Motors shares its knowledge under a Creative Commons licence, once seen as a wild experiment by more established players. Local Motors finds itself the subject of great interest from major car companies who seem to be scratching their heads on how to survive. These are the takeaways that make this company so fascinating.

- It fundamentally changes the relationship to supply and demand by rethinking and redesigning the process from conception to production.
- It harnesses a distributed knowledge network which is both hyperlocal and superglobal.
- It makes excellent use of open source and Creative Commons in the business.
- It makes a clear point of being green and being sustainable.
- It innovates through engaging enthusiasts who are passionate about car design and engineering. In one year 44,000 designs were submitted to Local Motors, and 3,600 innovators have shared their knowledge and insights.
- It is high velocity: this company can design and build a car five times faster than a conventional manufacturer can.
- It uses competition as both risk mitigator and innovation accelerator.
- It is lightweight; built to be adaptive and flexible.
- It is less capital-intensive than its conventional peers. Normally, it takes $200m to take a car from conception to full-scale production. Local Motors achieved the same result with $1.5m. That is 100 times less capital.
- It fosters regional development. Rather than building another car plant, Local Motors is building micro-factories, so that money flows into local communities, and creates local jobs.
- Finally, learning is seen as a constant daily process, and so the organisation is a learning organisation: learning to evolve and to grow and learning what works and what doesn't.

Local Motors is a great example of a lightweight, flexible and adaptive system that can work at velocities that are unprecedented, and where sociability is embedded into the very fabric of the process. The company is built around community; it is also a media platform in its own right, and it has identified mutuality as a business strategy. In fact it gets one to question the nature of what an organisation looks like in the 21st century, this one being less machine-like and more like a village. People have lived and worked in villages since the dawn of civilisation. The corporation, writes Charles Handy, is a youthful concept, little more than a century old. 'One could argue, too, that the notion of a lively village, with its unabashed humanity, is a more appropriate way to look at what the corporation should be in the 21st century than the constrained and impersonal entity it has been.'[170] As Handy wrote in *Gods of Management: The Changing Work of Organisations*: 'Villages are small and personal and their inhabitants have names, characters and personalities. What more appropriate concept on which to base our institutions of the future than the ancient organic social unit whose flexibility and strength sustained human society through millennia?'[171] But such innovations are not confined to the motor industry.

170. 'The paradox of Charles Handy', *Strategy and Business*, http://www.strategy-business.com/article/03309?gko=f3861.

171. Charles Handy, *Gods of Management: The Changing Work of Organisations*, new edn of 3rd revised edn, Arrow Books, 1995.

Funding innovation: democratising financial capital

GDP = Population x Total Factor Productivity, so TFP = Innovation. Therefore the only way GDP is going to grow without population growth is the need to remain innovative.

Ah, the thorny old issue of innovation, where does it come from? How do you incentivise it? How do you fund it? And how do you harvest it? I have become convinced that innovation and entrepreneurship are the key to the GDP question, particularly as we see larger, established companies failing faster. So what takes their place? The truth is this, that 80% of growth, or regeneration, new jobs and inward investment are generated by new companies. Not that you would think that from reading the financial papers. It is these people through entrepreneurial endeavour that are largely building the future, rather than trying to protect the past.

And, of course, innovation needs to be funded. For the last 50 years a large chunk of those funds have come from the venture capital community. But, in the same way that other parts of the industrial model are flagging, VC funding is no different. The G04Venture monthly report, March 2010, stated that 'Professional venture capital funds have become less relevant to the financing of innovation for the time being', and that 'the market is wondering whether professional VC managers add sufficient value'. The report also pointed that as VC funding became less venture focused, read 'risk averse' and 'poor deal flow', many entrepreneurs have had to become 'creative' in terms of fund-raising to feed the innovation machine. In fact more money is raised through friends and family than through conventional VC funds.

So it does not surprise me that when faced with a form of institutional failure, in this instance, funding for start-ups, the ability to access funding and engage in an entrepreneurial community is also being redefined. In the same way that Local Motors challenges the economic and organisational orthodoxies of the automotive industry – a company called GrowVC is doing the same thing with funding. Although The Grow Venture Community has been described as the kiva[172] of start-ups. Grow Venture Community is better defined it as a platform and ultimately an ecosystem that enables a community of practice to come together, to share knowledge and information, and in so doing to accelerate innovation. We envisaged that although physical place is still important, the ability to connect people, skills, knowledge and money to each other was what made GrowVC special.

---

172. http://eu.techcrunch.com/2010/02/15/grow-vc-launches-aiming-to-become-the-kiva-for-tech-startups/. Kiva enables people globally to invest what is to them small amounts of money – £10.00, £25.00 upwards – in people who live and work in areas of the world that previously would not have access to any form of entrepreneurial funding, Africa, Bangladesh, the Philippines etc., and Kiva has been hugely successful, transforming the lives of people; it has raised some $100m to invest in entrepreneurs around the world in emerging economies.

GrowVC is a funding model for technology start-ups which draws financial investment and intellectual capability from a global network that forms a specific community. As the company themselves say, the next Silicon Valley is not a location, it is a platform and community on the internet, that wants to be open, collaborative, ethical, transparent and highly effective. Not unlike other companies that have harnessed tools and technologies to remake their world afresh. And it works like this: those that join get access to a global service for entrepreneurs, funders and experts. Joining GrowVC, and the basic features, such as building a person profile, are free. Premium features come with subscriptions ranging from $20 to $140 per month, depending on how much money the start-up company is seeking or how much the investor is looking to invest. For unlimited service investments, the monthly subscription fee is $90 per month. The fund is aimed at start-ups that need $10,000 to $1m USD.

100% of the membership fee feeds into a community fund that invests back into 'promising start-ups' which are members of the platform. GrowVC makes its money by investment transaction fees and ROIs. In many ways GrowVC supports Paul Romer's observation that 'the most important ideas are, ideas about how to support the production and transmission of other ideas'.[173]

The fund is managed by GrowVC but all the investment decisions are left to members who determine how to invest their portion of the fund into other start-up companies that they feel have the most potential. The most successful decision-makers get financially rewarded when the community fund begins earning a return on investment. Like all good ideas, they can be divisive. Reading the range of comments generated by a post at TechCrunch, some felt that GrowVC was robbery in all but another name, whilst others were cheerleaders for offering up alternative ways of raising funding.

With these comments, a gentleman wanted to know if the service was available to entrepreneurs based in Africa, to another, who flamed the entire idea. From my own personal experience, I have every sympathy in seeking out an alternative solution to entrepreneurialism and fund raising, as I believe it to be necessary. GrowVC also challenges the orthodoxies of a linear world, for example the legal framework of investment and how it is controlled. Each country has its own laws on investing, so what happens when the company straddles multiple countries and continents? There is a growing awareness that funding by micro-payments from individuals that form a virtual investment community has become a significant trend, as a space and place (virtual silicon valley), so that people interested in entrepreneurism can find each other. These new frameworks for organising will begin to

---

173. Paul Romer *Economic Growth* in the *Fortune Encyclopaedia of Economics*, ed. David R. Henderson, New York Time Warner Books, 1993, p. 33.

ultimately challenge the conventions of who funds who and who benefits from that transaction. Then the question arises: can the velocity of innovation and commercial development be increased as a consequence of a new type of investment ecosystem?

One way this is being co-evolved is through an open approach to the business itself. GrowVC already have an early version of an open API for other companies to develop applications and services, which enable the development of new funding and business models.

In its first year of operation GrowVC had over 9,000 members from 200 countries, approximately 1,400 start-ups, total investment of $20m and deals were done. It launched the first local network at the end of 2010 in India and within 12 weeks already had 1,000 members combined with the cooperation of local angel networks and VCs; and it launched a China chapter shortly afterwards, in Chinese of course, a Spanish version platform is in the works. And GrowVC finds itself constantly approached by individuals who, although working within the VC community, and are well paid, feel stifled. GrowVC like Local Motors offers them a way to put something back into an industry they still feel passionate about, but which they feel can no longer adequately serve the market it was created for. So from a connected community perspective, the platform and business help build teams and, through its ecosystem and community, to find partners, people and other actors who can play a meaningful role in the life of a company start-up.

There are something in the region of 70 companies that offer a crowdfunding service which represents an ecosystem that has emerged over the last five years. This ecosystem will grow and is going to increasingly offer a viable alternative to funding entrepreneurial endeavour; Europe, Latin America, North America, the BRIC countries all have at least one or two funding platforms that represent the evolution from investing via orthodox venture funds to an entire open entrepreneurial ecosystem. And as the ecosystems start to link up to each other, they will evolve into an entirely new industry standard. Networked investing is simply a response to the failure of an outdated way of doing things, and it may well be that people are ready for it. GrowVC and other players represent a fundamental redesign of how VC funding happens now and in the future.

Democratising financial capital

In this process of the democratisation of venture funding, and the creation of a new innovation ecosystem (to accelerate deal flow, that creates more companies, that creates more jobs), it has been reported back to me that an increasing number of Americans believe this could be the re-invention of the American Dream. This is achieved by breaking down the barriers between who can and who cannot engage in wealth and value creation as an entrepreneurial activity. In the same way that debates raged a few years back about who had the right to create journalism, film, books, photography, etc., 'the professionals vs. amateurs', companies like GrowVC offer the opportunity where anyone and everyone could be or should be funding start-ups. Although funding entrepreneurship has always been defined as high risk, the recent track record of our entire financial system makes that seem like an oxymoron. Such is the pressure for change that the Wall Street Journal[174] reported that,

> Federal securities regulators are weighing demands to make it easier for fast-growing companies to use social networks such as Facebook and Twitter to raise money by tapping thousands of investors for very small amounts of shares. The Securities and Exchange Commission is looking at adapting its rules to encourage Internet-age techniques for small companies raising capital. The issue is part of a wider review by the agency into whether to ease decades-old constraints on share issues by closely held companies. If all goes well, small companies can raise cash relatively cheaply, while investors get a stake in an innovative business with limited downside risk. The SEC is now considering calls to relax its rules to make it easier for companies to use crowd-funding without having to undergo the full panoply of disclosure and other legal requirements required by the securities laws for share issues.

If countries, regions, cities and towns want to accelerate innovation, if they want to give entrepreneurs the best possible chance to succeed, then they need a platform like GrowVC, which is best described not by the misnomer of 'crowdfunding', but by a global community of practice which is redefining the possibilities of entrepreneurship. Through local chapters in China and India, for example, early stage entrepreneurs that would never before gain access to global information and knowledge can now do so. It is but one small example of understanding the possibilities of being an open platform and ecosystem rather than a closed one.

Microfinance in London – a leg up for the excluded

Companies like GrowVC, have challenged the fixed orthodoxies of the business of venture capital; it is indeed a necessary response to the needs of entrepreneurship, jobs and growth. But you still need money to invest, and although we talk about money and banking every day, and we are assailed with until recently anyway an unremitting avalanche of offers for credit and loans, it's a curious fact that over 3 billion people cannot take out a loan from a bank, and of course that locks many

---

174. 'SEC books up for internet age', Wall Street Journal, 9 April 2011.

people into a life sentence of poverty. Faisel Rahman comes from a Bangladeshi family and lives in Dalston, London. Inspired by working with the World Bank in Bangladesh on a large scale (in terms of capital invested) microfinance programme, he asked this question: why was it that the poorest people in Britain – the people most in need of some financial assistance, most in need of fair rates of interest – were also the people who were denied access to bank accounts? This is a land where people at the edges of society that banks deem untouchable can only get finance from loan sharks or money lenders at rates between 600 to 2500%+. Six million adults in Britain do not have access to a bank account; of these at least four million each week borrow from 'doorstep lenders'.

Tim Adams writes:[175]

Rahman spent a lot of time talking his idea through with people in the financial industry. He was told that microfinance might work in the developing world but it would never work here. That the poor would not save. That bad debtors would never become prompt repayers. That he could never develop the idea at scale. In the face of this scepticism Rahman obtained a grant for a few thousand pounds from the overdraft of a charitable trust and secured it against his credit card. He then opened the doors of Fair Finance to business.

Such resistance does not surprise me, it's a little like my friend who could not understand that his iPod could play on shuffle, and hence struggled with listening to Harry Potter as a consequence.

More significantly, it demonstrates the system failure of banking; spreadsheets cannot deal with the unpredictability, the messiness, of human lives. It avoids what the system perceives as unnecessary risk. What Rahman is doing is looking at alternative relationships between banks and the communities they serve.

Not only has Rahman helped people get out of appalling debt, which requires more than the average input someone would get at a local branch of any UK high street bank, he has helped over 150 entrepreneurs start businesses that otherwise would have been impossible. And in fact he is expanding his business to 8–10 more sites in London. Default rate on loans average at 6% – interest rates run at 35% but that is still lower than credit card companies. Rahman has demonstrated that his business works, and can even provide investors in the bank with a modest rate of return. Can the business ultimately grow from a small-scale operation into something that could have a real impact on the lives of many disadvantaged in the UK? As of yet, we don't know – but Rahman demonstrates an alternative, more lightweight, more compassionate, humanistic view of the world.

---

175. Tim Adams, 'Microloans in Hackney', *Observer*, 21 March. 2010http://www.guardian.co.uk/society/2010/mar/21/microfinance-faisel-rahman-muhammad-yunus.

Rahman is not the only person trying to find a means to break the self-perpetuating cycle of money, banking, loan and sharking, with all its consequences. Maria Nowak has been working for nearly 20 years in France to develop what the European Commission argues is perhaps the most successful microcredit organisation in Europe[176] focusing on helping people out of exclusion. ADIE, the organisation she created, is the 'association for the right to economic initiative'. Rather than using the benefits system that supports those that fall out of the market economy, the ADIE model looks at how the excluded are enabled to return and contribute to society, not as dependants but as wealth creators themselves. I like the idea that you treat people not as victims of society, but with the potential to give something back.

In 2003 ADIE had 5,000 clients, which by 2006 had grown to over 9,000, and as of 2007 it has 22 regional offices, 119 branches across metropolitan France, 350 staff members and 1,100 volunteer mentors. This rapid growth has been achieved without compromise on who they serve and why, if anything, ADIE has gone deeper into the needs of the socially excluded. For ADIE, microcredit develops human capital by building self-confidence and entrepreneurship. Now what high street bank claims to do that?

How markets thrive: commerce, culture, community, connectivity

In redesigning companies to be more sustainable, we must move away from the idea that markets are places where companies produce and consumers consume – or you read, but you don't write. There once endeth the relationship. In the context of a world where socialness and social communication is affecting the commercial effectiveness and even livelihoods of companies, where innovative companies have already started to accommodate the inherent nature of people, we need to draw upon some important ideas as to what makes all this work. It's what Stowe Boyd likes to call Social Business.

We need to accept that we are a highly participatory species, and there are some bonding agents we need to understand. It is the interweaving of commercial, creative, individual and collective responsibility and reputational needs that enables true markets to thrive. It is the marriage between what Tomi Ahonen and I described in Communities Dominate Brands[177] as the four Cs of commerce, culture, community and connectivity. Culture becomes sticky when its participatory read/ write commerce is more sustainable when we can all be commercial participants, read/write and revenue can be shared, community is only created by being participatory, read/write and connectivity is the means to this happening which

---

176. http://ec.europa.eu/employment_social/equal/news/200711-odent4_en.cfm.
177. Ahonen and Moore, Communities Dominate Brands, p. 201.

allows people to connect up to each other. We can all contribute, we can all 'read' and 'consume something', but importantly, we all have the possibility and opportunity to 'write', to contribute. And in amongst all of that, markets form around three simple things: knowledge and information exchange, commerce and cultural activity which becomes a form of communion.

If I use the example of market towns which existed before the industrial revolution, these market towns are separated by 15 miles, forming a human social network, because a man or woman can walk 30 miles in a day. So a little bit like the Choupal, if I went to market on market day and I lived in the north and my friend Ami lived in the south, I would be pleased to see my friend, I would want to exchange news and information, like the Choupal in India. I would need to trade, act commercially, and I certainly would want to enjoy some entertainment, have some mead, watch a mummers' play and maybe enjoy some dancing – all cultural activity.

If we take that truth and move to today, walking down Main Street in Santa Barbara, when they shut off the main drag for the Thursday farmers' market, reminds me of these things. There are musicians, and other forms of entertainment, like the snake man, a great curiosity for children, and then there are the traders. I watch people stop and chat, buy some produce and sling a few dollars into the busker's collection box. I see the same thing in Cambridge's market square. So when I came across a company called Threadless, that enables anyone to design a T-shirt, upload that design and then lets people that are interested chat about the design and vote for it and the winner of that week gets $2,500 and a dollop of kudos, I thought: 'market day'. Threadless succeeds by engaging its customers; they 'read' and they 'write', they succeed reputationally and commercially, they have fun, and only 5% of people that buy Tees from Threadless are not involved in one way or another in the Threadless community.

Max Chafkin[178] says:

Trust and trustworthiness at Threadless is the company's most important asset because its vast online community is managed collectively. Threadless employs no moderators, and no single person or group is charged with keeping the community happy. Nor, technologically speaking is the social network itself especially advanced. It lacks many of the features found on Myspace or Facebook. There are no virtual friends, no messaging features, and no status messages. Users' profiles are made up of their blog postings and their submissions. One of the really smart things Threadless has done is to get its designers of T-shirts to wear their designs and photograph themselves.

---

178. 'The customer is the company', Max Chafkin. Inc., 1 June 2008.
     http://www.inc.com/magazine/20080601/the-customer-is-the-company.html.

It is simple but it is also very powerful from an identity perspective. What Chafkin describes is Kevin Kelly's prediction of how economies would evolve, with distributed cores and co-evolved customers. But it also says something else – it speaks of the deep human need for belonging and identity; it describes the multidimensional nature of humanity as well as offering a new pattern of commerce and organisation. For Threadless, the benefit was seeing it grow from 70,000 members at the end of 2004 to more than 700,000 in 2009. Sales in 2006 hit $18m – with profits of approximately $6m. In 2007, growth continued at more than 200%, with similar margins.

'I believe that a desirable future depends on our choosing a life of action, over a life of consumption. Rather than maintaining a life-style which only allows to produce and consume, the future depends upon our choice of institutions which support a life of action', wrote Ivan Illich in 1973.[179] The question is: who is going to build those institutions? The answer quite simply is us: you and me. Lukas Gadowiski the founder of Spreadshirt said to me,

> It's a strange feeling looking out at the desolate remains of old factories and bleak funnels of Leipzig's formerly prosperous industry district, but at the same time it is also very inspiring for me. To see how fast more than a hundred years ago huge companies have been built, which most of have disappeared by now – for whatever reasons – is telling you a lot about the dynamics of economics and entrepreneurship. This scenery fires my imagination and shows me that things often happen faster and on a bigger scale than one would ever have thought of. There is one thing worse than having too much sense for imagination, and that is not to have enough.

I met Lukas in 2006 when he was 29, a Polish immigrant living and working in Leipzig. He was running a company called Spreadshirt. Spreadshirt is a virtual place where you can for free create your own shop – you then design your own T-shirt graphics and upload that T-shirt design to your Spreadshirt shop. You set the price of your T-shirt design. Once an order is received (minimum quantity – one), Spreadshirt prints that design, does all the financial transaction stuff, taking a percentage of each sale, and dispatches the orders. From literally nothing, with no marketing budget and no venture capital backing Spreadshirt created a community of over 200,000 Spreadshirters around the world in four years. In my view, it's a complete redefinition of economics: what we make, where we make it, who we make it with and how we distribute it. It's a redefinition of society born out of the inadequacies of a one way, mass consumer culture. And Spreadshirt revenues stood at €21m, as of 2008.

---

179. Illich, *Deschooling society*, p. 52.

Let's say you're an out of work graphic designer, or a frustrated one. You can, for free, create your own Spreadshirt shop, upload as many designs as you like, join in with a global community, and if you are really successful perhaps put yourself through medical school, by the proceeds of your creative efforts. 'We did not build Spreadshirt' said Lukaz. 'The community built Spreadshirt.'

Etsy.com also fits rather neatly into the idea of the socially networked economy, though slightly differently. Etsy is what I would like to describe as a mass niche community of passionate interest. It is 'mass' as its community is global, and it is 'niche' because it serves a very specific niche area. Etsy's mission is to enable people to make a living making things, and to reconnect makers with buyers. 'Our vision is to build a new economy and present a better choice: buy, sell, and live handmade', they say. Essentially, Etsy is an online marketplace for buying and selling all things handmade. Etsy connects buyers with independent creators and shop owners to find the very best in handmade, vintage and supplies.

Setting up shop looks pretty easy, customisation, straightforward, and there is a thriving and happy community. Etsy shoppers are looking for handmade goods, vintage items and craft supplies. Reach the ideal customer for your products when you sell on Etsy is their mantra. And back to the idea of a continual learning environment: you can chat with other Etsians, share tips and marketing strategies on an Etsy Team or even attend an online workshop in their Virtual Labs. The Etsy community spans the globe with buyers and sellers coming from more than 150 countries. Etsy sellers now number hundreds of thousands.

Open source sauce

> The tools and governance principles of the open source software community, in some modified form could yield new approaches to community organisation and problem solving.[180]

You may be aware of the concept of 'open source', but let's nail the definition. According to Wikipedia, open source is an approach to the design, development and distribution of software, offering practical accessibility to a software source code. Some consider open source as one of various possible design approaches, while others consider it a critical strategic element of their operations. Before open

---

180. Pekka Himanen, *The Hacker Ethic: A Radical Approach to the Philosophy of Business*, Random House, 2001. According to Himanen, the three main features of hacker ethic are: [1] enthusiastic, passionate attitude to the work that is enjoyed [2] creativity, wish to realise oneself and one's ability, often in teams that are formed spontaneously (project orientation) [3] a wish to share one's skills with a community having common goals, along with the need to acquire recognition from one's 'tribe'; one is motivated by inner zeal rather than external awards: the fruits of one's work are donated to everybody for their advances and further developments.

source became widely adopted, developers and producers used a variety of phrases to describe the concept; the term open source gained popularity with the rise of the internet, which provided access to diverse production models, communication paths, and interactive communities.

The Open Source Initiative (OSI) was formed in February 1998 by Raymond and Perens. With about 20 years of evidence from case histories of closed and open development already provided by the internet, the OSI continued to present the 'open source' case to commercial businesses. It sought to bring a higher profile to the practical benefits of freely available source codes, and wanted to bring major software businesses and other high-tech industries into open source. The effects of an open approach, however, has today much wider ramifications.

From a literacy perspective, how utterly contradictory is the logic of the word 'open' to the word 'closed'. Open with no end, no rules, no control is a reflex when straight lines thinkers are not articulate enough to comprehend the true potential of working in an open philosophy of innovation and economics. Yet as we have seen in this book, open source code, open innovation, open business models, open legal frameworks are attractors, innovation accelerators and even risk mitigators. Such an approach can deliver a number of important benefits, for example, leaner running and more adaptive organisations. The key is to understand how open source models of operation and decision-making allow the concurrent input of different agendas, approaches and priorities, and differ from the more closed, centralised traditional models of organisation, economic production and innovation. Then, from a design leadership, and organisational perspective, one can start to calibrate open source thinking and behaviours into organisational capability.

Open source a common language

In looking at new models of manufacture and commerce, in a networked context I came across a project in Rotterdam called c,mm,n (c,mm,n wiki). Like Local Motors, it has a very different agenda and mission statement to that of a legacy industrial giant. C,mm,n (pronounced 'common') is an open source community for what they describe as 'sustainable personal mobility'; c,mm,n busies itself with investigating how we will move around in the future. C,mm,n's community is open to anyone with 'a creative, intelligent and enterprising perspective on mobility issues, and who wants to help create a better world'. It is argued that only through applying open source legal frameworks and structures will manufacturing, and, I hold, even our economies, ever be truly sustainable. What this means is that just like open source software, the product is 'open to all'. The c,mm,n car blueprint and the mobility concepts that have so far been derived from the c,mm,n project are freely available under an open source licence. This allows the potential for large-scale collaboration, not unlike Linux software programming. This approach has already been applied to, and worked for, many different, social, political, commercial and scientific endeavours. So there is no reason the same principal cannot be applied to our non-linear future. Under the open source legal framework, everyone is free to use and modify the design, the only condition being that any designs that are realised from the c,mm,n project are returned to the community as open source information. It is through harnessing our collective intelligence and scaling the cooperative nature of humans that we can accelerate innovation so that it becomes, in a sense, frictionless, affording a degree of velocity that would even have Captain Kirk grinning like a Cheshire cat, or, as Eric Raymond would say, 'With many eyes all bugs are shallow.'[181]

C,mm,n explains that the c,mm,n platform can be utilised to create new business services, for example one could build a rental or lease-hire business.

But of course this presents once again a significant cultural challenge for companies who believe that power is about toll gates combined with copyright, or IP control, that is that they need to educate the public about copyright law rather than the other way round. Plus saddled with massive debt, eyes fixed on the quarterly numbers and institutional shareholders breathing down their necks, to step away from an entire way of doing business would seem madness. Clay Shirky argued in a post from 2009, 'Revolutions create a curious inversion of perception. In ordinary times, people who do no more than describe the world around them are seen as pragmatists, while those who imagine fabulous alternative futures are viewed as radicals', he continues, 'When reality is labelled unthinkable, it creates a kind of sickness in an industry.' How on earth do you migrate from an old model to a new one? It takes more than a small dose of courage and vision. But it can be done. Perhaps by pointing to such projects, we can help others leave the world of linear thinking, and linear business models and embrace the world of no straight lines, with all its flexibility that's required in the networked economy. Interestingly, Jay from Local Motors, which also operates under an open source model, tells me that a fair few manufacturing companies have approached them wanting to know the secret sauce of their model. Jay says he's really happy to do that, but of course anything that is shared must be shared with the community. Clearly the ideological chasm to cross is just too far for some.

---

181. Eric S. Raymond, *The Cathedral and the Bazaar*, O'Reilly, 1999.

Networked research and innovation

Science like other industries faces significantly interlinked challenges; how is science going to be funded in the future, and how does one accelerate scientific breakthrough? The funding of science innovation and where that funding comes from and where it is spent. Private science research and innovation is feeling the grit in its wheels.

John Martin writing in the *New Scientist*[182] believes the recent financial crisis has significant implications for pharmaceutical research. He argues that the running of large pharmaceutical companies carries a social responsibility that's as heavy as running any bank. But he sees the unwritten contract between big pharma and society being neglected. Martin's big question is this: 'Is our health now too important to be left to big pharma?'

For example, the colossal amounts of money spent on cardiovascular drugs; Pfizer spent about $6bn, Eli Lilly $3bn and GlaxoSmithKline $2.5bn over the last decade, but have delivered very little in terms of innovation. The cash spent is the negligent equivalent of the misuse of funds by the banking industry. And the mountains of cash accumulated from the sales of medicines has come mostly in the UK through the National Health Service. It's Martin's estimate that on average each top 20 pharmaceutical company has access to about $7.5bn in cash. The big question is: could the cash piles of big pharma be utilised in more efficient ways for the public good? Martin makes the observation that it is insane to increase spending on R&D with such paltry rewards. His point is that eventually there's nowhere left to go – the cash is spent and there is nothing to show for it.

Many innovative ideas that have changed society have arisen from the combination of curiosity and academic freedom found in universities. Surely releasing some of that cash into a new paradigm of networked co-creation could unleash innovation. This is where small amounts of funding can produce big results. In recent years, university research has been exploited by industry to produce new drugs, such as blood clot-busting 'tissue plasminogen activator', courtesy of the Catholic University of Leuven in Belgium, notes Martin.[183]

Big pharmas have big bucks, and universities have the raw resources of human endeavour. Combine that with an openness to new ideas, a flexibility to adapt and a capacity to work with people from other cultures, and guess what you might get. So the question is ... is there a model for encouraging large-scale scientific problem solving? Yes, and it comes from an unexpected and unrelated corner of the universe:

---

182. John Martin, 'Big banks, big pharma, big problems', *New Scientist*, 12 October 2009.
183. Martin, 'Big banks, big pharma, big problems'. 'Efficacy and safety of tissue plasminogen activator 3- to 4.5-hours after acute ischemic stroke. A metaanalysis', http://stroke.ahajournals.org/cgi/content/short/STROKEAHA.109.552547v1.

open source software development, argues Karim Lakhani, an Assistant Professor at Harvard Business School.[184] His research leads to these conclusions:

- Practices in the open source software community offer a model for encouraging large-scale scientific problem solving.
- Open up your problem to other people in a systematic way. A problem may reside in one domain of expertise and the solution may reside in another.
- Find innovative licensing ways or legal regimes that allow people to share knowledge without risking the overall intellectual property of the firm.

Martin writes that on the one hand we have an unproductive big pharma which is cash rich, and on the other a cash-poor university system that has produced fistfuls of Nobel Prize winners. The way forward is obvious: inject the money into university research. Experience tells us this can have major benefits. One of the most successful initiatives in the last decade has been the spin-out of small biotech firms. Biogen sprang from MIT and Genentech from the University of California, San Francisco. Martin argues that 100 new companies could be created from British universities alone over 10 years if big pharma money were blended with a proactive way of recognising patentable inventions and managing university science. What Martin and Lakhani are describing is a more open collaborative approach to research, innovation and commercialisation, something that Will Hutton agrees with.[185] His view is that those economies prepared to stay open and create national innovation architectures that support a diversified landscape of vigorous firms, institutions and technologies will repeat the amazing feat of the British industrial revolution at the end of the 18th century. But such innovation ecosystems will not be created spontaneously; there is a need to develop an ecosystem that can respond to these dilemmas by designing answers that today do not exist. Boston in the USA is a case in point, in interviewing many people that represented the diverse ecosystem that enables academia, innovation, entrepreneurship and commerce to successfully co-exist.

But on top of that situated ecosystem, there is now the possibility to apply open source collaboration, Karim Lakhani writes,

> open source collaboration is a very different model for innovation and product development than most firms are used to … In open source communities we see a vast degree of openness in which everybody can participate, but also the practice of broadcasting your work to everybody else. People continually broadcast their problems, others broadcast solutions, and the person with the

184. Q&A with Karim R. Lakhani, author Martha Lagace, 'Open source science: a new model for innovation', Harvard Business School, 20 November 2006. http://hbswk.hbs.edu/item/5544.html. Lakhami is also editor of *Perspectives on Free and Open Source Software*, MIT Press, 2005.
185. Will Hutton, *Observer*, Sunday, 23 September 2007.

problem is not always the one with the solution. Oftentimes, somebody else can make sense of both what the problem has been and what people are proposing as solutions, and can come up with a better answer.

This concept is exemplified by the Polymath Project[186] initiated by Cambridge mathematician Timothy Gowers, which works on massively collaborative mathematical research projects, and has resulted in several papers being published in journals. This trend has been named as open science.

Competing to innovate

An aspect of open collaboration literacy which may seem counter intuitive is that of competition. Competitions can attract people passionate about solving real world problems; these need to be open access attracting a true divergence of knowledge, and have a fine pedigree. The Longitude Prize was an act of Parliament (the Longitude Act) of the United Kingdom passed in July 1714 during the reign of Queen Anne. It established the Board of Longitude and offered a monetary reward for anyone who could find a simple and practical method for the precise determination of a ship's longitude. Today, competitions provide the ability to shift risk as they have always done, and generate wider interest through networked communication technologies. But why do we compete? We compete not for money *per se*, but more often we respond to the call of a higher order purpose and something we are passionate about which when tapped is a deep human motivation – we seek transformation.

Let's take a contemporary example; TopCoder is a company which administers contests in computer programming. TopCoder hosts fortnightly online competitions – known as SRMs or 'single round matches' – as well as weekly competitions in algorithm design and development. The work in design and development produces useful software which is licensed for profit by TopCoder. Competitors involved in the creation of these components are paid royalties based on these sales. The software resulting from algorithm competitions – and the less-frequent marathon matches – is not usually directly useful, but sponsor companies sometimes provide money to pay the victors. Statistics (including an overall 'rating' for each developer) are tracked over time for competitors in each category. TopCoder runs other types of competitions. This example is called a Experimental Marathon Match – NASA's Integrated Medical Model Team were confronted with a problem so they reached out to TopCoder setting a challenge: write an algorithm that will optimise a space flight medical kit for astronauts.

---

186. http://polymathprojects.org/about/. http://polymathprojects.org/.

This Experimental Marathon Match event had over $25,000 in prizes. In addition, 10 participants will get VIP access to one of the few remaining NASA shuttle launches and all contestants who actively participate will receive a limited edition, personalised TopCoder/NASA T-shirt. Competitions create in a sense a false deadline, but what they do is focus the mind. NASA, Local Motors, Threadless, TopCoder, Innocentive, YourEncore are all contemporary examples of unleashing innovation through the framework of competition that are transformative. What in gaming terms is called an Epic win.

Of course there are different reasons for creating competitions such as the Pulitzer for journalism, the James Dyson prize (an international award that encourages next generation industrial designers) or the Ansari X prize, which offered a purse of $10m and inspired companies to spend $100m overall to win that prize.

Before 1991, 97% of the value of big prizes was dedicated to recognised prior achievement like the Nobel or Pulitzer but since 1991, 78% of new prize money has been dedicated to solving specific goals. In effect, the unleashing of innovation. However, there is a widely held view that in the UK at least there is little political cultural or business appreciation of the importance of competition in stimulating innovation. Yet no matter what industry you are in, creating open innovation competitions can be a means of accelerating innovative solutions. Companies like Local Motors use competitions to help it run leaner, but also to accelerate innovation; Threadless exists and thrives because of competition. Competition can bring long-term social and regional development benefits such as the Eden project in Cornwall, that brought £1bn into the local economy, which directly created 500 jobs and supports and additional 3,000 locally, and the Saltire Prize in Scotland could bring economic autonomy and sustainability to a region via harnessing wave energy to the production of electricity.

Harnessing collective intelligence, motivating people through commercial and reputational rewards and connecting individual knowledge up to the network means there's a different way of innovating and a different way of making money. If big pharma provided access to its vast cash pile and invested in the right way, it would also put the pedal to the metal in terms of rapid innovation and development. But it's not only big pharma that could benefit. More importantly, the entire industrial approach towards patents and intellectual property ownership as a means to economic salvation is myopic and gets in the way of real innovation that could serve humanity better – it is a mindset issue, a philosophical issue and a human issue.

Chapter Four

Gutenberg is a moblogger: economic, organisational and societal transformation through mobile communications

THERE IS ANOTHER ASPECT OF OUR NON-LINEAR WORLD which plays an important role in what comes next. We are inevitably moving towards a society where our mobile devices become the remote control for our daily lives. Any technology that allows us to better connect, communicate, share knowledge and information and get stuff done will be widely adopted.[187] Some of the stories already presented suggest the changes to people's lives big and small that mobile communications will usher in. Perhaps my favourite is the Austrian dairy farmer who brings his cows in for milking by calling them on his mobile phone. The lead cow has a mobile device attached to her collar.

We are but at the beginning of our journey of transformation which will take some time, generations even, to play out. Vint Cerf, one of the founders of the world wide web, has a view that much has already been achieved to create a better world: 'It has provided access to information on a scale never before imaginable, lowered the barriers to creative expression, challenged old business models and enabled new ones.' He continues: 'It has succeeded because we designed it to be both flexible and open. These features have allowed it to accommodate innovation without massive changes to its infrastructure.'[188]

Gutenberg is a moblogger

When discussing or teaching disruption, I ask the question whether the church ever saw Gutenberg coming. The church was a powerful monopoly controlling all before it by ensuring that knowledge, the protein for innovation and creativity, was safely kept out of the hands of feudal man and woman.

---

187. McGuire's Law: the utility of any activity increases with its mobility. http://mcguireslaw.com/.
188. Vint Cerf, 'If you thought the internet was cool, wait until it goes space age', *Observer*, Sunday, 17 August 2008.

Power was knowledge, and knowledge could only ever be accessed by joining the church. Gutenberg, busy in his garret in Mainz, had no idea what he was unleashing upon the world, yet were Gutenberg to be alive today, he would be creating technology so that he could be taking pictures and shooting videos with his mobile; he would be blogging and vlogging via his mobile, paying for his car parking spaces via his mobile, getting his library books renewed via SMS, dating on Flirtomatic and getting his healthcare from the 3G Doctor. When technology becomes successful, it becomes ubiquitously invisible and so our mobile devices become our personalised remote controls for life.

The numbers of mobile devices in the world, currently some 5 billion, with 80% of the world's population living within range of a mobile network, including the Masai and the Bedouin, is extraordinary. Never in the history of the human race have so many people been able to connect to each other – the scale is simply unprecedented. In developing economies, people are finding innovative ways to use mobile technology. Grameen's microfinance and village phone programmes in Bangladesh and elsewhere are known and respected around the world, but there are many less famous examples. During the Kenyan elections, Mobile Planet provided its subscribers with up-to-the-minute results by text message. And in his Presidential election campaign, Barack Obama did not miss the opportunity to mobilise his supporter network through mobile connectivity. Writing in the *Observer*, Cerf states: 'As the cost of mobile technologies fall, the opportunities for such innovation will continue to grow. We're nearing the tipping point for mobile computing to deliver timely, geographically and socially relevant information.' He goes on to comment on how researchers in Japan have proposed using data from vehicles' windscreen wipers and embedded GPS receivers to track the movement of weather systems through towns and cities with a precision never before possible. 'It may seem academic', he adds, 'but understanding the way severe weather, such as a typhoon, moves through a city could save lives. Further exploration can shed light on demographic, intellectual and epidemiological phenomena, to name just a few areas.'

So welcome to BIG WE, a place where 5 billion of us are connected by meshes of the connective tissue of mobile communication networks. To give that some context, there are four times more mobile phone subscribers than internet subscribers. They also outnumber PC owners 3:1, and television owners 2:1. Philip Sugai, Marco Koeder and Luovico Ciferri, argue in their book *The Six Immutable Laws of Mobile* that the mobile device has superseded the car as the true symbol of freedom. The six immutable laws of mobile are[189]

---

189. Philip Sugai, Marco Koeder and Luovico Ciferri, *The Six Immutable Laws of Mobile Business*, Wiley-Interscience, 2010.

- Value over culture.
- The law of the ecosystem.
- The empowering nature of mobile (at the point of inspiration).
- The value of time zones.
- Mobile-specific business models are essential.
- The future is Simplexity.

The six immutable laws of mobile business

These laws relate to the fundamental principles for creating sustainable commerce. These laws provide guidance for the development, management and marketing of advanced mobile content and service offerings, which can be applied to both developing and advanced mobile markets around the world. The laws are based upon an in-depth analysis of one of the longest-established and most profitable mobile markets in the world: Japan. What is currently emerging around the world today has already been tried and tested in Japan four to seven years ago. Japan accounted for over 35% of all global revenue for advanced mobile data services in 2008 and now looks back at 10 years of (successful) mobile-web experience.
 First it is necessary to cut through the many myths and the hype surrounding Japan's mobile dominance to identify the most important laws that will guide the success of mobile businesses around the world.

The six core laws that apply to most mobile markets in the world are the following.

IMMUTABLE LAW #1 – value over culture
Japanese culture has had no significant impact on the success of the mobile internet in Japan. The secret of success is not about the culture but about servicing the following four categories: interaction, entertainment, expression and transaction. There are common needs amongst people that a good service needs to fulfil. This has not so much to do with a specific culture but with providing true value to users.

IMMUTABLE LAW #2 – the law of the ecosystem
Within a sustainable ecosystem, the roles of the various players must remain in collaborative balance. This concept of mutuality was unique to the Japanese mobile industry. In comparison elsewhere, when mutuality is not part of the businesses ecosystem, the only certainty is that the entire ecosystem can (and usually will) fail (the travails of global handset manufacturers and telcos in general are testament to that). To attract the best and to create an ecosystem rich in diversity, DoCoMo, the operator in Japan, keeps just 9% of subscription revenues,

passing 91% to content companies. This is almost counterintuitive for many – how or why would your share such large amounts of revenues? Because the mobile internet would flourish only if the right content and services were developed and deployed in a way that consumers could easily understand and adopt. To deliver only the very best experience, one has to incentivise and stimulate the ecosystem of third party developers to give their creative best – to do that one revenue shares. The answer is that for DoCoMo 9% of something very big is always going to be bigger than 91% of something very small. Japan's ecosystem is called iMode. Apple's iTunes/iOS is modelled entirely on iMode though it does not share revenue with app developers and content providers in the same percentages. Google's Android platform and ecosystem adheres to similar principles; however, Google has envisioned an ecosystem on an entirely different scale and will provide revenues to match. Eric Schimdt, Google's CEO, believes that in the near future Android will deliver $10bn per year to the company.

IMMUTABLE LAW #3 – mobility empowers
The mobile device is becoming the remote control for life. It is a key to a new empowerment, by being life-enabling, life-simplifying and navigational (help me navigate through the complexity of my life). Through mobile devices, users can connect to other people, to their environment or to services in a new way, which we are already seeing. People, organisations, industries, communities of interest are in need of services that can help them to either embrace or escape their current situation. For organisations, mobile devices will redefine what they perceive as assets, and how they create and provide access to those assets. This will provide new revenue opportunities and an increasingly distributed marketplace.

IMMUTABLE LAW #4 – the value of time zones
Research from the six laws project has shown that 70% of mobile use in Japan happens at fixed locations. This mirrors studies of mobile usage in other countries. This ultimately means that mobile content use is not location but time-specific. Instead there should be two approaches to content irrespective of location: one is about short bursts of varying duration and the other one about longer, dedicated attention representing different usage 'time zones':

1. In-Between-Time where content and services must be concise, easy to access and understand and easy to drop and pick up again later.

2. Golden Time where dedicated usage is longer term, and larger blocks of time are available to focus on content and services. Users here explore and engage more, and for longer periods. In this time zone, content and services can have more depth and breadth.

IMMUTABLE LAW #5 – mobile-specific business models are essential
It is interesting to note that the mobile platform was the main driver for Web
2.0 in Japan. Over the past 10 years, the mobile internet was midwife to a range
of new innovative business models that are now starting to impact on the rest
of the world. Significantly, many of the most successful mobile services in
Japan did not depend on advertising revenue as their sole source of income,
which has helped them to develop more valuable services for their customers
and stakeholders. Making money from people creating their own content,
virtual goods sales, freemium and subscription-based models have been
part of the mobile world long before these terms were coined in the west.

IMMUTABLE LAW #6 –the future is Simplexity
'Simplexity' – what does it mean? Having gone from a world that was linear
(simple), we now live in a world that is non-linear (complex). Managing
the complexity of our lives is and will increasingly become challenging.

Increasingly, technology products are also becoming more complex.
This is the stage of complexity where your VCR, for example, comes with a
manual the size of the New York phonebook. But as technology becomes more
sophisticated there is a new evolution: Simplexity, this is where the front end,
or the user interface, becomes very simple but the complexity in the backend
increases. Take the Nintendo Wii, the DS: even your gran or grandad can use it.

Simplexity is a powerful way of opening technology to the masses and
(hopefully) to the benefit of the masses: the iPhone/iPad's touch interface using
natural gestures, intelligent car systems, location-based services, intelligent
agents and intelligent concierge services on mobile devices. Simplexity also can
mean reducing the complexity of a device in terms of cost. Less is more as long as
the intelligence in the backend (or cloud) is strong enough. Simplexity will and
does help the elderly or even developing countries (mobile phone as a banking
tool using rather low-tech phones and SMS but a complex procurement system
in the backend). This is just a small glimpse into the world of Simplexity.

Simplexity will be how we as people will be truly empowered through our
mobile devices and beyond.

But this is only the beginning. The global mobile revolution has just begun
and so-called 'mobile phones' are only the first manifestations of this revolution.
We will see a broad range of new intelligent mobile devices in the near future. For
the short term these are devices like the iPad and other tablets, connected e-book
readers like the Kindle or portable game consoles like the Nintendo DS with a
built-in SIM card. We are facing a multiverse of devices intermingling with a

multiverse of services and platforms. In terms of mobile network technology, LTE (Long Term Evolution = 100mbit/s broadband for mobile) is just around the corner providing new ways to access and engage in our world via mobile devices.

Also, reality as we know it will change. Through location-based technologies, meta tags, intelligent agents and augmented service, it will be possible to add an extra layer of information to our existing environment and allow us to interact with it in new ways. Here, Simplexity will play a core role. How can the complexity of our everyday life be simplified in a meaningful way and how can technology and digital services help to empower people?

If it is done right there will be an enormous potential for mobile devices in the future. And this future will be Simplex for sure.

We now live in a world where we are constantly searching for information to help us make and take decisions and transactions; it is defined as an intention economy. We have evolved from a world of 'Push' to one defined by 'Pull'. Commerce, governance, organisational adaptiveness, education and societal flexibility will increasingly be based upon the rapid interactions of people to people, and people to organisations via information and communication flows on platforms enabled by mobile communications. Mobile connectivity enables us to connect to the past, the present and the future; it increasingly allows us to signal our presence – like we do on Skype, by giving a variety of permissions, and notifications about our presence and status; 'Skype me', 'online', 'do not disturb', away, offline or invisible and our proximity; I am close by. It means the ways in which we can connect, share, organise and distribute all types of information, which can be reconfigured, shaped, crafted and designed for specific individual or group needs and purposes – there is not a single organisation on this planet that will not be left untouched by the mobile communications revolution. Underpinning all of this change, the hidden matter that will have an overarching effect on business and society are the massive flows of data that aid, how information is harnessed, shaped, refined and delivered to be perceived as relevant. Mobile connectivity is a vital interface to the world of non-linearity. So what does that look like and what do those ideas mean in practical terms?

The future of work: txteagle

A few years ago I came across Nathan Eagle when Nathan was mentioned in an article about mobile and data research being conducted out of MIT. Recently Nathan re-emerged on my radar screen with a company called txteagle. txteagle is based in Kenya, which is 75% literate, is English-speaking, has 16 million phone subscribers, yet half the population is unemployed. Nathan's txteagle business is founded in what I would say is a compassionate view of the world – the Stephen Heppell view of the 21st century.[190] In working on and adapting an existing SMS system for blood donors in Kilifi, a local district hospital on the coast of Kenya, Nathan saw an opportunity to develop a new way of connecting up literate but unemployed people in Kenya via mobile technologies to work that would generate much- needed income[191].

This is what txteagle does

txteagle receives a task-related piece of work from a client, and divides that piece of work into micro-tasks that can be completed on a mobile handset. Those micro-tasks are then sent to people living in villages all over the world. It could be a piece of fact-checking, translation or the transcription of audio recordings: a user would listen to a short clip, write it down by hand, and then copy it into an SMS reply. Eagle's studies have shown that this task can be completed in less than two minutes, and he believes that a proficient user could earn about $3 an hour doing the work. Nokia is also involved with a project to train a speech-recognition engine on Kenya's local languages, which in fact does not require people to be literate. When that task is completed, the person resends the piece of work back to txteagle who reconfigures the micro-tasks into the completed piece of work, and that gets sent back to the client. The mobile worker, is paid via a mobile payment system called MPesa.

This project carries with it some transformational ideas. The idea that one can find and reach out to a distributed workforce, via the mobile on an international scale, has many ramifications and possibilities. One for me is the lightweight nature of the business combined with the ability to enable what is considered a third world country to plug into an entirely different economy (the knowledge economy) in a new and novel way, enabling access to a revenues previously thought impossible. txteagle says there are 2 billion literate, mobile phone subscribers in the developing world living on less than $5 a day[192] and there are companies all over the world that are inundated with many small tasks that need to be done. To Nathan, connecting these two separate but needy groups seemed obvious. Nathan states: 'We can now enable these tasks to be distributed and completed via a mobile phone anywhere in the world'. The *Boston Globe* points out the opportunities,[193]

---

190. Stephen Heppell said that the 21st century is the 'learning century', the century where we learn to help each other.

191. http://txteagle.com/story.html.

192. http://www.slideshare.net/natecow/txteagle-etecho9.

193. 'The end of the office and the future of work', http://www.boston.com/bostonglobe/ideas/articles/2010/01/17/the_end_of_the_office_and_the_future_of_work/?page=full.

The jobs – short stretches of speech to be transcribed or translated into a local dialect, search engine results to be checked, images to be labelled, short market research surveys to be completed – come in over a worker's own cell phone and the worker responds either by speaking into the phone or texting back the answer. The workers can be anyone with a cell phone – a secretary waiting for a bus, a Masai tribesman herding cattle, a student between classes, a security guard on a slow day, or one of Kenya's tens of millions of unemployed.

There are over 100 local languages in Kenya; for, say, a mobile phone operator localising software could be hugely beneficial. From citizen journalism to highly location specific surveys, txteagle offers up an unprecedented opportunity for people previously tied to the land and locked into poverty, to plug into the global economy. If 2 billion people were to go from earning $2 per day to earning $2 per hour what kind of impact might that have? In a sense this is a rhetorical question; the order of magnitude would be unprecedented, it would be transformational. This picks up on a very interesting point, which is that the nature of the organisation, as well as work, is being redefined, partly by economic pressures but also by our need to no longer work as we once did. We possess the ability to redistribute wealth via the connectivity of communication networks, such as txteagle. txteagle also takes the view that the work these individuals do leverages their unique knowledge; txteagle does not want to become embroiled in what Nathan describes as labour arbitrage – the commodification of people and work – which in his view is neither ethical nor sustainable. Recently, txteagle has been working with the United Nations on a survey that looks at specific countries disaster preparedness. Normally this costs $5m, has 7,000 respondents and takes place in 33 countries, txteagle is able to undertake and complete that survey at a fraction of the cost and deliver money back to those that complete the survey via their mobile.

OK so that's Africa, some would say; blink and walk away. But what if we took Nathan's txteagle capability and used that in the UK – where we have a mobile penetration rate of 120%, yet millions still do not have internet access and where swathes of the population unable to find work live on the £39.50 a week job seekers' allowance, locked into a life of poverty, poor physical and mental health. In a recent Channel 4 programme, four television personalities were asked to live on a job seekers' allowance, and a documentary was made of the result. One of the personalities spent some time talking to a woman who had been an accounts clerk, had been made redundant, was in her fifties and could see no way out of the grinding poverty she was in. Essentially, there were no jobs where she lived, not that she hadn't tried. In explaining how she has to count every single penny until the next security cheque arrived, it became all too much for her, she broke down on camera, the tears hot torrents streaming down her face. Self-consciously she kept saying, 'I am so sorry' and wiping the tears away on the back of her hand.

There are times when the mediated medium of television can have a visceral effect. As I sat there watching this, I reflected on a gentleman from local government I had recently met with a view to helping local authorities work through some of the challenges they were about to face and who in my mind had no interest in really what I had to say, or what I knew. I wondered whether this lady had a mobile phone? What if we applied something like the txteagle platform in Britain – to enable this lady to work in a new way? She could be earning maybe enough to ease her out of the near poverty-like conditions she is currently in. Without a great deal of money being spent on infrastructure, people in the UK could be given back the chance of a life better lived with a bit of dignity. For me, that seems worthy of some consideration. Would it be fair to say this would be a no straight lines solution to what was previously seen as an intractable problem?

The transformative power of mobile money

In researching how mobile money, m-money, or m-banking is going to play an important economic role, I turned to my good friend and mobile industry expert Tomi Ahonen,[194] who helped me understand that in the western world, we have credit cards, debit cards and bank accounts, and, for us, mobile payments offer some improved convenience. It won't really change our lives. But most people on the planet do not have access to a bank account. Banking is very poorly developed in all African countries compared to the industrialised world. There are significant challenges to getting banking services working in Africa, ranging from the high costs of opening an account to very limited bank branches and services and remarkably bureaucratic requirements to verify identity – on a continent where identity documents are not always available. For them, cash can be a very serious issue. Imagine being poor in Africa, earning a dollar a day – 40% of Egyptians earn less than 2 dollars per day, and Egypt is one of the more affluent African countries. If you earn a dollar a day, and are paid once per week, that six dollars is a fortune. The streets are not well lit, there aren't many cops around, but there are plenty of AK 47 Kalashnikov assault rifles to help the criminally inclined to increase their wealth. Estonia saw they had crime related to parking meters. They eliminated cash; now all payments are in some digital form (credit cards, debit cards or mobile phones – most are on mobile) and the crime related to parking has been eliminated. Then, in Sweden, bus drivers were being robbed for the change that

---

194. Tomi Ahonen, 'The insider's guide to mobile 2010', http://www.lulu.com/product/ebook/insiders-guide-to-mobile-free-edition/14591083.

they carry in cash, and the Swedish authorities looked at what happened in Estonia, and decided, good idea. By eliminating cash as acceptable payment on buses (you can buy monthly tickets or pay by debit card – or pay by mobile) the robberies stopped.

For many people living on this planet in big and small ways mobile money is simply transformative. Instead of having to walk half a day to meet someone to pay them, payment is made by mobile payment system. And as more money comes into and moves around an economy, economic growth becomes a by product of that activity. Four years after introducing mobile banking and mobile payment into Kenya, 25% of the total Kenyan economy is transmitted through mobile phones. Even if you lose your phone, mobile money is the most secure form of digital payments, more safe than credit or debit cards, and can be re-enabled by the banking and operator authorities within minutes. All you need is to borrow a friend's phone, go pick up a prepaid SIM card and call up the operator and say your phone is lost, please disable the mobile wallet on that phone number and transfer it to this new one (and give your mother's maiden name and your shoe size etc.) – easy! A plastic card takes days even if it is American Express.

Kenya has a 37 million population, yet there are only 3 million bank accounts. The local mobile banking system M-Pesa is, however, used by 1 million Kenyans. At least 25% of banking customers in Kenya have shifted to mobile phone-based banking. No wonder people get their full salaries submitted onto their phone. But perhaps even more radical is the development of mobile voice minutes and SMS text messages becoming a new currency. People in many countries now shift minutes from one customer to another so mobile is effectively becoming a new equivalent of money. M-Pesa has brought transformational change to the Kenyan economy. In three years from its launch, half of all banking accounts in Kenya were mobile banking accounts. In four years, mobile banking has captured 25% of the total economic activity in Kenya. No wonder Susie Lonie and the team at M-Pesa won the *Economist* award for this innovation in 2010. In Africa M-Pesa trades $150m a day more than Western Union does, which, whilst transforming people's lives, it is ironic that in the west we cannot learn from such an insight. txteagle pays all its workers via M-Pesa. This transformational service is now rolling out across Africa the Middle East and India; what could it or mobile banking do for the rest of the world? Does it enable the opportunity for the redistribution of wealth?

Literacy, poverty and regional development

Poor literacy remains a decisive barrier to the economic empowerment of many people in the developing world, according to a programme running at the

University of California, Berkeley.[195] The Berkeley initiative argues that, while technology cannot replace learning through engaging with qualified teachers of language, it can nevertheless provide learners, especially those who are disadvantaged and lack access to other educational opportunities, with the foundation for further growth in listening, reading, writing and conversational skills. And although desktop computing works in urban areas, it is mobile devices which offer significantly a greater opportunity in rural places. Because many children in developing regions have limited time to attend school regularly, when they need to work for the family in the home or agricultural fields, learning in the out-of-school settings made possible by mobile technologies can increase unprecedented access to literacy. Informed by educational theories on language acquisition, Berkeley students are designing a suite of mobile-learning applications that target conversational skills, listening comprehension, phonetic decoding and sight-reading. These applications will run on mobile devices, the fastest-growing technology platform in emerging economies.

Berkeley is using rural India as its testing ground. In India, the number of people using mobiles has risen from 10 million in 2002 to more than 700 million at the end of 2010.

In Africa, Worldreader.org, an NGO, is providing Kindles to children to enable them to access books, which are prohibitively expensive in that continent. With the support of Random House and Amazon, Worldreader conducted the first-ever trial using e-readers in a sub-Saharan classroom at the OrphanAid Africa School in Ayenyah, Ghana. The intent is to increase children's literacy by providing for the first time access to books, which brings for the very first time access to ideas, thoughts, dreams and knowledge. If Gutenberg's lesson is that access to information ultimately brings a more civilising and perhaps fairer world to life – and help fertile minds to be more creative and mercantile – the argument must be to accelerate communications connectivity, and I think the question must also be asked – does such innovation need to stay in Africa?

The spoken web

The means by which people in rural areas can learn on mobile devices is increasingly being called the spoken web. Guruduth Banavar, director of IBM's India Research Laboratory (IRL),[196] believes that this enfranchises and enables local communities to create and distribute locally relevant information and content, as well as connecting people with e-commerce sites using the spoken word over the telephone

---

195. http://bigideas.berkeley.edu/node/101.
196. http://www.pcworld.com/businesscenter/article/150938/ibm_testing_voicebased_web.html.

instead of the written word. The research lab expects its technology to be relevant to a variety of users looking for information and wanting to engage in transactions. These would include farmers who need to look up commodity prices, fishermen in need of weather information before heading out to sea, plumbers offering their services and retail businesses like grocery shops that can list products, offer order placement, have personalised targeted advertisements or set up reminders.
IBM sees three clear benefits for those locked into a life where the key to the door marked 'a better way of life' is called communication:

- It enables the underprivileged to create, host and share information and services produced by themselves.
- It provides simple and affordable access mechanisms to let the masses exploit IT services and applications similar to the ones that are currently available to worldwide web users.
- It provides a cost-effective ecosystem that can be made available over the infrastructure that exists today to create and sustain a community parallel to the web.

Hand-held learning journeys?

In the US a Texas university initiative which gave an iPhone to every one of its first-year class demonstrates that individual mobile computing will become a fundamental tool in future learning. Writing at Smart Mobs, Judy Breck quotes the response of one of the students: 'My professor will ask a question about something and I don't know what it is, but right here on my phone, with just one touch, I have Dictionary.com, I have a Wikipedia app. I can look it up. I know what they're talking about, because it's right there.' I think this is interesting, as it would enable children to start to make their own learning journey. Often, there are several ways in which a piece of information can be shared and more importantly understood in context and absorbed. In a conventional classroom, this is a challenge because of the scale of the class, but with the right tools, children could find their own way to understanding what dusty old Mr Thompson was trying to teach them. Repeating the same information in the same way does not necessarily enable a child to learn.

Personalised and participatory healthcare

Today's advancement of eHealth products and applications and their wider level of implementation among several countries across the globe have made policy makers and other stakeholders to assess carefully future developments, taking into account the need to build seamless information exchange networks across regions and countries. 'Mobile could be a game-changer. But only for those who get in the game', says Susannah Fox, of Pew Research Centre's Internet & American Life Project.[197] In *Participatory Health: Online and Mobile Tools Help Chronically Ill Manage Their Care*,[198] one of the observations made was that patients seek ongoing conversations with their doctors; the report states:

> Beyond merely searching for health information is patient 'engagement' with such information and its sources, both online and elsewhere. The Edelman Health Engagement Barometer,[199] launched in October 2008, identified about 22% of American adults as 'health info-entials' – that is, people who most actively seek health information and discourse and want to be able to talk about their health needs with others. What motivates these people toward those parties with whom they seek health engagement is trust, authenticity, and satisfaction. And among all sources of information and contact, health information seekers expect 'conversations with my doctor' to be the most important connector for health engagement.

The Pew Project found an even stronger correlation between mobile platforms and the use of the internet to seek health information: 89% of people with wireless internet connections seek health information online, compared to only 40% of consumers who use only a wired internet connection. A difference may also be found in the quality of the interactions: According to Fox, writing in 'The Social Life of Health' information: 'E-patients with mobile access to the internet are more likely than those who have tethered access to contribute their comments and reviews to the online conversation.'[200] This behaviour was also identified in *The Mobile Difference*, where the Pew Project reported that wireless access is associated with deeper engagement and participation in online communications.[201]

We need eHealth developments that are improving the right of access to quality healthcare regardless of personal condition and geographical location, allowing the selection of the appropriate health resource from anywhere at any time. So what might be the benefits of using a mobile device for health services?

- It's a completely personal device.
- It facilitates highly personal health services.

197. http://www.pewinternet.org/.

198. Jane Sarasohn-Kahn, *Participatory Health: Online and Mobile Tools Help Chronically Ill Manage Their Care*, California Healthcare Foundation, September 2009.

199. Edelman Health Engagement Barometer, 'Health engagement in the era of public influence', October 2008, www.engageinhealth.com/docs/edel_HealthBarometer_R13c.pdf.

200. Pew, 'The social life of health', 2009. http://www.pewinternet.org/Reports/2009/8-The-Social-Life-of-Health-Information.aspx?r=1.

201. John Horgan, *The Mobile Difference*, The Pew Internet and Life Project, 25 March 2009.

- It can help ensure the fidelity of patients.
- It's always turned on and carried or within arms' reach.
- It facilitates wireless body area networks.
- It facilitates the gathering of contextual information.
- It ensures it's there in unexpected emergency scenarios.
- It provides assurance that care is at hand.
- It facilitates push services as well as pull.
- Its built-in micropayment means it enables lower costs to deliver services and supports low-cost, pay-as-you-use health services.

For example, a service called 3G Doctor allows people to create and maintain medical histories on their phones. All the allergies, current medications, past treatments and names of doctors and hospitals are now in one place. For those with complicated medical histories, this could be no less than a life-saving service. We are starting to see a range of services made available via mobile platforms, which enables the collection, storage and analysis of wellness-related data, collected from everyday life. Remote diagnostics and patient management technologies in telemedicine have been highlighted as being one of the key components of healthcare for the 21st century.

In the UK, welfare economics was built from a vision of utility geared towards the individual. Amartya Sen[202] points out that it was Lionel Robbins[203] in the 1930s who heavily influenced welfare policy in turning away from an interpersonal understanding of health and well-being. If we look at modern medicine, and the healthcare system outside of acute care and intervention, what we're describing is our desire to claw back some personal control and autonomy, personal accountability and responsibility. When knowledge is taken from us, we lose something more than that knowledge – we lose a piece of ourselves. And when we think about how that's happened to us in all walks of life, it's clear how we seek alternative ways of accessing and harnessing information. What is emergent is an alternative version of a truly supportive ecosystem built around human scale, and human need, only made possible by the mobile-web ecosystem.

Hyperlocal help networks: Japan

This ability to help each other is manifest in a mobile service in Japan called Otetsudai Networks, which literally means 'help networks'. It's where anyone can register and fill in the kinds of skills they have available, say window-cleaning or

202. Amartya Sen, *The Idea of Justice*, Allen Lane, 2009, p. 277.
203. Lionel Robbins, 'Interpersonal comparisons of utility: a comment', *Economic Journal* (1938).

washing dishes or loading boxes at a warehouse. Then there are temporary employers who have short-term needs, for example a shopkeeper has a sudden illness and the one assistant has to leave the shop early. The shopkeeper needs someone who is reasonably qualified temporary help for his store. He only has to detail a need (four hours this afternoon selling shoes at the store in this address at this shopping mall; cash register operation skills needed, pays x per hour). Then those who are near that location, who have indicated that their status is available to do temporary work, will get the alert.

It allows for negotiating. If you don't like the hourly rate offered, you make a counter offer of what you'd be willing to do the job for. The shopkeeper may get a couple of responses, someone who agrees to the amount but can only do two hours and another who's willing to do four hours but wants higher pay. The user interface shows users' local area, with little purple stickmen. Kanji characters give brief descriptions of what these 'can do'. Commerce is made through the data traffic.

Help networks and local newspapers

Local newspapers in Europe and the US are in deep crisis. Half the UK's 1,300 local newspapers will close between now and 2013, destroying 20,000 media jobs. It's not that journalism is redundant in this time of epochal change, but its business model most certainly is. News organisations have singularly failed to truly experiment, and have been negligent in not asking themselves the most important question they should have all asked: how do we fund good journalism in the 21st century? In the meeting with the Johnston Press chief executive that I detail in the preface, I argued for a new way to create additional and sustainable value for both readers and advertisers – the funders of journalism. There were enough examples of innovative ways of creating timely and relevant services which via digital communication technologies would [1] attract more people – a bigger audience [2] attract more advertisers – greater revenues. Unfortunately, this did not happen and the result is the parlous state of that company and indeed many others today. Frankly, I think there's no going back. It appears that even when entire industries are under deep duress, they suffer from some collective cultural and rational myopia – an inability to embrace an alternative vision of how to organise and make commerce. And there are many reasons for that malaise. One being which CEO, with one eye on his pension, is going to stand up to the board and the institutional shareholders and say, 'the business model that has enabled us to work at a 40% operating profit for the last 250 years no longer works'. But of course the endgame of that course of action is ultimately tragic.

Yet, what if local newspapers truly understood that markets are conversations and that stimulating the flows of trusted communication between people creates commerce, like help networks in Japan trade thrives when people are connected in the conversation of sharing valuable information? So why not adopt and adapt help networks into 'classifieds for the 21st century? For sure, it's a non-linear approach but it's already a proven business model. As John Martin pointed out in the big pharma story, it's often the non-linear approaches that deliver innovation to create commercial success.

Augmented thinking for local newspapers

Let's take this thinking a little further, and introduce the concept of augmented reality (AR). Think about it like this: an ordnance survey map represents multiple layers of information, derived from various studies of an area. The map is valuable to me, as it enables me to navigate to various destinations or to take a number of critical decisions on my journey, whether by foot or otherwise. This information is 'augmented' and its value is derived from the unique augmentation of that information. Traditional notions of what constitutes 'value' are made redundant.

Robert Rice, an AR pioneer, explains his particular view of AR: 'I prefer open systems that are extensible and expandable, which also facilitate the development, creation, design, and deployment of content, applications, and so forth by other people. If you intelligently empower the end-user, you accelerate market penetration and user adoption.'

I like the word empowerment. If you are empowered, what happens? You just might come back for more. Rice sets some ground rules. AR is not somewhere you go, he argues. It's everything around you and is therefore enhanced, augmented, intelligent, interactive, and dynamic. AR is local, not global. It's neither 2D nor 3D, having other dimensions and axes, like time, context, and location. AR is also not an extension of the web but is something completely different so thinking about it in the same way that we think about the internet or web pages as far as methods, business models and interface is a fundamentally wrong approach. On the internet, you can be anyone, but AR is going to be accessed via a mobile device in most cases and will have unique identifiers that will be personal to the user, like a smart phone. With AR, moreover, consumers can no longer be considered as just a credit card number and a shipping address. AR will leverage the power of who you are, where you are, what you're doing and who is nearby.

If we extend the concept of help networks, I could be looking for a plumber. Let's say his name is Joe. The service I use to find Joe should provide me with these important pieces of information about Joe,

- His identity – he is who he says he is.
- His reputation scoring – one to five stars, based on customer feedback.
- Recommendations – who recommends Joe?
- His schedule – what his diary looks like.
- His proximity.
- His fees.

The service has aggregated filtered and organised collections of data which enables me, in this instance, to make better-informed decisions about my various commercial transactions. It could be that such a service applies the right type of reputational pressure on Joe to always deliver on his promises. Word of mouth is responsible for 70% of decisions on purchases; as the ticket item increases, word of mouth becomes stronger in its influence. This insight should inspire entrepreneurs and commercial strategists to rethink how economics works in today's world.

All aspects of our non-linear world come into play here: the commercial imperative to create trust, the need for transparency, feedback loops, the enabling of collaborative platforms, the engagement of a community of interest, interfacing with information and with each other without interference, locality, proximity, deep context, permeable flows of information, the harnessing of collective intelligence, blended reality, co-evolved customers, collective and individual accountability, presence, embedded sociability and mashups of data. Of course, such a service requires dynamic data flows, but data and refined data flows are the mitochondria of a networked economy.

So previously paid-for classified ads evolve into services that become life-enabling, life-simplifying and navigational, in that they need to be helping customers navigate through the complexity of their lives. Such an approach turns commercial propositions into valuable human-focused services.

It's in the unique augmentation of data into information that a different form of value is created for us (the sixth law of mobile – Simplexity). Now in some respects that is not entirely straightforward. However, an article in *New Scientist*,[204] described how mobile navigational and location-based services that claim to offer additional information to the user can only deliver if the maps they render and present are in three dimensions and not two. One practical way of achieving this is by accessing the vast repository of data that resides in flickr.com. To achieve the sub-metre positioning accuracy that really good AR demands, mobile devices will have to analyse scenes, not just record images. Building 3D maps from multiple data sources can also deliver greater accuracy. Microsoft's Photosynth software can create composite 3D images from a bunch of 2D images, while huge public

---

204. Jim Giles, 'Augmented reality gets off to a wobbly start', *New Scientist*, 23 September 2009.

image libraries such as Flickr could provide the raw data.

The sheer complexity of meshing something like Flickr's entire database, all of its gazillions of images, all the metadata that's attached to each and every one of those images, is nothing less than mind-bending. And the revenues that would flow to Flickr, as a consequence of such an enterprise would be significant. However, Flickr would need to understand that, within a networked and participatory economy it would need to share those revenues. For this to work, people need to be prepared to share not only their images via a Creative Commons, or a commercial Creative Commons licence, but allow their individual data to be put in the pot of metadata.

Designing the organisation as a platform

Now and in the future, the organisational and commercial architect will understand that organisations will be built as a combination bricks and mortar and communication of technologies – in this way the organisation evolves from a static, fixed entity into a blended dynamic form which offers many benefits, such as being more lightweight, and adaptive, leaner, and which can, as previously stated, evolve new assets and create and find new markets for those assets in a global marketplace. Let's take an institution that we are all familiar with, a museum, and explore how we can create something more vibrant, more immersive, more successful, both culturally and commercially.

When the idea of the museum was first conceived – a place to collect together and hold knowledge – it was an innovative act of creation which has benefited us in many ways, but today we must ask ourselves what does a museum look like, how does it stay relevant and how does communication technology enable the museum to evolve to become as innovative as when it was first conceived?

Museums and cultural institutions have assets; these are rolling exhibitions, permanent collections, archives, lots of stuff in storage and a retainer of unique knowledge stored through its staff and curatorial capabilities. Outside the museum exist 'communities of interest', motivated in engaging with the museum in a number of ways. The communities of interest may look like this: public corporations, universities/academia, business, other museums/cultural institutions. And their motivations may extend in a number of different directions: money, pleasure, self-improvement, status, professional information. And in many ways they are inter-related.

THE CULTURAL ORGANISATION ASSETS	COMMUNITIES OF INTEREST	MOTIVATION
Polling Exhibitions	Public	Money
Permanent collections	Corporations	Pleasure
Archives	Universities/ academia	Self improvement
Lots of stuff in storage	Business	Status
Implicit Knowledge: curators	Other museums / cultural institutions	Professional information
	Inter-related	

Thinking like a network

So the first thing the cultural institution needs to do is learn to think like a network. In a map of the internet and increasingly the mobile-web, we see many companies and organisations connected to each other, forming a large and diverse ecosystem. In this networked ecosystem, these large and small organisations are sharing things like data, interoperability, content, infrastructure and revenues. They are plugged or, better still, meaningfully interwoven into this ecosystem. Importantly, they provide ubiquitous access to their assets. Museums possess a set of assets, which are both physical and knowledge based, and it is highly probable that these assets that have limited access consequently limited benefit, educationally, culturally and commercially.

Becoming no straight lines literate

So what's holding these organisations back? I think it comes back to the idea of literacy. Everyone involved with museums and cultural organisations will understand the word curator, what it means and implies: curation = context = meaning + academic and critical recognition. Whereas, if we use the following language: ecosystems, platforms, mobile, communities of interest, the link economy, economies of scope, designing for the intention economy, designing for personalisation, designing for deeper engagement, designing with data, designing for short and long time frames, participatory cultures and tools, blended reality and embedded sociability, we will undoubtedly find wildly different views and perspectives on what they mean, even though a comprehensive understanding of this language equals survival plus critical and commercial success.

Conceiving the museum as a platform that blends the physical space with all digital communication has to offer, rather than bricks and mortar with a web presence and a bit of mobile stuff going on, fundamentally offers a different organisational, commercial and educational capability. How it fits into an ecosystem adds further opportunity, and how it connects all its assets with communities of interest is real NSL thinking.

Designing for the intention economy

We live in the 'intention economy' that economy is underpinned and built upon the foundations of data. Museums must ensure it has [1] defined what it thinks it assets are, and [2] that all its assets are findable, but not just in Hall A, they must live as products and services that can be found, downloaded or used on a mobile device in a village school in Africa, or the research department of a university in Manchester, or even in Mr Smith's painting studio in Sydney. This is a form of curation, filtering and sense-making. These bundled products and services may then be offered for free, or one-off fees, or via a subscription or even licensing model. If we consider the role of data in the intention economy, one primary reason Amazon is so fantastically successful is because of its user recommendation engine; you bought this or these so you might be interested in this or this or this? And of course Apple has copied Amazon with its Genius service in iTunes. So why would a cultural institution not do the same?

Design for service

Let's consider the 'digital curator'; the expertise of museums is its value proposition that could be used to generate income. Who might be customers of digital curation? Consumers, academics researchers, business professionals – all could have a compelling need to access specific expertise, as bundled digital services centred on the collection, specialist background information or even digital teaching packages. The Tate Britain offers £20 online teaching courses on artists' techniques and methods.

If we take archives, normally the archives are seen as physical, held in a place; the revenue model is constrained by the physical location and the proposition, cultural heritage management is constrained by legal frameworks of usage –

copyright and location. Core activity is management; resources are defined as archive knowledge though limited in its capacity because of access. The archive has no partners who can support the museum and the museum bears all costs.

Whereas if we perceive the museum as a platform, with a new model of cultural and commercial access, we can see something very different. The museum as a platform offers the opportunity of ubiquitous access from anywhere in the world (it could be offering educational material to schools in Africa or elsewhere which can be accessed via a Kindle), its proposition is access supported by Creative Commons legal frameworks, it has multiple revenue models and its activities are based upon the packaging of knowledge, skills and information into relevant packages for the layman as well as the serious academic.

Design for customisation

The cultural institution must be able to customise its offerings: books, catalogues, project materials that previously would not have been possible, practically or economically. New production methodologies, print on demand, e-books, application technologies, for example, now exist which demonstrates a unique way of creating and customising. The museum as a platform needs to consider how such an approach becomes part of its access and assets strategy.

Lessons for organisations

I developed this thinking when asked to present to an audience on how mobile communication platforms, devices and capability offers new opportunities to cultural institutions. Yet I could not help think that my findings could be applied to almost any organisation. Or that there were similarities with other new and emergent organisational forms discussed in this book. The reality is that the museum or cultural institution that has been with us for a very long period of time can now be fundamentally re-designed, its role and capability enhanced in a universally connected world by understanding a new language of design that unleashes its assets to a wider and more diversified audience. That thinking could be adopted by a multitude of other organisations.

Embedded mobility is an organisational and commercial capability not a marketing/sales tactic. Designing for ecosystems + platforms + mutuality, communities of interest, participation, mass customisation, with alternate time frames and levels of immersion in mind, all lead to the creation of new value which is only possible when one can intuitively understand how these tools, processes and technological capabilities fit together.

Chapter Five

The big P and little p of transformation: once you have stormed the Bastille, you don't go back to your day job

As THE SHAPE OF OUR WORLD EVOLVES, we are also in political transformation, both in terms of the political relationship between the individual and commercial organisations and the large Politics of how we organise and run our societies. What should government look like in a non-linear world? Are we creating and running the right systems in the right way? Why is it too many people are disengaged with the process of democracy and civil organisation?

Data, democracy and identity

Where to start on this particular part of the journey through our non-linear world? The first step must address the issue of data; who would have thought even in 2005, that consumer politics and societal politics would revolve around data, who has it, who owns it and how it is used, combined with the legal frameworks that protect us as citizens.

The *Guardian* news brand now has a data blog, using data gleaned from a plethora of sources to create a different type of journalism. In January 2010, the London Datastore was opened, instigated by then Mayor Boris Johnson, releasing all of the Greater London Authority's data which under a Creative Commons licence publishes various data feeds from civil service organisations with the view that others could create a more transparent and collaborative form of democracy by allowing citizens to turn raw data into something that is useful for society. Duncan Campbell wrote that the move meant the release for the first time of 'huge realms of previously unavailable data' for everyone to see and use free of charge. And, for its part, the London Datastore website pledges that 'Releasing GLA data is just the beginning though and we'll be using our connections and influence to request and cajole other public sector organisations into following suit.' When data flows, things happen.[205]

---

205. http://smlxtralarge.com/2010/01/12/the-london-datastore/.

In the UK, the Ordnance Survey, which provides maps of the UK, has released all its data under a Creative Commons licence, after Sir Tim Berners-Lee, the inventor of the world wide web, advised Gordon Brown, then the prime minister, to make Ordnance Survey map data available for free because of its essential nature for linking together other sets of data. More controversially, the recent UK government has created the Public Data Corporation, which has many concerned about its mandate and agenda, Francis Maude outlined the pressure that the government is under, suggesting that many state agencies faced a conflict between maximising revenues from the sale of data and making the data freely available to be exploited for social and economic gain. Indeed, data from the Ordnance Survey mapping of the UK and even the MET office, plus 50 other main data sources, will be included in this new organisation – the big concern being raised is this then a commercial asset to be sold or to be a tool for better government?

For example, in Norway the government there has created a platform whereby an individual has access to all their personal data and transactions stored in one place. Each Norwegian citizen now has his or her own customised public service web portal called MyPage. The personal portal offers a dialogue with public authorities and makes it easier to find the services each individual might be looking for, without having any prior knowledge of which municipal or government office is responsible. Data becomes a core component of this parallel networked government whilst transparency is vital to the building of future long-term trusted relationships between individuals, communities and the state.

For most people, their introduction to this new and complex topic has come through news stories of various politicians and civil servants having lost laptops, on trains or elsewhere with sensitive data on hard drives. For example, Her Majesty's Revenue and Customs lost the records of 25 million people's names, addresses and bank account details when discs failed to arrive at their final destination, the audit office. Companies have had their servers hacked, notably Sony PlayStation that saw the details of 77 million subscribers swiped from its encrypted servers, whilst the US government is in a war of words with China over what is called Spear Phishing of individual Gmail accounts. Banks have sent the wrong information to the wrong people, and turning up the heat. News International finds itself currently in an unfolding and embarrassing scandal – the hacking into people's personal mobile phone messages to sell newspaper stories, which is a criminal offence. This story is important because it deals with many of the problems with our modern age; greed, power, corruption, doing whatever it takes to make money and the sovereignty of the individual. And finally, Julian Assange caused the world to literally reverberate with the 250,000 documents WikiLeaks published which brought to light the thoughts, behaviours and actions of western governments (notably the UK and the US), not necessarily with their best side showing.

Your destiny with data

What happens therefore to the data security, privacy and identity management once aggregated dynamic databases can be accessed and used? And the even bigger question is: how much of one's identity do people want to display as they navigate the networked world and how much of their personal information will they be prepared to give away, or even reveal, to get something of value back in return?

From an individual perspective, we leave continuous trails of data, plumes of bits of information. It's the personal exhaust from our digital interactions. These are the shadows and messy footprints of our daily lives. In the highly competitive world of marketing and commerce, this data is being recognised as increasingly important, with companies desperate to harvest, aggregate and refine it for commercial gain. Hal Varian, Google's chief economist, published a paper in which his research found that the peaks and troughs of Google searches would be predictive in the demand for certain goods and services.[206] Yet our destiny with data is complex. There are legitimate concerns about who actually owns this information, and when our identities can be pieced together via data flows, privacy becomes a key battleground. This requires companies to rethink key issues around trust and transparency. For example, the intense debates and community action that have resulted in Facebook having to learn what it can and cannot do with the data it holds has perhaps been an early indicator of how critical data has become to us all.

As we move through this wired-up world, we must also be aware of our identity in the public domain, or what some describe as 'presence'. People as an individual and citizen must become the owner and gatekeeper of their identity. Experts are trying to design a 'user-centric open identity network' or a new 'identity layer of the web' that would give us the ability to manage to some extent our identities – that is both our digital presence and offline identity. The idea is an identity system that is scalable (so it works everywhere), user-centric (so it serves people's interests, instead of being something done to them by external forces) and, importantly, customisable. This new system would recognise that each of us has multiple identities. We will be able to spoon out bits and pieces of our identity, depending on the social or business context we find ourselves in. From a commercial perspective, Doc Searls, a long-time promoter of digital identity who teaches at Harvard's Berkman Center for Internet & Society, believes such a system could be a viable alternative, described as the 'intention economy' that gives users control of their own attention and leads them to products, services, subjects and ideas that

206. http://static.googleusercontent.com/external_content/untrusted_dlcp/www.google.com/en//googleblogs/pdfs/google_predicting_the_present.pdf.

interest them.[207] It is evident today that there are many emergent trading platforms which are part of this trend.

Increasingly and over time we are leaving more pronounced digital footprints, especially given the rise of popular social networks.[208] It is our unique signature created out of the data trails left by a user's activity in a digital environment – which John Battelle calls the click-stream exhaust.[209] According to the Pew internet report,[210] there are two main classifications for digital footprints: passive digital footprints and active digital footprints. A passive digital footprint is created when data is collected about an action without any client activation, whereas active digital footprints are created when a user deliberately releases personal data for the purpose of sharing information about himself. In a digital context, many interactions, such as creating a social networking profile, or commenting on a picture in Flickr, leave a digital footprint. In a mobile context, complete data records are the transactional data that constitute the user's digital footprint.

However, the mere availability of transactional data alone is not enough since privacy and data protection rules will apply to the usage of data. There's a paradox with privacy. On one hand everyone fears losing it. Scott McNealy of Sun Microsystems famously said that consumer privacy is a red herring: we have zero privacy and we should all get over it.[211] But the alternative view is of the need to respect the sovereignty of the individual whether that be in a commercial or civil context. Esther Dyson argues that we need more granular control over our data. She believes that the notion of privacy doesn't fully capture the challenges of the current environment online:[212] 'We need to stop talking about privacy and start talking about control over data', she says. She argues that, in the future, users are going to want more granular control over their data, making detailed decisions about what gets shared with whom. 'Users may be overwhelmed when first setting up an account, but when they get more comfortable with an application, they will exert more control.' On the other hand, we all have an incentive to contribute data about ourselves, while reflecting on the manner in which we want to be seen, so as to be more visible within a digital context. For instance, even if you do nothing else

207. http://cyber.law.harvard.edu/people/dsearls. Alan Moore, 'Life and commerce in the connectivity of the cloud', http://smlxtralarge.com/2009/05/16/life-and-commerce-in-the-connectivity-of-clouds/. J. D. Lasica, 'Rapporteur', 'Identity in the age of Cloud Computing: the next-generation internet's impact on business, governance and social interaction', Aspen Institute, Communication and Society Program, 2009.

208. Ajit Jaokar et al., *Social Media Marketing: How Data Analytics Helps to Monetize the User Base in Telecoms, Social Networks, Media and Advertising in a Converged Ecosystem*, Futuretext, 2009.

209. http://battellemedia.com/archives/000647.php.

210. http://www.pewinternet.org/report_display.asp?r=229.

211. http://www.wired.com/politics/law/news/1999/01/17538.

212. www.pewinternet.org/pdfs/PIP_Digital_Footprints.pdf.

except create a profile on LinkedIn.com, you are immediately visible on Google, hence, you are contactable. The linking of disclosure of data and transparency will become a key currency in how data is collected, used and managed by buyers and sellers. And we will need to learn how to manage our own data and the implications of revealing that data to third parties whoever they may be. We may want to be found, and we may not, we may want certain engagements with a whole range of companies, organisations and individuals; data, and more importantly refined data, the black gold of the 21st century is the means by which that will happen.

Data as the interface in the intention economy

There are a number of emerging initiatives that empower the customer. One such initiative is called Vendor Relationship Management at Harvard Law School. According to their site Vendor Relationship Management (VRM) is the reciprocal of Customer Relationship Management (CRM), providing customers with tools for engaging with vendors in ways that work for both parties. CRM systems have been inefficient and clumsy mechanisms to try and keep customers or extract more money from them in a linear fashion, with emphasis on management not customers or relationships. Many companies take a very Roman view of their property rights over of their customers,[213] they like to say they 'own' the customer but no one has the right to own me, but that's the conflict for linear-minded companies. But people are increasingly becoming aware of being gouged by both corporations and governments, once again we arrive at a place where power relationships are being renegotiated.

We need markets that can work for both buyers and sellers – people need products and services and products and services need people, it's just that in the 21st century we help those people and those products and services to find each other when they need each other the most, by using data to fine tune those relationships.

The goal of VRM is to improve the relationship between demand and supply by providing new and better ways for the former to relate to the latter. In a larger sense, VRM intends to improve markets and their mechanisms by equipping customers to be independent leaders and not just captive followers in their relationships with vendors and other parties on the supply side of the marketplace. For VRM to work, vendors must have reason to value it, and customers must have reasons to invest the necessary time, effort and attention to making it work. Providing those reasons to both sides is the primary challenge for VRM.

---

213. The Romans were the first to introduce a legal framework of ownership that modern law and concepts of ownership are based upon.

VRM principles include:

- Relationships are voluntary.
- Customers are born free and independent of vendors.
- Customers control their own data. They can share data selectively and control the terms of its use.
- Customers are points of integration and origination for their own data.
- Customers can assert their own terms of engagement and service.
- Customers are free to express their demands and intentions outside any company's control.

Making VRM work

We're just beginning to see the emergence of a range of businesses that can truly address this issue. For example, Qustodian is a company that enables people to interface commercially with companies, and to better manage those relationships, via their data, which in this instance lists an individual's lifestyle and commercial preferences; this is a filtering sense-making process; Waitrose rather than Tesco, BMW rather than Audi, Wendy's rather than McDonald's, Whole Foods rather than Walmart. And of course the most natural way to interface with a range of companies that you want a 1 to 1 commercial relationship with is via the mobile-web. Users of the service provide information and data that's unique to them and consent in receiving information that can enable them to make and take commercial transactions and decisions. This is managed through what Qustodian call a 'Yoad'. Qustodian will help you create and manage your Yoad and share income generated by it with you. A Yoad is the database storing your profile information and lifestyle preferences for use by commercial traders to determine whether they should be communicating with you. Crucially your Yoad remains yours whilst Qustodian is the custodian of your data. The concept and reality of the ownership of data, with the interrelated memes of trust, transparency and disclosure, are what Qustodian believes are the keys to the future of sustainable business. As Agustin Calvo, a co-founder, explains when he describes his thoughts on why the ownership of data is so fundamental, 'Who owns my wife?' he asks,

> Nobody. Because it is not about ownership, it's about RELATIONS; the willingness to have a relationship, maintaining the relationship, adding value to it, gaining from it, giving and receiving ... There is no discussion ... my yoad is by definition mine, just like my wife is herself. But my wife is only one relationship, whilst with brands and companies, managing my yoad helps me

have relations of value and mutual benefit with whom I want, when I want and for what I want to have from that relation, by enabling me to have conversations with them, started by them, by me or by context, which can end (or not) in transactions.

Research not only with Qustodian but with other companies demonstrates that enabling people to navigate, aggregate and curate information in this way, albeit for commercial purposes, is something of great value to them. Further, on the basis that we trade for mutual benefit Qustodian also plan for open APIs so that others can help co-develop the platform, the business and also share in financial benefits of doing so. Qustodian shares a third of its revenue with its members, which is mobile law #2, the law of the ecosystem. Qustodian understands that only if the experience is a good trading experience people will use the service.

Qustodian is not built on search-based enquiries, but instead on people and their context, their data and their networks, matching them with companies who have goods, products and services to sell in a manner that is fairer and more equitable. The company launched last year. It's an innovative commercial model; it also understands something else very important: community. Qustodian is also building its business through networked communities of passion – established situated communities that have many reasons to connect and communicate with each other. In 2010 Qustodian invited Athletico Madrid onto its platform, offering its service for the club to share news and information with its passionate fan base. Qustodian knows that ultimately in that thriving marketplace as well as knowledge and information being traded, commerce will become a natural part of that market. As data expert and Stanford Professor Andreas Weigend believes, our world

> has shifted to a model of collaboration and explicit data creation. Successful firms develop systematic ways to encourage and reward users who contribute honest data. A good system does not try to trick customers into revealing demographics or contact information that is useful for the company. Rather, it rewards users with information that is useful to them.[214]

Bill of Rights

In a similar vein to Doc Searls and his VRM principles, privacy advocates have realised the implications of personal information being available on social networks. In response to these developments, a document called the Bill of Rights for the Social Web was released by Joseph Smarr, Marc Canter, Robert Scoble, and

---

214. Andreas Weigend, 'Now, new, next', *Harvard Business Review*, 20 May 2009. http://blogs.hbr.org/ now-new-next/2009/05/the-social-data-revolution.html.

Michael Arrington.[215] It publicly asserts that all users of the social web are entitled to certain fundamental rights, specifically ownership of their own personal information, including their own profile data, the list of people they are connected to and the activity stream of content they create; control of whether and how such personal information is shared with others; and freedom to grant persistent access to their personal information to trusted external sites. Sites supporting these rights shall:

- Allow users to syndicate their own profile data, their friends' list and the data that's shared with them via the service, using a persistent URL or API token and open data formats.
- Allow users to syndicate their own stream of activity outside the site.
- Allow users to link from their profile pages to external identifiers in a public way.
- Allow users to discover who else they know is also on their site, using the same external identifiers made available for look-up within the service.

The overall goals are concise and clear. In practice, this means as a user you have certain freedoms:

- If you're on Myspace and your friend is on Facebook, you should be able to contact them, share links, find out their friends.
- If you leave a social networking site, you should be able to 'take' all your data with you, including your contacts, friends and the content you have created. In practice, of course, this is not easy to implement and there are a number of initiatives created to address this problem because user data is not portable

As we can see, data will play an increasingly defining role in our lives, in so many ways. Evolving trading models, platforms and capabilities, redefining individual sovereignty and way we will interact with organisations commercially. It will also impact on the running of governments and the services that we as a society rely on, and how they may well be created in the future.

The political consequences of our non-linear world

John Keane in his book *The Life and Death of Democracy*,[216] describes the origins of democracy and by default how we manage to fundamentally get on with each other, evolving the democratic process over time to act as a control mechanism over power relationships that affect us through the myriad spectrums of local, regional, national and international life.

---

215. Bill of Rights for the Social Web. http://opensocialweb.org/2007/09/05/bill-of-rights/.
216. Keane, *The Life and Death of Democracy.*

Keane explains that, contrary to popular opinion, the belief that western powers have a God-given right to bring western democracy to the world is false. In fact, the ideas and language that formulated early democracy do not originate from Greece but from the east, from Mesopotamia, the lands of Syria, Iran and Iraq. And today the future of democracy will be decided in the Asian areas of the world including China. And there is no doubt that communication networks will play an equally significant role in deciding in what the next stage of our human built world looks like.

Democracy brought a secular sense of humility to the world as a mechanism to humble the powerful and to keep unbridled power in check. Democracy, argues Keane, brings a sense of equality to all human beings and a visceral sense of the possible. 'For democracy to be possible, people have to be sure that they themselves are the source of power of the institutions that govern their lives.'[217]

Like other institutions, including businesses and universities, democracy is also caught up in the process of 'glocalisation', And of course this brings pressure to the political outcomes of what happens next. Like many others, Keane notes that communications abundance is having a profound effect on people's visceral sense of being the true source of power, and explains that it is through proliferating communications media that we have now have the tools and capability to 'monitor' power far more closely. And I cannot help thinking that it is when ordinary people either engineer a participatory response to unfettered power – the Solidarity Movement, founded by Lech Walesa, the Velvet Revolution in the former Czechoslovakia, the Singing Revolution in Estonia, or more recent events such as the toppling of the Communist party in Moldova in 2009, or in northern Africa dubbed 'the Arab Spring', where leaders were prised from the rock face of their positions of power – or organise as a collaborative body co-determining budgeting for local communities in Brazil, for example. I see a connection in the power of networked communication with humanity as a species that is capable of achieving the sublime through high levels of organisation, participation and collaboration.

The consequences of that have significant implications. Since 1945, many of our pressing issues (often contrary to state interests) have been forced into consciousness not by 'political parties, elections, legislatures and governments', but mainly by people checking and confronting political power that 'run parallel to – and are often positioned against – the orthodox mechanisms of party-based politics'.

I wonder whether we are once again after a period of time taking matters into our own hands. Charles Malik,[218] was renowned as someone who profoundly believed in the principles of human rights. How do we, asked Malik, gain the rights of humanity on a global scale? Indeed, Malik believed that if humanity felt that the

---

217. Keane, *The Life and Death of Democracy*, p. 709.
218. Keane, *The Life and Death of Democracy*, p. 733.

various institutions of governance failed us we would take matters into our own hands – and we did. Yet in many ways, that was still confined to regions and countries. Is it possible this time around that through communications connectivity the scope changes? 'This new galaxy of media has no historical precedent', says Keane. It is

> a new world system of overlapping and interlinked media devices that integrate texts, sounds and images and enable communication to take place through multiple user points, in chosen time, either real or delayed, within modularised and ultimately global networks that are affordable and accessible to many hundreds of millions of people scattered across the globe.[219]

Politics as a consequence has become viral, even visceral, which implies that traditional frameworks of governance have become somewhat outdated, and consequently ineffectual. Therefore, Keane concludes, in the age of networked communications, organisations that are constantly monitoring the motives and actions of various powerful parties, 'combine into something of a Gestalt switch', which makes us think differently about how we perceive power and who wields it. In today's world, says Keane, the powerful are more often 'feeling the "pinch" of the powerless'.

Nicco Mele at the Harvard Kennedy School argues that governmental institutions in America are not failing, they have failed. California is essentially bankrupt and is attempting to rewrite the constitution as it cannot within its existing legislative framework solve its crisis. Over a long period of time politicians have failed the people they serve; corruption, negligence, and institutional failure is as evident as the failure of Flint Michigan. Mele also argues that people were shocked by the incompetence of George W. Bush, and the consequence was the extraordinary events that led to the election of Barack Obama to the American presidency. Ordinary Americans yearned for order, discipline and sanity, something missing from the George W. Bush era. But order, discipline and sanity has not materialised in the way America had hoped; the rise of the Tea Party movement, although positioned as anti-Obama and anti-Democrat party, has its roots tapping into a deeper frustration of the failed institution of American governance at a local and state level. It is without doubt a volatile mixture. And, more importantly in Britain and throughout the European Union, it is recognised that structurally government big and small cannot afford business as usual, but has also not delivered properly to the people they serve. So once again we face a design challenge.

---

219. Keane, *The Life and Death of Democracy*, p. 738.

What happens next will not happen by divine right. The good shall not inherit the earth; professional politicians have not delivered us a secure and safe world, and we cannot leave it to those who, motivated by a mixture of rage and fear, wish to enforce more fundamental ideologies on us all. So we have to work at it – individual and collective accountability demands us to become participants, because as like any road map there is no one superhighway to the future, but a series of interlocked roads and other topographical features that will challenge the ultimate outcome for us all – we are at a dramatic moment of how do we get from here to there? Cynicism and disaffection are but two examples as distractions to the bigger prize. By the end of the 1990s, Poland, France, the United Kingdom, Hungary and the Netherlands had the lowest turnouts ever recorded for voting, and so did the numbers of people prepared to join a political party decline.

Disaffected and cynical, why vote in a postcode lottery? Why vote when there is no one to vote for? Keane says the question arises of where we can apply our vote to be meaningful; remember the second Pop Idol in the United States which first introduced text message voting was the biggest texting event in the world at that time: 7.5 million people, and 30% of that 7.5 million had never sent a text message before. This is significant statistic – getting people to change their behaviour around technology is always challenging. So this demonstrates the deep human need and motivation to participate, albeit in a wannabe pop star show. It's a long way from the Putney debates between Oliver Cromwell, his new model army and the Levellers at the Church of St Mary the Virgin, Putney, in October and November 1647. The Leveller programme included religious toleration, reform of the law, free trade, an extended franchise, rights guaranteed under a written constitution and a government answerable to the people rather than to king or parliament.[220]

That said, the first ever televised election debates in the UK of 2009 certainly stimulated perhaps in recent times almost unprecedented heated and engaged discussion about what type of democracy and government the UK wanted next. And those conversations flowed in bars, cafés, the workplace and through social networking platforms. It is ironic, then, that due to our antiquated voting system, some people were turned away from polling stations denying them of their democratic right to vote.

Today, political parties are beset with the issue of how to reach and connect with their citizens; now fearful that cynicism becomes the one-way street to irrelevancy, people are looking for something where their contributions are recognised, and increasingly demur from the pre-packaged micro-wave politics which has created a form of political obesity with all its nefarious problems (just

---

220. Geoffrey Robertson, *The Levellers: The Putney Debates* (Revolutions Series), Verso, 2007.

consider the case of Silvio Berlusconi). And yet at the end of this sad tale of woe I see a green shoot of optimism, in that, it is the actions of people individually motivated and collectively organised where there exists the potential for something new – unprecedented, as Keane reminds us. As Nicco Mele told me, people are learning to get what they need from each other, when faced with institutional failure. And it was Jean Monnet,[221] who believed it is when small actions can access the true point of leverage where those very small steps become snowball-like in their effect.

It is this lightness of touch that inspires me, but one I wonder whether our politicians have sight of, or sensitivity towards how to design and create such outcomes? To illuminate, 'Minnesota Works Together' is a system of collaborative engagement that enables people in the state of Minnesota to navigate effectively from 'me to we attitudes', particularly in enabling everyday people and those elected or engaged professionally with civic duties to find common ground, in 'defining problems and finding policy solutions'. There is much wisdom in such mechanisms, argues Keane, yet his tone is mournful. It seems that at an infrastructure level the opportunity has been more miss than hit. And of course the whole hoo ha around social media and the utopianism associated with the internet and all things digital becomes the dense fog that dissipates the ability for many to miss the landscape of the true opportunity. There are many voices that argue for the 'rejuvenation of local government', and the 'redesign of town halls, so that they felt and functioned much more like open public spaces', and more 'extensive use of participatory budgeting' – something that I believe has been badly overlooked at all levels of political life.

Consider a world where we are exhausted by the penetration of all things market driven into the arterial life of democracy, combined with fatalism, disaffection and the violence which has been done to others in the cause of democracy – why should we care? It makes you stop and wonder, and its here that we feel the sense of optimism – Renaissances are historical acts of rebirth, Richard Sennett has argued for it and paradoxically the idea that we can all have a hand in shaping our world anew has witnessed a recent surge of energy and 'creativity'. The true idea of democracy is that we can just get on with each other, even in complex multifaith and culturally diverse societies. The rough and tumble of humanity is what it's all about and it is this capacity to collectively solve problems that is what makes us unique.

> The radical implications is clear; democracy is a universal ideal because it is a basic precondition of people being able to live together on earth freed from arrogant power fed by talk inspired by principles like God, History, Truth, Man Progress, the Party, the Market, the Leader of the Nation.[222]

---

221. Keane, *The Life and Death of Democracy*, p. 822.
222. Keane, *The Life and Death of Democracy*, p. 852.

It is an eternal unwinnable struggle, yet it is also one that if we, in Keane's words, 'abandon', then we do so at the peril of humanity itself.[223] The idea that we are all equals, capable of making and taking decisions to better survive or get along, is central to this argument. Keane says democracy was a sensational invention, the idea that people would not allow themselves to be led by those that assumed the position of total authority. The idea is that 'when democracy takes hold of people's lives, it gives them a glimpse of the contingency of things. They are injected with the feeling that the world can be other than it is – that situations can be countered, outcomes altered, people's lives changed through individual and collective action'. And we are now using communication networks to achieve that ideal today. Democracy is, Keane argues, 'the best human weapon against hubris and folly, that are inevitable consequences of concentrations of unaccountable power'.

People power in politics

So how do we make the powerful feel the pinch of the powerless? By renegotiating our relationships to each other, renegotiating our relationship with commerce and business and renegotiating our relationship with government. The story of the incredible events that led up to Spanish election of 2004 is a case in point.

Spain was preparing for a peaceful 'change of guard' after the 14 March 2004 elections. The ruling Popular Party (PP) was comfortably ahead in the polls, and the incumbent prime minister was bound to deliver the government to his recently chosen successor. Instead, on 11 March the country woke in horror as ten bombs blew up in commuter trains, the first right outside the Atocha station, killing almost 200 and injuring more than 1,500 souls.

Panic spread throughout Spain and the world. After five painful hours, the prime minister accused the Basque terrorist group of the atrocity; it was the proof that his party's hard line against ETA terrorists was justified. Meanwhile, a cassette tape recorded in Arab was found in an abandoned van, suggesting connections with Al-Qaeda. In fact, by 21:30 an Islamic group claimed responsibility for the attack, justifying it on the Spanish government's support for the invasion of Iraq.

During the next day, as more evidence linked to the attacks was discovered, the government continued to point the finger at ETA, which issued a statement denying any knowledge or involvement in the act. Such was the sense of collective and national outrage that by the evening, all over Spain, 11 million people gathered in city squares shouting: 'No to terrorism.' Saturday, 13 March, should have been a day for contemplative reflection before the elections. Instead, as evidence

---

223. Keane, *The Life and Death of Democracy*, p. 867.

contradicting the government's version kept appearing, many started to wonder about the honesty of the officials' declarations. Simply put, had the terrorist attack come from ETA, it would benefit their political agenda; had it come from Al-Qaeda, it would be a severe blow.

At around noon, the first SMS with the simple message: 'The government lied. Pass it on' started to appear on people's mobile phones. No one really knows who started it, but there were soon other SMSs and emails with similar messages circulating throughout Spain. By 23:00, there were more than 10,000 people gathered in front of the PP Madrid headquarters, according to Euronews, while similar rallies sprang up in all of the main Spanish cities. The PP accused the PSOE, the main opposition party, of starting the rallies to pressure voters the following day. The PSOE knew it had it not been the instigator of the SMS chains, but had actually kept quiet because it knew the government was wrong in its ETA argument. But the PSOE refused to challenge the official version for electoral purposes. Later on, the PSOE realised it was indeed the main beneficiary of the phenomenon, but it maintained that at the time it had no control of what was happening on the streets.

Spain's political parties and media tried in vain to find the source of the messages and some say they still are doing so. Most of all, everyone was baffled by the remarks from people present at the rallies that some claimed to have received the same message from five different people. Even traditional PP supporters joined the rallies because it was not a political gathering from only one side of the society, but a quest for truth. And whoever started the chain of events, the consequence was that the outcome of the elections were irrevocably altered by the sheer amount of networked communications and SMS messaging during the weekend.

From political militants to people on the street wanting to know the real truth about the attacks, it seems like at least one person in every Spanish family received one or more SMS message, and was sufficiently motivated to literally 'pass it on' to acquaintances. Young users were particularly active, with many saying that when they received the text message, they sent it on to everyone on their contact list. This was to be the first time when the results of a national election could be ultimately traced to the activity of a minority of well-connected individuals. Amidst this snowball effect: the alpha-users and their communities arrived in politics.

The power of self-motivated crowds connected in spontaneous action suggests some interesting challenges for governments. If 11 March signalled the first attacks to be triggered by a mobile phone, the 14 March elections in Spain were the first ones decided by SMS. Politicians bemoan the lack of voter engagement but in the future they may well wish that things had remained just like that. In my lifetime I never thought I would see the end of the Cold War and the fall of the Berlin Wall. Now, I'm not so sure that ultimate top down-control is even possible where communications connectivity can radiate truth into the wider world in seconds, or that indeed we want it. Although that will also have its own dynamics and consequences. What we've seen in recent years is the use of networked participatory communication networks being deployed to challenge authority.

In 2006, 20,000 high school students of Mexican race used Myspace to organise a mass walk-out from classes in Los Angeles to protest against a proposed immigration law. The planned legislation would have made it possible for the parents of these children to be deported as illegal immigrants. But the speed, size and scale of the demonstration scared legislators out of passing any immigration laws. These young children were successful in their political goals. These children hadn't joined Myspace to undertake political activism but they knew it was a communications media which they instinctively used as a collaborative tool when they needed to organise themselves.

But it's not only in the west that this communications revolution is altering our lives. The use of networked communications is widespread, and the attempts by governments around the world, in a variety of ways, sometimes ingenious (China, Korea), and sometimes brutal (Libya, Burma, Syria, Bahrain), to stifle free speech, extensive. Iran is a case in point. Life under the rule of the Iranian ultraconservatives is constrained and highly regulated. What has erupted are the independent voices of people expressing their views via blogs, Twitter and other social networks. In Iran in 2009 it was reported that there were more than 60,000 active blogs or weblogs; this is the place Iranians call 'Weblogistan': a land of free speech. A formidable number of independent voices for a country accustomed to tightly controlling the press. The Open Net Initiative reports that the growing popularity of the internet has led to increasing government scrutiny. Everyday people become dissenting voices online, as well as human rights activists, bloggers and online media outlets; they have all become the target of government regulatory action and are subject to arrest, imprisonment and torture.[224]

The collision between these two sides of Iran – hardline versus those that want a fairer world – represents an important battle over the freedoms they seek and are entitled to. The outcome in part will dictate the future shape of Iran, but more critically it may well be that networked communications will increasingly be used as a political tool, heralding a new species of protest that's potentially entirely irrepressible. In *We Are Iran*[225] by Nasrin Alavi, Lolivashaneh, a former Iranian blogger states:

224. http://opennet.net/research/profiles/iran.
225. Nasrin Alavi, *We Are Iran: The Persian Blogs*, Soft Skull Press, 2005.

I keep a weblog so that I can breathe in this suffocating air ... In a society where one is taken to history's abattoir for the small crime of thinking, I write so as not to be lost in my despair ... here I feel that I am in a place where my calls for justice can be uttered ... I write a weblog so that I can shout, cry and laugh, and do the things that they have taken away from me in Iran today.

Mahmoud Ahmadinejad's landslide victory in early 2009 brought a wave of massive protest demonstrations, organised through Twitter, mobile communications, blogs. This became known as the Green Movement. The reaction was violent and bloody, and so the movement resorted to the ancient Iranian custom of dissent, the shouting at night from the rooftops.

My next door neighbour is an immigrant who came here in 1977. He just received a SAT phone call from his brother in Tehran who reports that the rooftops of night time Tehran are filled with people shouting 'Allah O Akbar' in protest of the government and election results. The last time he remembers this happening is in 1979 during the Revolution. Says the sound of tens of thousands on the rooftops is deafening right now. It's almost four in the morning in Iran.[226]

However, that does not represent the whole story, as whilst the online world bubbles away, in 2006 women in Iran formed the One Million Signatures Campaign. Its purpose was to challenge the laws that discriminated against women in a variety of ways. The campaign intended to raise one million signatures as a means of protest which would apply pressure for reform. Yet again, Iran has responded by applying the means of violence, detention and physical punishment, but the women in spite of everything and supported by a global community still pursue their claim.[227]

Today, when people have a high need to force political change, combined with a collective sense and awareness of why and how to act, they have the means at their disposal which did not exist when the Berlin Wall came down. Digital networked communication tools can harness information, and people can coordinate collective action that, as Kevin Kelly believes, unleashes involvement and interactivity at levels once thought unfashionable or impossible. Egypt and the recent tumultuous events is a case in point. The then President Mubarak, in seeking to control the unfolding drama of people-powered protest, shut down the internet; in so doing he hoped to both stop the coordinating flow of information between protestors and draw a veil over the prying eyes of the watching world. In a weekend Google engineers created and had operational a system called speak-to-tweet (twitter.com/speak2tweet). With three available international phone numbers, protestors could still send information

226. http://www.huffingtonpost.com/2009/06/13/iran-demonstrations-viole_n_215189.html;
    http://www.huffingtonpost.com/2009/06/14/iran-updates-video-live-b_n_215378.html.
227. http://en.wikipedia.org/wiki/One_Million_Signatures.

out into the world using Twitter, via leaving updated information as a voicemail using normal telephony. As the old cliché goes, necessity is the mother of invention.

More significantly, Howard Rheingold questions how such activity influences the sense of civic duty young people will feel in the future by the consequences of their actions. 'Ordinary people can be instruments of the sublime', wrote the author and playwright, Alan Bennett. And once you've stormed the Bastille, you don't go back to your day job – right? We often cite the apathy of youth and their disengagement with the world around them for not being interested in civic-related concerns or even politics. In part, this is true in as much that, in many ways, we have the civic mindedness educated out of us, and are deeply cynical of the true motives of those that represent us. On the other hand, I believe people possess the capacity to engage with the world when they know that their actions will lead to positive outcomes.

System reboot for civil society

As networked communications and their associated tools and capabilities have intertwined with participatory cultures, it has become clear that the barriers to getting stuff done through a collective approach has become once again possible; it offers up new organisational models that would allow social institutions and social services to operate in different ways, embedding them into our local communities in more lightweight and meaningful ways.

Many people have argued that government and industry should take advantage of these innovations to create more people-powered organisations. Now, in the face of serious crises in both the economy and the political system, and in the middle of a recession that calls into question whether we can even afford 'business as usual', it's time to take a serious look at how we can leverage human talent, energy and creativity to begin rebooting the system to create sustainable, affordable, long-term mechanisms for public engagement.

Lee Bryant argues that in order to make better use of government spending to make it go further, government procurement should be treated as a stimulus fund and used to deliver social and economic benefits as well as products and services. Secondly, he believes people power should be harnessed to improve existing democratic and public services. Don't just create a service and leave it to languish, he urges. Instead, enable constant flows of feedback to constantly and incrementally improve the effectiveness of that service.[228]

It is within human collective action that we identify a new pathway to success. Henry Jenkins writes: 'In a networked society, people are increasingly forming

---

228. Lee Bryant, 'People power can reboot Britain', *Independent*, 22 June 2009. http://www.independent.co.uk/opinion/commentators/lee-bryant-people-power-can-reboot-britain-1713007.html.

knowledge communities to pool information and work together to solve problems they could not confront individually. We call that collective intelligence.'[229] This is what Bryant alludes to.

Bearing that in mind, in the next decade with the problems we collectively are confronting, we will need to be radical about power, realistic about money and relentless on innovation.[230] Equally, we need some collective, participatory imagination to realise our possible future. The big question, though, is how to achieve any of this? In the US, federal Chief Information Officer Vivek Kundra has outlined plans for pursuing these ideas. In the UK, Bryant observes that we have a late 20th century government in its final phase, so we should not expect too much. Perhaps it's better for all of us to simply get on with it and create our own structures and services; as he says, the 20th century is over.[231]

Let's reconsider the role of literacy here, and with historical precedent of the French Revolution, it was the language defined and used by pamphleteers and journalists that started to describe a new way of governance and society, that defined what came after the bloodiest days of the revolution. And it was this language that gave the aftermath of the physical revolution, its means of action, by which it evolved new systems, institutions and a way of life. So what if we imagined a language not of modern management, but one that embodied more humanistic life-giving qualities? Perhaps at that point people would be happy to re-engage in public life.

Such is the distrust in current government that when 'DIY government' is mentioned, there is a great deal of sneering at such initiatives. But it's the only way we can build our own version of a society that's strong, lightweight, adaptive, socially cohesive and enduring. It's only when people get to put some skin in the game, when they feel that their actions count, when they are recognised as meaningful, when it is understood that the needs of one place are very different to those of another, that they then take ownership. David Osimo in Public Services 2.0,[232] says that we are already on the journey whereby the idea and notion of a participatory and engaged society 'is moving from the periphery to the centre of policy debate'. He adds:

> Yet it is also clear that web 2.0 initiatives are still exceptional and marginal in the government context, and that progress is too slow so that the gap with web-based innovation is widening, rather than closing up. Governments are not in a position to decide on the direction of this evolution, as progress is being shaped by broader underlying forces, such as generational trends and

229. Jenkins, *Convergence Culture*, p. 235, also see pp. 20, 22, 26–7, 52–4, 57, 100, 127, 129, 200, 245. Also see: http://p2pfoundation.net/Convergence_Culture.
230. http://liambyrne.co.uk/.
231. Lee Bryant, 'People power can reboot Britain', *Independent*, 22 June 2009.
232. www.epractice.eu/en/library/298783.

citizens' expectation. But government can influence the speed and nature of this change, and make sure that it is less traumatic and confrontational, and more shared and inclusive.

Co-creation

So the idea evolves into what is described as co-produced government.[233] C. K. Prahalad and Venkatram Ramaswamy, writing in 'The co-creation connection',[234] explain the difference when one engages with the principles of co-creation. Whereas the traditional company-centric view says that the consumer is outside the domain of the value chain, they state that the consumer-centric view says the consumer is an integral part of the system for value creation. Similarly, while in the traditional model the enterprise controls where, when and how value is added in the value chain; the model centred on the consumer accepts that consumers can influence where, when and how value is generated. Where value is created in a series of activities controlled by the enterprise before the point of purchase in the traditional system, a consumer-centric approach says that the consumer need not respect industry boundaries in the search for value. And finally, while in the company-centric system, there is a single point of exchange where value is extracted from the customer for the enterprise, the consumer-centric one allows that the consumer can compete with companies for value extraction. The other advantage of the consumer-centric view, they say, is that there are multiple points of exchange where the consumer and the company can co-create value.

However, as we have seen already, co-creation can and is having a dramatic impact upon how many different types of organisation and institution there are – it is in many ways an ancient knowledge, and perhaps is only once again seeing a resurgence because the current system is faltering. So to go forwards we need to go back as there are lessons we can draw upon.

Curitaba: whole system solutions for complex problems

There is no doubt that the trilemma we currently face is forcing the debate. And so how we frame problems and how we effectively resolve them is going to make a significant difference. A lesson learned many years ago in a Brazilian city called Curitaba. In *Natural Capitalism*, the authors point to how if we try to cope by naming and solving problems one at a time we lose perspective of the true goal. By focusing on small parts of a wider ecosystem, we think we are creating efficiency,

---

233. David Boyle and Michael Harris, *The Challenge of Co-Production*, NEF and NESTA, 2009.
234. Booz Allen Hamilton Inc., 'The co-creation connection', 1 May 2002.

when in fact we can't see the metaphorical wood for the metaphorical trees.

> Faced with congestion, their answer is to widen streets and build bypasses and parking garages. Crime? Lock up the offenders. Smog? Regulate emissions. Illiteracy? Toughen standards. Litter? Raise fines. Homelessness? Build shelters, and if that seems to fail, jail the loiterers. Insufficient budget to fund all these competing priorities? Raise taxes or impose sacrificial austerity, to taste. Disaffected voters? Blame political enemies.[235]

Curitaba is a city in the south-east of Brazil that was able to extricate itself from seemingly insurmountable challenges that had inflected onto every part of the city, its infrastructure and its people. The story of Curitaba is enlightening in how the city creatively addressed those problems – from a systems and networked perspective understanding they were interlinked and that a designed approach would bring greater and more sustainable benefits. The networked interventions, were cognisant of the interconnectedness of Curitaba's problems rather than trying to resolve complex problems in a siloed manner; this was the means by which Curitaba was able to address the future direction of the city and its people.

But we must go back to the 1960s and 1970s. At that time Curitaba was a city with significant infrastructure, social, economic, educational and health challenges. The architect of Curitaba's miraculous turnaround was a man called Jamie Lerner who, as the authors in *Natural Capitalism* write, was 'informal, energetic, intensely practical, with the brain of a technocrat and a heart of a poet', not unlike Richard Sennett's Craftsman. So how did Lerner do it? How did he inspire and enable Curitaba to pull itself up by its bootstraps and become a thriving vibrant city? Being trained as a planner and an architect, Lerner significantly identified the problems of the city as interrelated, and so sought solutions reflecting that. He also recognised that the people of Curitaba must feel included, listened to and involved. Indeed, Lerner believed that 'If people feel respected, they will assume responsibility to help solve other problems'.

And Lerner also stipulated that solutions had to be four things. They must be simple, fast fun and cheap. Lerner was of the view that people are willing to hope for and engage in creating a better world when they see visible change. In such circumstances, the only way to achieve this was to get things done at speed. He realised that the credibility of his office would come from creating a municipal park in three weeks, launching an extensive recycling programme a few months after its initial conception.

---

235. Hawken, Lovins and Lovins, *Natural Capitalism*, p. 285.

Consequently, the six mayors that followed treated Curitiba not as a political football but as a design problem, those six mayors twenty-eight years (and counting) of good management have generated a flow of interconnected, interactive, evolving solutions – mostly devised and implemented by partnerships among private firms, non-governmental organisations, municipal agencies, utilities, community groups, neighbourhood associations, and individual citizens. Curitiba is not a top-down, mayor dominated city; everyone respects the fact that while it is served by leaders, many of the best ideas and most of their implementation come from its citizens. It encourages entrepreneurial solutions.[236]

What are the lessons here for us? In *Natural Capitalism*, the authors identify that it is

by the strength of good design, treating a wide variety of needs not as competing priorities to be traded off and compromised but rather as interlinked opportunities for synergies to be optimised. In Curitiba, its results show how to combine a healthy ecosphere, a vibrant and just economy, and a society that nurtures humanity.[237]

Today, local government still thinks in a linear fashion; it is almost as if local government is not part of the local community – it provides by pushing out 'services' to the community that should 'consume' them or indeed retracts them when it can't pay for them. The lesson of Curitiba is that there is indeed a more sustainable approach, and this is found in Prahalad's and Ramswamy's ideas around co-creation.

From eGov to weGov

Over the past few years, government big and small has felt its way into an increasingly complex society – eGovernment was about fixing the existing system through technology, which was exactly the same as the commercial sector. Conventional wisdom was that the problem was technological, not a cultural one that was impacting business models from top to bottom, or in fact from the bottom to the top. It is now recognised that there exists a new framework where people-powered public services redefine the role and function of government. This becomes more lightweight, flexible, adaptive and sustainable – part of the human operating system of our non-linear world. We need, therefore, a step change that Stephen Goldsmith, in *The Power of Social Innovation*, explains is necessary and natural when decision-making is built upon systems of participation. He says:

---

236. Hawken, Lovins and Lovins, *Natural Capitalism*, p. 308.
237. Hawken, Lovins and Lovins, *Natural Capitalism*, p. 308

A leap forward in the quality of life in communities will occur more frequently when government opens the door for catalytic social progress spearheaded by the many ... who make changes daily in their communities. Together these acts can play a part in turning clients of the state into active, participating and productive citizens.[238]

And as a report from the Ash Center for Democratic Governance and Innovation at Harvard Kennedy School concurred, no one can now afford to go it alone, with the rising costs of services and the ability for government to manage an increasingly complex society just too difficult.[239] Yet the demand for better services still remains a constant pressure.

Better thinking, better world

The ability to co-create, co-design and work in a more participatory manner matters. There is a need for new ways to better understand social trends, norms and networks if government is going to remain relevant and able to help enact behaviour change. It demands a culture of openness which in itself is a form of resilience. It certainly needs to be a more adaptive one; this is achieved by empowering everyday people to lead and make change. Government needs to lay the foundations of this society, enabling inclusion through using open data and networked communications technology. Then it needs to foster culture change inside and outside of government, adopting a more networked form of leadership. Finally, it has to catalyse and nurture innovation.

Today we seek creative leadership that seeks out a new form of what government in the 21st century could be. The idea of aggregating the work of others and sharing that work by using the networked communications and convening power of government to redistribute that knowledge makes enormous sense, which means government becomes a trusted point of reference – no bad thing when you are tasked with being responsible for running the country. Data plays once again a key role in delivering real benefits by allowing access and interfacing with government in a user-centric way, while the costs of set-up and administration are kept low. But of course the value is now two-way; the report argues that such a networked, communicative system improves government's ability to 'listen, learn and (re)act

---

238. Stephen Goldsmith, *The Power of Social Innovation: How Civic Entrepreneurs Ignite Community Networks for Good*, Jossey-Bass, 2010.

239. 'From the "now wave" to the "next wave": public service delivery in a networked world'. The report was written by Dominic Campbell of FutureGov, Stephen Goldsmith, Daniel Paul Professor of Government, Harvard Kennedy School, Zach Tumin, Executive Director for Leadership for a Networked World , Harvard Kennedy School, 2009.

appropriately'.[240] It is in these ways that we can see how the state can be faster, leaner, better, more effective and more relevant. There is a growing awareness in North American and European governments over the past 18 months of better understanding how to implement social technologies for social change.[241] But to be clear, this is not and never has been about technology – it is all about people, people that make community, society, nations, continents. The technology is the tool; it is how we hold it, and use it, that is important.

Pattern recognition in emergent systems

A pattern is emerging: an international groundswell of people increasingly committed to being the midwives of bringing into this world ways in which we can deliver a more sustainable regenerative society predicated on the idea that humanity is pretty good at working out how to get along with each other. As Micah Sifry observes:[242] 'From Wikipedia to Craigslist to Amazon to Google, the web keeps rewarding those actors who empower ordinary users, eliminate wasteful middlemen, share information openly, and shift power from the centre to the edges.' We must also bear in mind that one does not replace the other but becomes part of the bigger whole, a parallel ecosystem so to speak. Carrie Bish says that in a parallel approach, when people often revert to an 'either or' argument, 'parallel structures' do seem to work. You don't destroy or change what's there, you just resolutely go about building an alternative. We're starting to see the effects of this today in every industry and organisation – our networked world has provided a platform for parallel structures and better alternatives have emerged. I think the same could be achieved with public services. Many of them no longer meet people's needs, so rather than trying to change government from the inside there is a good chance that building new public services outside of its walls may be the answer.

---

240. 'From the "now wave" to the "next wave": public service delivery in a networked world'.
241. Dominic Campbell, 'Socialised Government: the rise of micro service uninstitutions', 28 September 2009. http://personaldemocracy.com/blog-entry/socialised-government-rise-micro-public-service-uninstitutions.
242. Micah Sifry, '"You can be the eyes and ears" – Barack Obama and the wisdom of the crowds', in Daniel Lathrop and Laurel Ruma (eds.), *Open Government, Transparency, Collaboration, and Participation in Practice*, O'Reilly, 2010.

Chapter Six

Crafting a new pursuit of happiness: re-ordering work and play

REFLECTING ON HOW A TRUE SENSE OF authentic participation changes our sense of engagement with the world, it's time to turn to the idea and language of craftsmanship, and its integral role in the connection between I + We. This is part and parcel of the unfolding of ideas and language that can help us describe the possibilities of a regenerative and open society that so many now argue for.

Social philosopher Richard Sennett's book *The Craftsman* is an exploration into the idea of craftsmanship. His journey begins with the basics of technique and personal expression that define the mechanics of craftsmanship. Then he applies that philosophy to how craftsmanship could be at the epicentre of social good in modern society. Sennett's view is that craftsmanship is an innate capability in nearly all of us, and that 'nature furnished humanity at large with the intelligence to do good work (craft skills)'.[243] The consequence of which was we became engaged citizens. He writes: 'Our species ability to make things reveals more what we share. Learning to work well enables people to govern themselves and become good citizens.'[244]

It is this deep thinking around the deep social constructs of craftsmanship which allows us to envision how as humanity and individuals we are able to re-engage meaningfully with each other, and feel respected within a wider group. I + We = social cohesion. 'Man seeks those tools that once again can be the bringer of peace and be a maker not a breaker of civilisation, man uses and applies those tools for the collective good', argues Sennett.

Every single one of us a craftsman

Steve Ireland, who was regional director of the BBC North East for many years, has begun to undertake a project called *Our Life*, along with his business partner

243. Sennett, *The Craftsman*, p. 241.
244. Sennett, *The Craftsman*, pp. 268–9.

Rob Hallam. Steve's perspective is that with low-cost media and communication production tools at our fingertips, young people can be helped to re-engage with the world around them by learning to become 'craftsmen and craftswomen' with all the good brought forth through in this instance, the craft of communication. This has some significant outcomes. By learning how to shoot video, edit, interview, construct a story, be critical of information and think about the ethical implications of their storytelling, young people discover what is important to themselves and in doing so they acquire a different type of literacy. This literacy enables people to be more thoughtful, to be able to critique and produce cultural content. The more of us that become part of doing more, engaging more, creating more, the greater we are constructively shaping civil society. We enrich society through individual and collective actions and doing so enriches us too. This all means that we will contribute, commit and engage more, as there is more context, more meaning in what we do. Initially, the troubled housing estate that Steve went to, and the kids he worked with there were reluctant participants but they were sufficiently interested to turn up. Over a couple of weekends Steve and a small team enabled these children to perhaps consider for the first time a different type of engagement with the world, to look at it critically and produce a piece of media communications that was created entirely by them. Sennett makes the connection between recent technological developments and the ancient model for craftsmanship. People aspire to be good craftsmen, but such people have been ignored and misunderstood by institutions, and as a consequence they become depressed and withdraw inwards on themselves.

There is something in making and creating that viscerally brings people into the world. In doing so we become more aware, more open, more engaged. Life becomes essentially more meaningful.

Working well

Reflecting on the craftsman analogy, Sennett explores how and why people will work well, which is opposite to the capitalist-held view that the motivation to work well is defined not by the need to do good work, to collaborate and find meaning in that work, but by pure competition. But the combination of craftsmanship and participatory cultures demand by default that we must work together collectively to high standards. This results in a sense of mutual and self-respect, argues Sennett. My own personal happiest working experience was in Finland in the marketing communications company Hasan & Partners. The company's culture required me to apply my skills as thinker, art director, typographer, graphic designer, storyteller, teacher and at the interface with clients. If I could not have worked effectively in any of these disciplines then my time there would have been shorter, and ultimately less fulfilling. It was demanding but, as a consequence of my personal commitment to work well, I produced good work and developed a lifelong respect of those that I worked with. When I returned to England in 1995 to work in a major advertising agency in London I underwent something of a culture shock. I was no longer in the craftsman's studio. I was, to my mind, in a factory.

Adam Smith declared in The Wealth of Nations that in a factory 'the man whose whole life is spent in performing a few simple operations ... becomes as stupid and as ignorant as it is possible for a human creature to become'. Craftsmanship in the 21st century provides us with a framework to reverse this trend. Sennett tells us that the craftsman constructs authentically. His honesty is communicated through his work, which then holds an inherent eternal truth. And the craftsman represents all of us with a desire to do something well, concretely and for reasons for other than material profit. It's the unleashing of this deep motivation that we seek.

The axeness of an axe: systems design

Reflecting on Sennett's thoughts and observations about craftsmanship what has axe-making got to teach us? Well quite a great deal, if we are prepared to be open to what Gabriel Branby, chief executive of Gränfors Bruks, has to say. Branby's story starts with him buying Gränfors Bruks; discovering the company was in crisis financially, he also realised that the inequitable way in which people were paid showed in personal motivation and the end quality of the product. So he sought to find a way that would bring his workforce together as a community, in which they all believed they were sharing equitably, married with a refined production process and an ethical approach to business.

Branby's story is about how one designs and builds a successful company predicated on quality; a quality of product achieved through systems thinking that also incorporated a process to bring out the ethical and committed craftsman in his entire workforce. These committed craftsmen and women are able to produce the best axes in the world. Which is why we have to ask what is the axeness of an axe? 'The axeness of an axe? What on earth does that mean I hear you ask? Well it's about starting with the essence of something, stripping things down and taking away anything that is superfluous.'[245] Take away unnecessary materials and production processes and add knowledge, Branby explains. At his factory in Sweden, Branby has a collection of over 2,000 axe heads. In wanting to learn about the axeness of an axe, Gabriel travelled extensively through his homeland of Sweden

245. Leonora Oppenheim, 'The Do Lectures – the axeness of an axe', Treehugger, 9 September 2009. http://www.treehugger.com/files/2009/09/the-do-lectures-axeness-of-an-axe.php.

and further afield talking to people that use axes on a daily basis. Branby gathered extensive information on axes – their usage and design. That knowledge ultimately informed both the business design and the manufacturing process he employs.

Responsibility for 'The Total'

Branby thinks in systems; he calls his worldview and philosophy 'The Total', as it encompasses ethics, business, production process, products and the world in which we inhabit. For him, 'What we take, what we make and what we waste' are in fact all questions of ethics. We have, he says, an unlimited responsibility for 'The Total', a responsibility that we try but do not always succeed in taking. One part of that responsibility is the quality of the product and how many years it will endure. Rather than designing in obsolescence, Gabriel designs it out.

This philosophy in making a high-quality sustainable product is a way to pay respect to the axe and its user, and to nature, which provides the raw material. A high-quality product in the hands of those who have learned how to use it and look after it will very likely be more durable. This is good for the owner, but it is also beneficial as part of a greater whole; increased durability means that we take less (decreased consumption of material and energy), that we need to produce less (which gives us more time to do other things we think are important or enjoyable) and that we destroy less (so there is less waste).

Gränsfors axes are forged by craftsmen, smiths motivated to do good work, who are able to forge axes with such precision that no supplementary work is needed to stone, grind, smooth or paint the axes to hide mistakes in the forging. The forging craft is allowed to take its time. The smiths do not work by the piece. They take care and do the right forging from the beginning. A smith at Gränsfors Bruks has nothing to hide and is proud of his or her professional standards. When the craftsman or craftswoman is satisfied with their work and has personally accepted the axe, the head is marked with their initials next to the company's crown. These are the craftsmen and craftswomen of Gränfors Bruks.

What do I take out of this? I could say that was a nice man taking about axes, but what relevancy did it have to me? I could take the view that I don't make axes, so there is no relevance to me but that is the means by which we become closed, unable to be open, to be adaptive, and always be in beta as a craftsman must always be, so there is another way of framing this story. I see a story about whole systems design that includes, people, nature, sustainability and an ethical belief that manifests itself into a truly extraordinary product that has shaped an entire company. There are lessons here to learn about innovation, to seek innovative ways to create.

And this has been achieved through learning deeply about anything and everything to do with axes that stripped away all the things that gave nothing of value to the axe and added knowledge. Gabriel gave meaning to his workforce and a motivation in which they were commercially but equally personally dedicated to give their creative best – an engaged craftsman is a committed craftsman, ergo an engaged workforce is a committed workforce.

C. Wright Mills, a mid-20th-century sociologist stated:

> The laborer with a sense of craft becomes engaged in the work in and for itself; the satisfaction of working are their own reward; the details of daily labor are connected in the worker's mind to the end product; the worker can control his or her own actions at work; skill develops within the work process; work is connected to freedom to experiment; finally, family, community, and politics are measured by the standards of inner satisfaction, coherence and experimentation in craft labour.[246]

But craftsmanship does not only exist in the manufacture of ancient tools in an analogue world, it exists with the production and creation of computing software, Linux being a useful point of connection.

Linux craftsmen and women

The story of Linus Torvalds and the creation of open source software has passed into post-modern folklore. But Linux, as the source code became known, is a direct descendant of both participatory collaborative cultures and craftsmanship, plus the fundamental need of humans to find meaning in the things they do. Moreover, it represents a new way of working, understanding deep human motivation for the work they do and organisational capability. Sennett asks how quality of knowledge can co-exist with free and equal exchange in a community. But in Linux, the process of skill evolution is speeded up; change occurs daily. Linux programmers are a modern tribe that ascribes to the philosophy and practice of craftsmanship. They represent the very opposite to straight lines thinkers who are unwilling to do anything until all the goals, procedures and desired results for a policy have been mapped in advance. The open collaborative model of organisation has much to teach us. The latter represent a closed knowledge system and, as Sennett points out, closed knowledge systems have tended to have short lifespans in the history of handcrafts. For these modern-day craftsmen and women, leisure is not passive consumerism but active and participatory. Their world recombines the needs of

---

246. Quoted in Sennett, *The Craftsman*, p. 27.

humans to collaborate, experience collective joy, express identity and make some money as they go. In medieval times, when written contracts between adults had little validity, when informal, but implicit trust instead was the underpinning of economic transactions, 'the single most pressing earthly obligation of every medieval artisan was the establishment of a good personal reputation'. Authority means more than occupying a place of honour in a social web. For the craftsman, authority resides equally in the quality of his skills. Victor Papenek believed that the process of design had become 'the most powerful tool with which man shapes his tools and environments and, by extension, society and himself'.[247]

In 2006, Henry Jenkins produced a report on media literacy for the MacArthur Foundation. It states that it has identified 'a set of core social skills and cultural competencies that young people should acquire if they are to be full, active, creative, and ethical participants in this emerging participatory culture'.[248] I think this lives in craftsmanship because the authority of the craftsman, resides in the quality of his skills, such as:

- **Play** – the capacity to experiment with your surroundings as a form of problem-solving.
- **Performance** – the ability to adopt alternative identities for the purpose of improvisation and discovery.
- **Simulation** – the ability to interpret and construct dynamic models of real world processes.
- **Appropriation** – the ability to meaningfully sample and remix media content.
- **Multitasking** – the ability to scan one's environment and shift focus as needed to salient details.
- **Distributed cognition** – the ability to interact meaningfully with tools that expand mental capacities.
- **Collective intelligence** – the ability to pool knowledge and compare notes with others toward a common goal.
- **Judgment** – the ability to evaluate the reliability and credibility of different information sources.
- **Transmedia navigation** – the ability to follow the flow of stories and information across multiple modalities.
- **Networking** – the ability to search for, synthesise, and disseminate information.
- **Negotiation** – the ability to travel across diverse communities, discerning and respecting multiple perspectives, and grasping and following alternative norms.

---

247. Victor Papanek, *Design for the Real World: Human Ecology and Social Change*, Pantheon Books, 1971.
248. Henry Jenkins, *Confronting the Challenges of a Participatory Culture: Media Education for the 21st Century*, John D. and Catherine MacArthur Foundation, 2006, p. 4.

'These skills will help young people work through the ethical dilemmas they face in their everyday lives. Such a systemic approach is needed if children are to acquire the core social skills and cultural competencies needed in a modern era', argues Jenkins.[249] I might add that these are skills that we all need to learn. Socrates sought to understand the meaning of truth, justice, beauty and decent society by questioning people directly about how they understood the meanings of those particular words. In many ways, craftsmanship as a concept and philosophy equally asks us those very direct and pressing questions.

Sensory re-engagement

The definition of sensory is: 'affecting animate nerve organs'. Synonyms for the word include: acoustic, audible, audiovisual, auditory, aural, clear, discernible, distinct, lingual, neural, ocular, perceptible, phonic, plain, receptive, sensory, sensual, sonic, tactile and visual. And my firm belief if that the sensory re-engagement is linked to craftsmanship, it locates us, identifies us and makes our experience authentic and real. There are three strands of sensory engagement: shared collective joy, playfulness and our physical environment.

Shared collective joy

It's dark, I am standing in a field with 100,000 other people, in front of me is a stage flooded in ethereal light and on it Jay-Z is rapping – the crowd is pumping and in the afterglow I look around me to see rapture on every face that surrounds me. The crowd is as one and I am at one with the crowd. This is transcendence of the secular kind, or is it? Is there something more spiritual here that cannot be defined by the ideology of any religion but that binds us a species in a more primordial manner? I have used the terms of participatory cultures, cooperation and collaboration, extensively in this book, but why is that so important? Human beings, as already mentioned, are designed to work in aggregates, which delivers amongst other things a benefit called collective joy, 'The capacity for collective joy is encoded into us almost as deeply as the capacity for erotic human love of one human for another', writes Barbara Ehrenreich in *Dancing in the Streets: A History of Collective Joy*. 'We can live without it, as most of us do, but only at the risk of succumbing to the solitary nightmare of depression', she concludes.[250]

In feudal times, although they were materially poorer than their modern-day

---

249. Jenkins, *Confronting the Challenges*. http://www.henryjenkins.org/2006/10/confronting_the_challenges_of_6.html.
250. Ehrenreich, *Dancing in the Streets*, p. 260.

descendants, feudal man and woman had 115 festivals a year to look forward to. In a late medieval carnival, for example, 'everyone had a role to play and a chance to distinguish themselves individually by the brilliance of their costumes, the wittiness of their jokes, or their talents as dancers or athletes'. Their collaborative and collective participation reaffirmed their identity, their personal sense of worth and their belief in the world.

However, from the 17th to the 20th centuries, thousands of acts of legislation were introduced which attempted to eliminate carnival and popular festivity from popular life. An eyewitness account describes the emptying of the common after the suppression of Sunday recreations. The common once 'presented a lively and pleasing aspect, dotted with parties of cheerful lookers-on', it was now 'left lonely and empty'.[251]

The reason we have wooden pews in churches is because as the church was establishing its authority throughout northern Europe, communities would turn up to church, standing room only at the time and may decide to have a bit of a party or use the space for one of their 115 festivals per year – much to the growing distress of the church. As the church and state asserted their authority, festivals that were once conducted in churches and then public squares became a thing of the past. Social historians believe that the repression of collective festivities was a by-product of capitalism which in many ways has existed until very recent times. The straight lines of our industrial world have deep foundations. Our desire to unshackle ourselves from that way of life has equally had a long gestation. Beneficially, our industrialised society for the first time lifted many of us collectively above a feudal existence, but it over time stripped us of a great deal of what makes us people. It transformed us into a disciplined, factory-ready working class. But in so doing we ultimately pared away culture from community, carved community from identity and separated us increasingly from each other. The working man and woman were reduced to units of production, and society became units of consumption to be measured and calibrated against industrial measurements of efficiency.

Protestantism, the co-joined twin with the new capitalism, 'descended like a frost on the life of Merrie Old England', mourned Max Weber,[252] and destroyed many, if not all, traditional forms of group pleasure. In Johan Huizunga's study *Homo Ludens*, he showed that in pre-modern Europe, adults enjoyed the same card-games, make-believe charades and even the same toys as their children. It was the demands of the industrial revolution that forced adults to put away their playthings. 'Modern work is desperately serious', Huizinga observed, adding that when 'utility rules, adults lose something essential in the capacity to think;

---

251. Quoted in Ehrenreich, *Dancing in the Streets*, p. 100.
252. Quoted in Ehrenreich, *Dancing in the Streets*, p. 101.

they lose the free curiosity that occurs in the open, felt fingering space of play.'[253]
This lament is echoed by Ehrenreich:

> The loss to ordinary people of so many recreations and festivities is incalculable
> and we, who live in a culture almost devoid of opportunities either to 'lose
> ourselves' in communal festivities or to distinguish ourselves in any arena
> outside work, are in no position to fathom it.[254]

Modern commentary on precisely this outcome comes to us via *The Office*.
On one level, it's a simple black comedy. But *The Office* is also a meditation on the
obsolescence of the traditional workplace – a place stripped of meaning – and the
crisis of post-modern man and woman struggling to find meaning in a world
where, as J. G. Ballard puts it, to be a consumer is to be a citizen; where ownership
of a loyalty card represents membership of humanity itself; and where spiritual
experience takes the form of retail epiphany. *The Office* is universally successful,
the question we have to ask is why is that? Good script writing – yes of course,
but more importantly I suggest, because, it touches something in us all.

'In supposing that competition between individuals brings out the best in us,
and that bringing individual rewards is deeply motivating, we miss the point that
collective action brings communal cohesion and a sense of belonging', argues
Sennett;[255] it is something not to be underestimated, our sense of ourselves on
this earth is built out of a sense of shared togetherness.

Craftsmanship, shared collective joy and the convergence of culture

Professor Henry Jenkins believes we are seeing the emergence of a new form of
participatory culture as we take media into our own hands, reworking its content to
serve our personal and collective interests and we are acquiring skills now through
our play, including our gameplay, which we will later apply towards more serious
ends. Craftsmanship is embedded into this participatory culture. The problems
arise when transparency is lacking, when information and knowledge is shared
unequally – the positioning of 'the expert' versus 'the others' can create resentment,
hostility and subtly poison an organisation to the point of petrification.

Most people want to believe that their lives add up to more than a random series
of disconnected events, argues Sennett, and the well-crafted institution wants to
respond to this desire, as Gabriel Branby did for example. Workers who have been
retrained by an institution are much more bonded to it than in-and-out workers,

---

253. Quoted in Sennett, *The Craftsman*, p. 270.
254. Ehrenreich, *Dancing in the Streets*, p. 99.
255. Sennett, *The Craftsman*, pp. 37, 52, 241–2

Sennett points out. 'In short, play inaugurates practicing, and practicing is a matter of both repetition and constant re-evaluation. There is an intimate relationship between problem-solving, and problem finding, technique and expression, play and work'.[256] Roland Deiser, an expert in organisational learning, points out that hierarchical power does not work between members of a network that co-creates.[257] Sennett contests that the capacity to work well is shared fairly equally among human beings; it appears first in play, and is elaborated in the capacities to localise, question and open up problems at work.

We easily dismiss play or playfulness, which is essentially how we learn. Play is by default the process of experimentation, failing and learning. But when we are living in a world which challenges our preconceived ideas on society, economics and the nature of any organisation, we can no longer expect to run at 100% capacity all the time. We need the time and space to play, try new stuff out, fail, learn and try again.

Participatory cultures in education

So how does that relate to education? Many schools have complex problems, such as children from families of low income, drug-related issues, abuse, unemployment and poor living conditions, as well as all the other flotsam and jetsam that life can sling at teachers. The challenges that these present can seem insurmountable. In the UK at least, pressure to achieve is applied by the slide-rule specialists in government to monitor national league tables (the mechanism by which schools are evaluated) and the efficiency machine of government monitors everything. But where are the kids in all this? Imagine you come from a family that has to deal with some or all of the above problems. How is that going to affect how you engage with the world around you? In September 2001, 30 young pupils from Elmwood Primary School in Croydon embarked on a unique musical venture, collectively learning a musical instrument. The children arrived in class and were presented with a range of woodwind and brass instruments from which they had to choose one. Instead of individual lessons, the entire class of beginners were taught together. Nine months later, the band performed to general acclaim on stage at the Fairfield Halls Croydon. But how was this possible? Normally, traditional music lessons take place outside the classroom, one-to-one with teacher and pupil. But this approach taught the whole class together and took them from beginner to concert in one term. It started as a way of getting more music taught but it has had much wider effects.

---

256. Sennett, The Craftsman.
257. Roland Deiser, Designing the Smart Organisation: How Breakthrough Corporate Learning Initiatives Drive Strategic Change, Jossey-Bass, 2009, p. 17.

Imagine you are Paul. He has a very complicated home life, and is behind his reading age, not because he's stupid but because, as Polly Toynbee has pointed out, some children are given a life sentence at birth. Paul has in fact low self-esteem and makes up for that by confronting the world in an aggressive manner; he struggles with anything and anyone that challenges him. Paul is in survival mode, though he doesn't know that. And he is fearful, though he wouldn't recognise that either.

Can you imagine giving this young boy a musical instrument, asking him to practise on his own, and then play in front of a group that may laugh at his duff notes? How is Paul going to react? Is he going to reach out and seize the day or is the more likely scenario that he going to feel so humiliated that his only response is to punch someone? It's a missed opportunity because he once happened purely by fluke to catch a piece of *A Lark Ascending* by Vaughan Williams on a TV commercial and for a fleeting moment his heart soared. He could still hear the tune in his head as he went to bed whilst his parents argued violently in the next room.

The ancient wisdom of participatory cultures

All those identity issues are avoided by a very simple decision that the class shares collectively in both success and failure. We all gratuitously point to Athena as the birthplace of democracy but as John Keane in *The Life and Death of Democracy* shows, it was the Phoenicians who understood the importance of democracy by assembly. Why? Because the Phoenicians were a seafaring culture and they had learned through hard-won practical experience that it is only through the cooperation of people collaboratively working together to build boats, sail in them through raging storms, fight in them and trade in them that they understood that democracy by assembly was the most effective model for group success. I see the DNA of what the Phoenicians understood in the Sound Start programme.

This kind of participation has got something going for it on so many levels. Paul said: 'If I wasn't doing this I'd be nicking cars.' And something else very interesting happened; the children involved in the Sound Start programme literally turned around to become very pro-school. Homework completion increased from 67 % to 97%, attendance and lateness became a thing of the past and there was a significant decline in children involved in 'disruptive behaviour' in and out of class.

It is this embracing of creation combined with participatory cultures that bring an equilibrium and a multiplicity of benefits into places and spaces that previously seemed lost to such ideals. The insight is we can organise education to be better, technology can be part of the story – but the bigger story is that we need to move from a process whereby teaching is information delivered by an authority, to one where students are drawn into creating, critiquing and discussing the world they inhabit. When we live in a world where there is an abundance of information, any student will question why that information is important; when young people have grown up only networking where authority in the peer group is earned, how can assumed authority of the teacher be credible?

The well-built environment and its networked benefits

Buildings matter, is the strongly held view of RIBA President Ruth Reed. Well-designed buildings represent, she says, the ability to bring architectural forms into this world that enhance our humanity in a multiplicity of ways, delivering, as Ruth believes, 'value to people's lives'. Value as in hospitals where people become healthier quicker, schools where truancy is significantly reduced, as is petty crime in the area, buildings that take less from us and nature, and public spaces which lift us up with a sense of belonging, of community, the bonding agent that creates for healthy societies,

> Creating community is only marginally about technology. What matters is the co-presence through time of bodies and the emergence of shared meaning as we interact with each-other in meaningful activities ... For hundreds of years, when the majority of the population was illiterate, participatory ritual and performance were the main ways that beliefs were shared within a culture.[258]

One of the problems that we face in falling in love with new technology is that we forget what already exists, what is clearly valuable and what we should not ignore. One of the biggest mistakes those in love with all things digital misunderstand about human beings is that although communication technologies are central in the process of transformation, we still are a highly situated species. Our physical environment, the houses we live in, the schools we go to, the places in which we work, the public spaces we share and hospitals we use all have a deep impact on us, and therefore a deep impact on society.

Downe Hospital – aiding the healing process

Research has proven that patients heal quicker in non-institutionalised spaces that have contact with nature, more specifically that the psychological aspects of an environment can reduce stress, speed up recovery, reduce the dosage of pain killers and reduce anxiety. Downe Hospital in Ireland was designed and built based upon

---

258. Thackara, In the Bubble, p. 109.

these principles. 90% of the beds have views over the rolling landscape of the Downshire Estate. In addition, healing is encouraged with extensive natural lighting, courtyard gardens, rather than the endless whitewalls of institutions. Art is extensively used throughout the hospital.

Downe Hospital won a prestigious RIBA prize in 2010. This is what the judges had to say:

> the new building departs from the original institutional form by breaking down the mass of an array of smaller wings springing from a central entrance. One benefit of disintegrating a large building into smaller architectural forms is the effect it has on the sense of wellbeing in the hospital's many rooms. All spaces are daylit and where possible naturally ventilated. This is not groundbreaking or heroic architecture, but it is a sophisticated response to a complex building type, which owes its success to straightforward design that is welcoming and offers a sense of reassuring ease to its users.

Like all hospitals it has a complex job to do, so it has a ten-bed observation unit; accident and emergency; outpatients; three 20 bed inpatient wards; coronary care unit; 25 bed dementia ward; 25 bed acute psychiatric unit; day procedures unit; rehabilitation – physio and occupational therapy; obstetrics and home from home birthing unit; radiology department; and children's centre.

The hospital is divided into three key environments: the patient environment, secondary healing space and a medical core. The patient environment encompasses all the patients' care areas throughout the hospital which includes wards, outpatients' departments and treatment areas; the building design ensures from all these areas patients and staff have uninterrupted views of the surrounding natural landscape, with the intention that this has a net benefit for aiding recuperation and healing, and for the staff that work there on a daily basis. The secondary healing spaces act as circulation, entrances, waiting areas, coffee shops, providing entertainment, contemplation, gardens and a sanctuary. The medical core is what it says on the tin, the place for intensive medical care, the place where critical care life-saving procedures are undertaken – but the medical core is enveloped in something that understands that, for many people, hospital is a stressful place, and to provide an environment that is designed around the needs of humans rather than the needs of utility and function is not an act of faith, it is in fact an act of good design. If people need less drugs, get better and recover quicker, that must ultimately have a net benefit on running costs and overall budget expenditure – surely that would be of interest to an economist?

Westminster Academy

Winston Churchill once said that we shape buildings and thereafter they shape us. In 2006 the Commission for Architecture and the Built Environment published a report – *Design with Distinction: The Value of Good Building Design in Higher Education*.[259] The report provided prima facie evidence that there is a direct correlation between building design and the recruitment, retention and performance of staff and pupils. The Westminster Academy provides strong evidence of the report findings.

In need of refurbishment, and a rethink on how the academy performed, head teacher Alison Banks pushed for a more transformational brief based around progressive and transformational education principals. It was also important that the school play an important civic role and hold a strong presence in the community. Conventional classrooms were combined with smaller breakout spaces, larger lecture-style spaces and even larger gathering spaces such as the main 'market place'. The plan of the building was developed to allow for future flexibility and to encourage better connections and movement between spaces. The CABE report states that the variety of learning spaces has accommodated the head teacher Alison Banks' educational vision of a school that encourages different ways of learning, from private study to team work and collaboration. The central space allows for whole school activities and involvement with the community. Other spaces range from the multi-functional long room, the large lecture theatre in the green room and the studio and lab spaces to smaller homerooms with u-shaped desk arrangements. Breakout spaces provide quieter areas for individual or group study. This hierarchy of spaces allow for a personalised learning programme, whilst offering adaptability for the future. But in fact there was a wider benefit; the new design attracted children who suffered from truancy to stay in school, petty crime in the neighbourhood dropped and so did anti-social behaviour in the classroom.

School buildings too often look like a utility and therefore, as many argue, that is how our children are taught as general fodder for a system that is becoming increasingly obsolescent. Learning is part of life – life should be a part of learning, so it should not be something we separate from the rest of the world around us. There is no doubt that technology plays a key role in the evolution of education; however, space and place are so crucial in determining whether education becomes a penance or a joy. Returning to the theme of community and environment, Gilda O'Neill a native of London's East End, and whose work described the changing social fabric of the East End wrote

---

259. http://webarchive.nationalarchives.gov.uk/20110118095356/http:/www.cabe.org.uk/publications/design-with-distinction.

People are often mourning the loss of a way of life in which they were part of a community that had grown organically over the generations ... Unlike the planners and architects who moved them around as if they were pawns in a chess game, they understand that communities are not created by ordering removal vans simply to transplant people from one location to another – not if they are to have a cohesiveness that makes sense to those who live within in them.

The idea of designing in community rather than editing it out seems to me part of what makes the Westminster Academy so important.

Community in place, space and time

According to a recent survey, 71% of adults used to play on the streets when they were young. Just 21% of children do so now. I used to love climbing trees, as do my son and his friends; I played out, all the time. Yet, there is a view that we have retreated from the public realm, and given it up to CCTV. Why should we do that? It's about questioning the current framework for public space and whether it is sufficient, while also giving permission for young people to play in public. If the world is less playful, then we retreat to places where we can play. Is the world more serious than 30 years ago, or is it my age? We need to be sensitive to the idea of what a public space is.

It's curious to think about all the places we travel through, where we are in transit, where we become transient, and the spaces that we travel through become meaningless – like a bus stop, says John Thackara. I think of many of the UK's old industrial cities and towns – hollowed out without the daily rub of humanity, and even those that have had the hand of modernism laid upon them, which become, as my partner likes to describe them, 'the depressing centre'. Sennett extrapolates what Thackara is getting at. 'When public space becomes derivative of movement', he writes, 'it loses any experiential meaning of its own. On the most physical level, these environments of pure movement prompt people to think of the public domain as meaningless ... they are catatonic space.'[260] That's a really big deal in my view and it reflects in many ways why public space bears witness to the tears in the fabric of society.

In *Communities Dominate Brands*, my central argument was that 'engagement' as a principle framework defined by human participation, attraction and involvement, intellectually, emotionally and physically, was the way forward.[261] Though I acknowledged that many tools of the communication revolution are digital, the

---

260. Sennett, *The Fall of Public Man.*
261. Ahonen and Moore, *Communities Dominate Brands.*

drivers behind them are very human. This for me is part of what Russell Davies was talking about in *Post Digital Design*.[262] Philosopher John Gray says: 'Being embodied is our nature as earth-born creatures.'[263] He means our DNA is part of and connected to the earth upon which we walk; we are not about to become full-time avatars any time soon. Philosopher Maurice Merleau-Ponty constructed a view that 'perception is a process in which an active body enters into a communion with its surroundings',[264] whilst Lucy Suchman says: 'Human activity is not primarily as rational, planned and controlled as we like to think. It is better described as situated, social and in direct response to the physical and social environment.'[265]

Merleau-Ponty and Suchman remind me of an extraordinary event called the Do Lectures. Founded by Dave and Claire Hieatt, they were conceived to bring together doers of the world to inspire people to take action. As Dick Dastardly says in *Wacky Races*: 'Don't just stand there. Do Something!' The event was held at Fforest Farm in West Wales, near Cardigan Bay. We all slept in shared tents and tepees; we ate together in a converted cowshed; the food was life enhancing and delicious and the lectures were held in a yurt. As the wind outside whipped around us, I listened to some extraordinary people who had done extraordinary things. I met people who enabled me to see the world in a different way, and I am going back for more. Play was collective: wood-chopping and bush-craft lessons, group runs in beautiful countryside and sitting in a pub made of slate, drinking the local brew and listening to Nick Hand telling me about his slow cycle journey around Britain,[266] as a fire gently gave off that lovely smoky woody scent that tells you that all's well with the world. Later, entertainment was the entire pub singing along to the amazing Katy Carr, with ukulele in hand, who sounds like Vera Lynn mixed with Edith Piaf, pulling out all the stops whilst singing 'Lily Marlene' – now that was priceless. Seven months later I am out walking near Cilgerren in Wales listening to Dave Hieatt on the phone talking to a potential speaker. Dave explains that rather than turning up doing a talk and leaving, the specialness of Do is when the speakers stayed, hung out with the people and discussed. Having been a speaker at Do last year, and having spoken at numerous events around the world, I could not have agreed with Dave more.

---

262. http://russelldavies.typepad.com/planning/2009/01/meet-the-new-schtick.html <http://russelldavies.typepad.com/planning/2009/01/meet-the-new-schtick.html>

263. John Gray, *Straw Dogs: Thoughts on Humans and Other Animals*, Farrar, Straus and Giroux, 2007, quoted in Thackara, *In the Bubble*, p. 63.

264. Maurice Merleau-Ponty, *Phenomenology of Perception*, trans. Colin Smith, Humanities Press and Routledge & Kegan Paul, 1962; trans. revised by Forrest Williams, 1981; reprinted, 2002 – quoted in Thackara, *In the Bubble*, pp. 170–1.

265. Lucy Suchman, *Plans and Situated Actions: The Problem of Human–Machine Communication*, Cambridge University Press, 1987 – quoted in Thackara, *In the Bubble*, pp. 105–6.

266. Slow Coast http://www.slowcoast.co.uk/.

I found my time at the Do Lectures fun, and challenging in that it led me to reflect deeply about the world I was living in. The Do Lectures were situated, meaningful and overall a powerful experience. If we consider other places, such as the Eden project in Cornwall, football or rugby stadia, or indeed even the Apple stores on high streets, these situated, sensorial environments are where we can meet, play and find greater meaning. So situated play + community = meaning? We cannot ignore our physical world. But we need a human world that responds to the sensory nature of humanity, not a machine world. As John Stuart Mill argued in his book *On Liberty* in 1859, 'Human nature is not a machine to be built after a model and set to do the work exactly proscribed for it.'

The American Jane Jacobs was highly respected for her insightful writings into how American cities worked, and what it is was that made them live and die. Jacobs lived on Hudson Street, New York, in the 1960s. The miracle of Hudson Street, according to Jacobs, was created by the way the streets and buildings of the neighbourhood were laid out and organised. Jacobs believed that when a neighbourhood is oriented towards the street, when sidewalks are used for socializing and play and commerce, the users of that street are transformed by the resulting stimulation; they form relationships and casual contacts they would never have otherwise.[267]

So our physical world matters, and will do so for a long time to come. It's easy for us to believe that our digital connections are decoupled from physical and energy systems. We're a culture that often forgets that, to think properly, our bodies need vitamins, sleep or a run around the neighbourhood. So the question we have to ask as we look around us is are we designing for community, social cohesion, for shared meaning? Yes, we can achieve much through digital tools and technologies but I fear too many today believe the virtual world is our salvation – it is not. Communication technologies are the tools that enable us to make some important and significant changes, but we must see that our physical world matters too, and that in fact we should not see the two as distinctly different.

---

267. Jane Jacobs, *The Death and Life of Great American Cities*, 1961; Modern Library edn 1993.

Chapter Seven

The open society; better ways of sharing knowledge, power and wealth

ACCORDING TO A STUDY BY THE Pew Internet & American Life Project [268] more than one half of all teens have created media content, and roughly one third of teens who use the internet have shared content they produced. In many cases, these teens are actively involved in participatory cultures. These are environments with relatively low barriers to artistic expression and civic engagement, strong support for creating and sharing one's creations and some type of informal mentorship whereby knowledge can be passed from the most experienced to novices, a bit like the way an apprentice learns in a craftsman's workshop. A participatory culture is one in which members believe their contributions matter, and feel some degree of social connection with one another. At the least, they care what other people think about what they have created. If a world is more playful, it is by default more cognitive. And if it is more cognitive, that means it's a 'read & write' culture as it's only through this interactive process that we as people become more knowing of the world around us.

This evolution of participatory culture can be witnessed in nearly every industry, in all walks of life. When there is enough interest in a topic, need or goal, momentum will generate to form a community. For example, the rise of fan fiction and the extraordinary output of, for example, the Potter Heads whose co-created and shared oeuvre exists as novels, blogs, stories, films, drawings and events. Or the large-scale organisational change of the healthcare system that is happening in Nova Scotia, which is being enabled through what Tim Merry from the Art of Hosting calls 'Participatory Leadership', whereby it is the participation of the people that are the true actors (nurses, clinicians, patients, etc.) within that healthcare system that are being hosted (guided) into co-designing, and co-creating how they are going to find the answers to their difficult and challenging issues. Both are examples of participatory cultures and participatory media that can also be described by what

268. Amanda Lenhart and Mary Madden, *Teen Content Creators and Consumers*, Pew Internet & American Life Project, 2 November 2005.

Professor Lawrence Lessig describes as a read/write culture. Participatory culture and its inherent creativity no longer lives at the periphery of society but now occupies centre stage.

The demand and creation of an open society

Lessig uses the term 'read/write culture' to refer to this ability. 'Read-only culture' refers to a culture in which we cannot participate, a culture that's really become ossified, a culture that's actually no culture at all. Using all the examples in *No Straight Lines*, we see that it is the combined acts of reading and writing that is the key component in how we, learn, organise, trade, govern, educate, design and act. It's so obvious that we miss the truth that there is an intensity of engagement that is missing from a read-only approach. Lessig points out that nearly everyone can write.[269] We believe our children must learn how to read and write, as this is the way they successfully access the world of knowledge, and the physical world around them. In the process of learning, we must appropriate other knowledge, other ideas, other cultures; we must absorb these completely to understand them.

However, read/write culture, participatory systems or co-creation have all in recent years placed significant stress upon legal frameworks that are in a sense the hidden architecture of authority, as our organised world has not been constructed with the levels of sharing and participation that our society now demands. Indeed, it has been constructed through the ownership of IP, copyright and patents; controlling of who can and cannot use, reuse, modify and share cultural work, designs, plans, you name it. This has become a huge battleground both ideologically and culturally. Current legal frameworks centred around ownership have become a form of commercial and organisational constipation. Many organisations and companies have spent mountains of cash on lawyers sending out cease and desist letters to those that they have deemed to have infringed their copyright, and in some extreme cases tried to have these culture modders incarcerated in prison. Copyright, intellectual property and licensing are all based on a bygone age when only big publishers could afford to produce and distribute new cultural material such as books or sheet music. But it evolved into a cultural mindset and economic model.

In the same way that we saw American radio rapidly migrate from a radio transmitter in a shack set up for the purposes and needs of the local community, with the Good 'Ol Boys playing a barnstormer to a national network,[270] supporting

---

269. Lessig, *Remix*.
270. Howley, Jenkins, McChesney, R. Williams, Lessig.

national stars, the loss of amateur 'yeoman creators', says Lessig, cheapens and flattens our culture, and, worse, ultimately alienates us.[271] At the same time, companies particularly in the mobile communications industry are suing each other over patent infringements as they jostle for market domination. In fact there is a direct corollary between the amount a company sues and its economic health. A *Financial Times* article headlined 'Claws & Effect'[272] noted that senior music industry figures, such as Lucian Grainge, head of Universal Music International, have been influential in mobilising Westminster to change the law on file-sharing. Labour MP Tom Watson wrote:

> Challenged by the revolutionary distribution mechanism that is the internet, big publishers with their expensive marketing and PR operations and big physical distribution networks, are seeing their power and profits diminish. Faced with the choice of accepting this and innovating, or attempting, King Canute-style, to stay the tide of change, they're choosing the latter option, and looking to Parliament for help with some legislative sandbags.[273]

Gerd Leonhard explains the implications of such an approach. 'In other words', he says,

> If the content industry can't get people to buy music or films, or other so-called content by offering relevant, fair and affordable new ways to do so, maybe the Government can help to force people back into buying the old-fashioned way; by the unit or copy? Rather than actually change the industry's business model, let's just change the consumers' habits – problem solved![274]

It has been well documented that large organisations have over many years built up large patent portfolios, as a form of protection. But ultimately, this slows down innovation and progress to a grinding standstill. And whilst all that is going on, a new marketplace is emerging where the entire process by which commerce is undertaken, and how we organise ourselves around that commercial activity, is a signpost to a new way of doing things.

271. Lessig, *Remix*, pp. 27–9. A view forcibly shared by Kevin Howley and Raymond Williams.
272. *Financial Times*, 28 August 2009. http://www.ft.com/cms/s/0/da18e7d4–9404–11de-9c57–00144feabdco.html?nclick_check=1.
273. http://www.tom-watson.co.uk/2009/08/filesharing-why-the-government-should-proceed-with-caution-and-what-you-can-do-to-influence-the-debate/.
274. Gerd Leonhard, 'Open letter to Lord Mandelson: here is how to solve the internet music problem – legalize it!', http://www.mediafuturist.com/2009/10/open-letter-to-lord-mandelson-the-way-to-solve-the-internet-music-problem-is-to-legalize-it.html.

Creative Commons for everyone

In *Pirates of the Caribbean: Dead Man's Chest*, the ship *The Black Pearl* must go into the Underworld to recover Cap'n Jack Sparrow. Jack is found, and now all *The Black Pearl* has to do is return from the Underworld to the world of the living. However, it's not entirely clear how that's meant to happen. The legend says that if *The Black Pearl* doesn't leave the Underworld before the setting of the sun, the ship and its entire crew will be marooned in the Underworld for all eternity. The trouble is that the sailing ship is sitting on a flat sea. In a wide shot, we see the sun setting, cut in half as its falls below the horizon line. Jack is looking at a map that's supposed to help him navigate out of the Underworld, and the situation is getting tense as the light begins to fade. Then Jack jumps up and begins to run from one side of the boat to the other. Slowly, the rest of the crew join in. 'What's he doing?' asks one of the crew. 'I don't know, I'm just copying Jack', says the other. The boat is rocking from side to side now at an alarming degree. What Jack has realised, his epiphany, is that the sun setting in the world they're in is the sun rising in the world they need to get to. Jack realises he has to do something completely counterintuitive, he must capsize the boat to survive. Those that have built very successful businesses with read-only business models believe that when one talks about sharing intellectual property, or revenues, one is being almost negligent. For them the notion of 'giving away' stuff leaves them dumbfounded. But sharing in participatory cultures is more complex, refined and interesting than that. Everything about a read/write culture, like iPod shuffle, is different to a read-only culture. For straight lines organisations, it's like a trifecta discombobulating the psyche of straight lines thinkers who run their read-only organisations and companies; it places great stress on how their organisations make money, and the way in which they think stuff gets done. Small grains of sand sometimes imperceptibly, incrementally, will change the shape of things; if you have grown up sharing, co-creating, creating, sharing, modding, uploading content to media platforms, how does that change your sense of yourself in the world?

Of course in this sharing, co-creative and self-expressive world questions arise over ownership, intellectual copyright and permission – who has the right to say its OK to use that material. For these reasons the Creative Commons was born. Creative Commons works to increase the amount of cultural, educational and scientific creativity in 'the commons' – the body of work that's available to the public for free which they can share legally, use and repurpose. What's important is that Creative Commons provides free, easy-to-use legal tools, available to all. Creative Commons tools give everyone from individual creators to large companies and institutions a simple, standardised way to grant copyright permissions to their creative work. Creative Commons licences enable people to easily change their copyright terms from the default of 'all rights reserved' to 'some rights reserved' which allows certain uses of their work whilst retaining the overall copyright of the material for the creator. Creative Commons licences are not an alternative to copyright. They work alongside copyright, so rights holders can modify your copyright terms to best suit your needs. And the organisation has collaborated with intellectual property experts all around the world to ensure that its licences work globally.

There is no doubt that when existing legal frameworks get severely tested, challenged or found wanting, we know that the world around us is in some form of systemic change. Our common wealth in the networked economy is and will increasingly be supported by Creative Commons frameworks. Companies are starting to reframe their approach to patents and IP via Creative Commons and the University of Rotterdam runs an open source mobility project where all intellectual property is shared under a Creative Commons licence. Flickr holds more than 100 million images produced under a CC licence, while more than another 150 million CC licences exist. The number is mushrooming, partly due to Wikipedia converting to Creative Commons licences in June 2009. At the most dramatic end of the spectrum, rock band Nine Inch Nails released their last album under a Creative Commons CC+ licence.[275] The group gave away its music for free under a CC BY-NC-SA licence, but found immediate and substantial financial return, as well as seeing long-term sales flourish. Nine Inch Nails achieved this by selling different versions of the same content. There was the initial free download of the first nine tracks of 'Ghosts', but fans could also purchase a $5 download of the whole album, a $10 2xCD set, a $75 DVD box set and finally, a limited edition $300 ultra-deluxe box set signed and numbered by Trent himself, all of it CC licensed.

Joi Ito, one of the founders of Creative Commons, said in an interview in the *Guardian* in September 2009:

> For me most people still don't know what Creative Commons is, but those people who are concerned about sharing and have run into the problem that Creative Commons solves, which is to lower the friction of sharing whether you're a producer or a government. The White House uses a Creative Commons licence. They all come to us for help. In that sense I think it's just a matter of time, and I think we've gotten to the point where, whether it's WIPO or RIAA or record labels, most of them ... understand now that we are not anti-copyright and we are not out to get them or to fight them, and we're really a technical standard and an interoperability standard, and we're really trying to help people to express their choices, not trying to convince people to make certain choices.

275. 'Nine inch nails releases Ghosts I–IV under a Creative Commons license', http://creativecommons. org/weblog/entry/8095. 'Trent Reznor on NIN's business models and the future of music', http:// creativecommons.org/weblog/entry/13915.

Commons-based action sustains humanity

In the same way that competition has driven innovation for millennia, understanding the commons from a broader perspective is necessary. The Creative Commons initiative has not been made by some crack pots, so high on utopian ideals that they have nothing to do with the real world. In fact, the commons as an idea and principal has been with us for as long as we have had settled communities. The commons, as an idea, is all about living a sustainable life. I live in a village, we have in our village a common, throughout the world there will always be common land, a place to be freely shared by all. Political scientist Elinor Ostrom was awarded the 2009 Nobel Memorial Prize in Economic Sciences, which she shared with Oliver E. Williamson, for her analysis of economic governance, especially the commons. Her work focuses on finding effective solutions to address one of the greatest dilemmas of humanity: the over-exploitation of 'common-pool resources'. If every person in a village has rights to fish out of the same pond, hauls that are reasonable at the personal level may lead in the aggregate to a depletion of stocks and no fish for anyone. So what is one to do?

Although this has been a millennial thorn in our side, we're very bad at commons thinking, a problem that's exacerbated by how our industrial society has framed ownership of goods, services and intellectual property. If that's contextualised around an emphasis on 'I' versus 'We', or exploitation versus sustainability, one can understand that we've got ourselves into something of a pickle. The response to trying to deal with big issues around 'commons thinking', how best to share, has been two-fold. First, we privatise. Secondly, we deploy external regulation. Both actually remove us further from our desired goal: the equitable distribution of wealth and resources.

Ostrom is considered one of the leading scholars in the study of common pool resources. In particular, her work emphasises how humans interact with ecosystems to maintain long-term sustainable resource yields. Common pool resources include many forests, fisheries, oil fields, grazing lands and irrigation systems. Ostrom's work has considered how societies have developed diverse institutional arrangements for managing natural resources and avoiding ecosystem collapse in many cases, even though some arrangements have failed to prevent resource exhaustion. Her current work emphasises the multifaceted nature of human–ecosystem interaction and argues against any singular 'universal remedy' for individual social-ecological system problems.

Ostrom's work, whilst looking at bigger world problems, challenges us to understand how a commons approach to a fairer society fundamentally changes how we engage with the world as individual agents or businesses. Let's take two examples.

In 2009, the Dutch government, in cooperation with the Dutch research institute TNO, conducted a survey into the economic effects of file-sharing on the music industry. The results are quite surprising as the survey concludes that illegally downloading music (which is allowed in Holland) has a positive effect on the music industry. If it would no longer be possible to download music, the sales of CDs would further decrease, the authors argue. Although there's a bitter dispute about this, Lawrence Lessig, in his book *Remix*, points to Dan Bricklin's piece 'The cornucopia of the commons'.[276] 'The networked architecture of Napster created value as a byproduct of people getting what they wanted in a vast interconnected database', he says.[277] In fact 57 million people were file-sharing when Napster was shut down. Surely the question begging to be asked is what underpins and drives such massive collaborative activity? And, what can I learn so that I can become commercially more successful? Markets, real markets, are not purely about transaction, they are inherently cultural.

Old world, new world: the economics of sharing

This is not new learning. As Lessig points out, research shows that when people were sharing analogue bespoke taped playlists, this increased music sales. It was the 1960s band the Grateful Dead, who pioneered ideas and practices that are only now being reluctantly embraced by corporate America. As Joshua Green pointed out in an article in the *Atlantic*,[278] by focusing 'intensely on its most loyal fans', the band 'established a telephone hotline to alert them to its touring schedule ahead of any public announcement, reserved for them some of the best seats in the house, and capped the price of tickets'. He adds: 'Only in the 1980s, faced with competition from Japan, did American CEOs and management theorists widely adopt a customer-first orientation.'

More significantly, the Grateful Dead did not attempt to prohibit the making and distributing of bootleg tapes, because they saw this a means by which they could freely market and promote the band. The band made their money by more people turning up at their gigs, and who bought the T-shirt. John Naughton, a true expert on technology and culture, wrote: 'the band anticipated by decades the "Freemium" business model now being touted by expensive managerial gurus. Stand by for a best-selling business book entitled "Management Secrets of the Grateful Dead". And if you want to know the future, ask a musician.'[279]

276. Dan Bricklin, http://www.bricklin.com/cornucopia.htm.
277. Dan Bricklin, http://www.bricklin.com/cornucopia.htm.
278. Joshua Green, 'Management secrets of the Grateful Dead', *Atlantic* (March 2010). http://www.theatlantic.com/magazine/archive/2010/03/management-secrets-of-the-grateful-dead/7918/.
279. John Naughton, 'Why Bowie and the Grateful Dead are the web's real visionaries', *Observer*, Sunday. 21 February 2010. http://www.guardian.co.uk/technology/2010/feb/21/the-networker-john-naughton.

Sharing as organisational capability

In the present day, the economics of sharing, in this instance music, has evolved into participatory and collaborative platforms. For example, SoundCloud is fast becoming the preferred streaming host for big name musicians. [280] SoundCloud is an online audio platform catering for music professionals enabling them to collaborate, promote and distribute their music. It provides an efficient and simple way for music professionals to exchange music they are involved with, allowing for easy collaboration and communication prior to a public release. Moby used it to air his new album, and, because SoundCloud allows people to listen to and comment on not only individual tracks but also specific parts of tracks, it is networked, collaborative and highly engaging of the people who use the service. On this participatory platform, there are clearly benefits for all actors.

Sharing can also build different types of economic models. Entrepreneur John Buckman explains in an interview[281] his post-digital thinking on how a Creative Commons + open source model built around sharing can be very profitable. First, there are significantly lower marketing costs through using Creative Commons and open source, allowing people to share your music or share your work. Under certain terms, you get your work distributed to a much wider audience. Buckman points to BookMooch, which allows people to physically share each other's books. BookMooch allows people to register their interest for a certain book; if someone has it, they send it to you. In running a previous business, Buckman says the mistake he made was that it was constructed within a linear framework: 'with me doing all the hard work and also really taking the business view that I was the producer and people were consumers of my content. But it had a scaling problem. If I want more music, more deals, I need to buy more attention, I need more staff.'[282]

Armed with this hard-won knowledge, Buckman designed and built a platform that enabled people to share their books. The consequence is the formation of what he calls 'accidental communities' of people who 'gather around something that really enables them, and people start to list all the books they want to read'. Jean Burgess and Joshua Green in YouTube point out that when YouTube was launched, it did so without having a clear definition of what it was; as a consequence, this 'under-determination explains the scale and diversity of its uses today'.[283] The sharing and swapping of lists results in $500,000 yearly in books sales from Amazon. That's a considerable amount for a company with no marketing spend. And Buckman observes that a system of people trading books directly with each

280. Chris Salmon, 'Full stream ahead', Guardian, Friday, 31 July 2009. http://www.guardian.co.uk/music/2009/jul/31/iphone-apple-spotify-streaming.
281. John Buckman, interview, 30 June 2008. http://blogs.magnatune.com/buckman/2008/06/index.html.
282. John Buckman interview.
283. Burgess and Green, YouTube.

other scales exponentially better than a centralised warehouse. As part of the reward system, traders of books and information get moochpoints from sharing and swapping books. As BookMooch scales up, this could be of huge value, with the creation of a knowledge database that could be of interest to publishers. And the tradable value of moochpoints could lead to public recognition of readers and traders who otherwise lead different, normal lives.

BookMooch, SoundCloud, the Grateful Dead, Creative Commons legal frameworks reveal the beating heart of what we are as a species: a meaning making species that thrives in conscious, meaningful communication. What is clear is that the people that created these businesses and capabilities were and are literate in how to create community, value and stimulate commercial activity by bringing together knowledge of what makes markets thrive, how to encourage participation both in terms of the legal frameworks of Creative Commons and the technologies of cooperation which manifest themselves as platforms. This literacy, Burgess and Green argue, does not belong to individuals, but is in fact a system that they say both shapes and enables participation. And as I touched on the point that participatory cultures are by default political because they challenge the status quo of the powerbases of companies, industries, and organisations, Green and Burgess also believe it represents a key political question on how this system is shaped [284]

The quiet revolution of cooperation

However, we are not limited to a digital only response to how we are seeking to renegotiate the way we want to live our lives. 'America is in the midst of a new revolution', writes Maria Armoudian:

> But this revolution is quiet, incremental, nonviolent, and travelling beneath the mainstream media's radar. The new American revolution challenges the current notions of dog-eat-dog capitalism through the building of a parallel economic system that shares, cooperates, empowers, and benefits fellow workers and community members. Over the past few decades, thousands of alternatives to the standard, top-down corporate model have sprouted up – worker-owned companies and cooperatives, neighborhood corporations and trusts, community-owned technology centers and municipally owned enterprises. In fact, today, involvement in these alternative models of business outnumber union membership as the means by which private-sector workers and community members are taking economics into their own hands. [285]

---

284. Burgess and Green, YouTube, p. 72.
285. Maria Armoudian, The Economic Revolution is Already Happening: A Q&A with Gar Alperovitz. 11 February 2009. http://shareable.net/blog/the-economic-revolution-is-already-happening-a-qa-with-gar-alperovit

This is a growing trend; it is a signifier that there is a movement away from the prescriptive ideology of how a mass consumer society sets out our lives from birth until death. In conversation with Maria, University of Maryland political scientist Gar Alperovitz, author of *America Beyond Capitalism*,[286] points out that in the US, 120 million Americans are members of cooperatives – about a third of the population. There are another 4,000 or 5,000 neighbourhood corporations, in which neighbourhoods own productive wealth to benefit the neighbourhood. Maria points to the fact that worker-owned cooperatives seem to be the most progressive and democratic models. They're usually non-profit making with profits circulating back to workers and communities, and coop practices of democracy in the workplace, with one person, one vote.

Alperovitz also refers to the Mondragón cooperatives of Spain.[287] These work by combining credit unions and service cooperatives such as grocery stores with industrial manufacturing cooperatives, research centres, and a university – all as one integrated unit. A cooperative corporation has its value invested in its people, an association of persons rather than an association of capital. That means one person, one vote rather than votes apportioned to the amount of capital invested. It also means that the individual workers own and control the company they work in. They are the largest worker-owned cooperative in the world, doing many billions of dollars in sales. They own and operate thousands of supermarkets, a travel agency with hundreds of units and gas stations. They also manufacture automotive parts, domestic appliances, bicycles and bus bodies.[288]

Across Britain, food coops are sprouting up in school halls, community centres, farm sheds or even your neighbour's front room – anywhere, in fact, where rent is free. So, are cooperatives the way forward to challenge the current system in which we live? Says Alperovitz:

> Ultimately there needs to be systemic change. But it is very important, and it's one thing that can be contributed. At this point, two central principles are developing in these 'schools of democracy' – they are changing who gets to own and benefit from capital, and they are changing the participatory process. And in addition to cooperatives, neighborhood corporations and organisations, cities and land trusts, state pension funds are being used in [socially responsible] ways.

286. Gar Alperovitz, *America Beyond Capitalism: Reclaiming Our Wealth, Our Liberty, and Our Democracy*, John Wiley & Sons, 2004.

287. Kevin A. Carson, *Organization Theory: A Libertarian Perspective*, Booksurge, 2008, ch. 15: 'Social organization of production: cooperatives and peer production'.

288. http://ukiahcommunityblog.wordpress.com/2009/02/02/cooperative-business/.

Constructing the open society

We are in the process of responding to our trilemma and in so doing are building a more open society which must be premised on the golden rule explained by Robert Putnam in *Making Democracy Work*, where he says that low trust levels lead to an inability for large-scale cooperation.[289] Charles Handy states: 'Trust sounds like a nice motherhood term; something no-one could be against, all warm and woolly. In practice, however, it's difficult and tough.'[290] Putnam based his thesis on researching how democracy in the south of Italy was so fundamentally different from its counterpart in the north of the country. He observed that, historically, southern Italian society had been run by the rule of tyrannos – top-down government that was monarchist, and dominated by the church. Such oligarchies seek not to encourage civic engagement, agoras or participatory democracy, as they are seen as a threat to their very existence. In contrast, northern Italian society thrived under the watchful gaze of the Enlightenment, which encouraged the very activities that its southern brothers attempted to snuff out. Are many of the governments, companies or organisations resisting the migration to a new way of doing things any different? Therefore, our new literacy requires us to become more familiar with the deeper meaning of a sharing economy, so we can then understand not the mechanics of cooperation, but the reasons which relate so critically to the I + We = Why? Lewis Hyde in his book *The Gift Economy* explores the idea of the reasons why we share and why that is so important to us. He says the purpose of the 'gift economy' is to establish and strengthen the relationships between us, to connect us one to another. It's the gift of exchange that brings social cohesion. Hyde talks about erotic commerce, derived from 'eros', which is based upon the tenets of attraction, engagement and union. In the gift economy, says Hyde, the more we share the wealthier we become, for it's the circulation of gifts within communities that multiplies our connections and strength of relationships. Contrast that to a market economy, where we perceive value by hoarding commodities, not in sharing them. The modern marketplace has had a devastating effect on this fundamental principle of trade.

> I have hoped ... to speak of the inner gift that we accept as the object of our labor, and the outer gift that has become a vehicle of culture. I am not concerned with gifts given in spite or fear, nor those gifts we accept out of servility or obligation; my concern is the gift we long for, the gift that, when it comes, speaks commandingly to the soul and irresistibly moves us.[291]

289. Robert D. Putman, *Making Democracy Work: Civic Traditions in Modern Italy*, Princeton University Press, 1993.
290. Handy, *The Hungry Spirit*, p. 187.
291. Lewis Hyde, *The Gift: Creativity and the Artist in the Modern World*, 25th anniversary edn, Vintage, 2007.

Through the process of social gifting we create deeper bonds of connection, a more implicit form of mutual connection and shared responsibility. The Dutch describe shared responsibility as the 'polder model'. a form of social organisation that enabled them to construct and maintain the dykes of Holland. Their view is that there can only be actors, and actors can only act together if they trust each other enough. It is a common saying that trust is a future bet on the contingent actions of others.

Max De Pree writes:

In much of our thinking and talking about how organisations work, the power of one word is regularly underestimated – trust. Trust is an enormous treasure for any organisation ... Trust doesn't arrive in our possession easily or cheaply, nor does it guarantee to stay around ... Trust requires respect – which means we take every person seriously. Trust multiplies with truth – without adjectives and not subject to redefinition by cornered leaders. Trust requires moral purpose, as well as keeping our promises. Demonstrating competence and making the nobler choice are part of how followers judge the character of leaders and whether to award them their trust. When leaders fail to see their obligations to be the initiators of reconciliation, trust begins to wane.[292]

De Pree argues that trust:
- Begins with a personal commitment to respect others, to take everyone seriously.
- Grows when people see leaders translate their personal integrity into organisational fidelity.
- Can take root and grow in the soil of the moral purpose of our organisations and personal commitments.
- Is built on kept promises. To be chosen means to be entrusted.
- In organisations, depends on the reasonable assumption by followers that leaders can be depended on to do the right thing.
- Requires leaders to hold the group accountable.

The language of No Straight Lines – participation, co-creation, networked economics, open source collaboration, Creative Commons legal frameworks – are all built upon the singular foundation of trusted relations. If we have so little trust left in the systems and organisations we designed and built all those years ago, it is time to find better more equitable alternatives; as Dr Frank Crane observed: "You may be deceived if you trust too much, but you will live in torment if you do not trust enough."[293]

---

292. Max De Pree, *Called to Serve: Creating and Nurturing the Effective Volunteer Board*, Wm B. Eerdmans Publishing Company, 2001.

293. Dr Frank Crane (1861–1928), Presbyterian minister, speaker and columnist, Everyday Wisdom, 1927.

As we can see, there is a model and framework which cannot be viewed only through the lens of 'new' and 'digital', but something which is moving at a far more structural level. Humanity is demonstrating it is capable of managing a fairer society through new systems of large- and small-scale cooperation. It demonstrates we all have a role to play, no matter how large or small. There is a meme describing the human operating system we are currently building; it is based upon [1] Compassion, Independence, Citizenship, [2] Adaptability, Speed, Ingenuity, [3] Scale, Justice, Vision. They resonate against each other.

Image from Nick Jankel.

Chapter Eight

Hacking the future: to be part of the future you have to create it

FOR MANY ORGANISATIONS, commercial and non-commercial alike, they are now faced with a design challenge, what is it that comes next? What does next look like and how do we create it? These are all very pressing questions. And of course, depending on levels of literacy and knowledge, will determine whether this participatory reconstructed world is perceived as a form of Communism as Steve Ballmer of Microsoft did, or defined, as Alan Rusbridger, Editor of the *Guardian*, as one built upon mutuality. All organisations will face different challenges in different ways; there are of course parallels but each alternative successful solution whilst adhering to common principles will be as different as the examples shared in *No Straight Lines*. The big challenge for all industrial organisations is that they are designed to operate at 100% efficiency – all the time, which is fine when everything else around you is in synch. But when everything is not in synch then running at 100% efficiency means there is no time to explore what next looks like. The net result an irretrievable road crash out of which few survive, as an increasing number of organisations and governments are discovering.

So we need the craftsman's approach to learning: the ability to play or experiment with an enquiring mind, an ability to bring together two unlikes in close adjacency and creatively explore what new forms of possibility might look like. To be happy to see stuff not work out as planned, and rather than seeing this as a personal (moral/ intellectual) or departmental failure, to learn from that experience; in fact testing to destruction is as important as success. This exercise however is a cognitive act. Organisations cannot farm this stuff out; they need to create the future if they want to exist in it. They are the actors which need to act. They need to explore what the future looks like to them. And the reason why this is important is because when we can't afford business as usual, and when we are currently in a cycle of almost continuous change, we are going to have disrupt ourselves before someone else does it to us – it's time to hack the future.

Hacking

Hacking as a term was first attributed to Stephen Levy as described in his book *Hackers: Heroes of the Computer Revolution*. The key points of this ethic are that of access, free information and improvement to quality of life. There are a couple of key points worth sharing. First, sharing is expected within the hacker culture and the principle of sharing stemmed from the atmosphere and resources at MIT. During the early days of computers and programming, the hackers at MIT would develop a programme and share it. Secondly, many of the principles and tenets of the Hacker ethic contribute to a common goal – the hands-on imperative. As Levy states: 'Hackers believe that essential lessons can be learned about the systems – about the world – from taking things apart, seeing how they work, and using this knowledge to create new and more interesting things.'[294] Thirdly, a common value for hackers and their work processes is that a sense of community and collaboration are present at all times.

In 'Civic hacking: a new agenda for e-democracy', James Crabtree references reciprocity. 'The opportunity is the construction of a civic space in which citizens talk to each other, rather than to the state', he states.

> An analogy will help explain this. If you are stuck in a computer game, what do you do? Gamers today – and remember around three in ten people play computer games – will go to a gaming community online, and ask others for advice. They will almost always find someone willing to help them overcome the challenge. Other gamers will help for a variety of reasons: they may get respect for their knowledge; their standing in the community will improve; or they may simply be in a good mood that day. But mostly they do it on the principle of reciprocity.[295]

And as Crabtree points out, hackers tend to work collaboratively. So sharing information is the key to development; the more sharing of knowledge within communities of interest or practice means that community, like a Linux, or an or a Local Motors community, becomes more capable – it can accelerate innovation, it can enable people to acquire new skills to apply to new challenges. Sharing good knowledge within a community is also creating a reservoir of knowledge – we are harnessing collective intelligence.

---

294. Stephen Levy, *Hackers: Heroes of the Computer Revolution*, Anchor Press, Doubleday, 1984, ch. 2.
295. Jame Crabtree, 'Civic hacking: a new agenda for e-democracy', 12 June 2007, http://www.opendemocracy.net/debates/article-8-85-1025.jsp.

What is harnessing collective intelligence?

It was Eric Raymond in his famous article *The Cathedral and the Bazaar* who shared with us the insight that 'with many eyes all bugs are shallow'.[296] What he meant was, as in the case of the Linux open source code, where many people are able to contribute their individual knowledge to a coding problem collectively – the ability to solve that problem rises exponentially. This process is also described as co-creation, an idea whose time has now come and moved centre stage. The result of the open source approach to harnessing and applying the knowledge and collective wisdom has been proven repeatedly in the fields of science (NASA Mars project, and Galaxy Zoo in the UK), R&D (Innocentive, a platform for solving scientific challenges, and YourEncore – a collaborative R&D platform), commercially with Local Motors in the US, TopCoder and politically with Ushahidi. These are but a small sample of a much bigger list.

Hacking a wicked problem

Let's seek out a wicked problem, and hack it; 80% of growth is from companies in an entrepreneurial community that begin their organisational life as start-ups. Yet these companies are the ones that often have the least access to high-quality resources that will enable them to establish a true path to economic success. And yet the pressure is on; the need to create a resilient and sustainable economy requires us to stimulate innovation – in fact we need to be relentless. And of course it gets ever more challenging as economic power shifts to the BRIC countries, whilst technology migrates us towards a global level playing field. In conversation with Jon Bradford, an expert in accelerating innovation based in Cambridge, our conversation arrived at a number of key issues around the challenge we face. In 2009, the world's economies and banking systems came to the brink of bankruptcy; whilst some countries have managed to step back from the brink, other countries have been effectively declared bankrupt only to be bailed out by the wider economic community. In either case, the fiscal constraints which bind economies in this 'new world' are substantially greater than those ever experienced before. Whilst the United Kingdom might not be technically bankrupt, it faces a national debt so big that we are forced to revaluate how our society functions and how we pay for it. From the NHS, to local services, prisons, schools – every single one of these faces monumental funding problems.

The engine room of any economy is dependent upon the capital which fuels its operation. The UK can no longer depend upon the fiscal capital upon which it has

---

296. Raymond, *The Cathedral and the Bazaar*. http://catb.org/ffiesr/writings/cathedral-bazaar/.

become historically reliant. Jon passionately believes the UK has no other option other than to rebuild its economy through a very potent asset, its latent intellectual capital – better explained as the experience, creativity and intellect of those that have been there and done it before. It is the combined intellectual capital of the entrepreneurial community that is more valuable than anything else we could possibly imagine. There are a number of substantial attributes that significantly differentiate fiscal and intellectual capital.

- Fiscal capital is limited to a small proportion of the population resulting from transfer of wealth between generations, whereas intellectual capital is spread widely through a population and cannot be passed from one generation to another.
- Fiscal capital is finite – once it has been passed to someone else it is gone, whereas, intellectual capital is infinite – passing on this capital to another does not restrict the ability to pass this on to another.
- Fiscal capital is not viral – giving it to someone does not make others feel better, whereas intellectual capital is much more viral – the transfer of knowledge has the ability to make a social impact on many others.

This pronouncement has been made repeatedly in the past, but this time circumstances are different and there is no alternative. Against that backdrop, government initiatives to foster innovation and regional development via the delivery of advisory services necessary to enable businesses to be successful have been patchy at best, and poor at the worst. Moreover, one could argue that entrepreneurship, the very commercial lifeline for this country, is being held back by an entire ecosystem and mindset. We just don't have a big enough, and dynamic enough, vibrant academic, innovative, commercial, entrepreneurial ecosystem, within the European Union. This is a view that is supported by Stanford Professor Burton Lee, a specialist on European entrepreneurship and innovation, as well as people such as Will Hutton, from The Work Foundation.

The problem that sits at the heart of this is that there is no joined-up thinking, no national means to share current or hard-won knowledge, or a designed process providing access to these mentors who represent this extraordinary pool of talent and wisdom that are able to get entrepreneurs to accelerate their thinking to better develop and build their companies. That benefit would bring commercial success, resulting in job creation, inward investment and real regional economic development.

Consider this: in the UK only three regions provide a net benefit to the exchequer, all other regions are a cost. Of course there are complex reasons for this; however, the goal should be that all regions move from a cost minus to a cost plus. So if we return to the mantra on being 'relentless', is it possible to create a platform and or a process that is lightweight, flexible, strong and enabling for all entrepreneurs to access, which could deliver on the needs and challenges of the early 21st century? And if so. what would it look like? Could we build a rapid learning system for entrepreneurial companies in the UK? The imperative to innovate and reinvent oneself, writes Roland Deiser, in these changing contexts has become ubiquitous and permanent.[297] The capability to learn is not just nice to have; it has become a key factor for commercial survival.

Is there a simple, cost-effective solution?

The answer is yes – and the means lies in harnessing the collective intelligence of all the people and companies in the UK that want to share their knowledge, passion and know-how in helping each other succeed. This ability to harness and aggregate people's knowledge is the key to accelerating economic success. It was the head of Hitachi's portable computer division who said: 'speed is god, but time is the devil',[298] so to increase speed we need to relinquish our penchant for hierarchy and red tape, and empower the periphery that creates a new learning architecture.

The hacker will have a hypothesis on what can accelerate innovation; he may well have identified a set of patterns which suggest the types of outcome he seeks. The hacker will collect evidence on how innovation can be accelerated and he will then go and explore those architectures and processes which perhaps adhere to the emergent pattern and insight. One such example is a learning platform called CompanyCommand.com that suggests a framework of how one could envisage an alternative process of enabling entrepreneurial companies to achieve the success that they deserve and we need.

Majors Nate Allen and Tony Burgess became friends at West Point in the 1980s and at the end of 1990s found themselves commanding companies in separate battalions in the same Hawaii-based brigade. Even in peacetime, company commanders are faced with significant and diverse challenges that can lead to them feeling isolated, which is exactly the experience that both Allen and Burgess went through. 'If I had a good idea about how to do something, there was no natural way to share it', says Allen. 'I'd have to pass it up, and it would have to be blessed two levels above me, and then passed down to Tony.'[299]

Living as neighbours, however, enabled the two company commanders to share their experiences informally with each other. 'At some point, we realised this conversation was having a positive impact on our units, and we wanted to pass it

---

297. Deiser, Designing the Smart Organisation, p. 12.
298. M. J. Ryan, The Power of Patience: How to Slow the Rush and Enjoy More Happiness, Success, and Peace of Mind Every Day, 1st edn, Crown Archetype, 2003.
299. Dan Baum, 'Battle lessons: what the generals don't know', New Yorker, 17 January 2005.

along', Allen explains to Dan Baum.[300] So Allen and Burgess decided to write a book about commanding a company entitled *Taking the Guidon*, and was posted onto a website. The result was an emergent conversation that became so rich that it brought into the world first CompanyCommand.com, then PlatoonCommander.com.

Explains Baum:

> The sites, which are accessible to captains and lieutenants with a password, are windows onto the job of commanding soldiers and onto the complexities of fighting urban guerrillas. CompanyCommand is divided into twelve areas, including training, war-fighting, and soldiers and families, each of which is broken into discussion threads on everything from mortar attacks to grief counselling and dishonest sergeants. Some discussions are quite raw. Captains post comments on coping with fear, on motivating soldiers to break the taboo against killing, and on counselling suicidal soldiers. They advise each other on how to kick in doors and how to handle pregnant subordinates. Most captains now have access to the Internet at even the most remote bases in Iraq, and many say they'll find at least ten or 15 minutes every day to check the site. They post tricks they've learned or ask questions like this, which set off months of responses: 'What has anyone tried to do to alleviate the mortar attacks on their forward operating bases?'[301]

At CompanyCommand nobody is as clever as everybody

CompanyCommand.com is populated by company commanders that have never been in the field of battle; there are company commanders in the field of battle and there are company commanders that have spent a lifetime in the army. It is the constant interaction between these three distinct areas that enables knowledge to be aggregated, shared and wisdom disseminated.

Roland Deiser in *Designing the Smart Organisation*,[302] writes:

> What makes the case particularly interesting is that the CompanyCommand project is much more than just another example of how communities of practice work. The initiative is not only extremely well designed; it also unfolds on the very unique background of an extremely hierarchal organisation, and it evolves into a comprehensive learning architecture that showcases the cross-fertilizing inter-play of informal grassroots processes and formal routines. The learning project has become a major transformational force towards a military organisation of the 21st century.

---

300. Baum, 'Battle lessons'.
301. Baum, 'Battle lessons'.
302. Deiser, *Designing the Smart Organisation*, p. 210.

The question we must ask ourselves is this: are there lessons for us to learn here? All this aggregated information results in a dramatic increase in the effectiveness of company commanders in the field who regularly use CompanyCommand. But this is not a one-off. The fact is when knowledge and information are harnessed into a very focused networked and collaborative manner, the results are always the same – an exponential acceleration of knowledge and capability. As Jon Bradford believes, it is the unleashing of the intellectual capital that is held in the minds of individuals which when aggregated and shared – the same as the dynamic of CompanyCommand – learning times and the ability to absorb information and turn that into action is transformed. But there are three keys points that I pull out of looking at CompanyCommand outside of a fluid learning community of practice: one is mentorship, the second is that Majors Allen and Burgess did not ask anyone's permission, the third is that it did not cost the earth to set it up and run. The hacker might also conclude there are other things he can apply here from other hacks – the gift culture that Lewis Hyde wrote about, the culture of participation, the high need and motivation to learn.

Springboard: rapid learning systems for entrepreneurs

Connecting the best and most able with the most willing
I am sitting in the Hauser Forum, in Cambridge, and today I am going to meet 10 entrepreneurial teams, and the 10 entrepreneurial teams are going to meet 10 mentors; tomorrow those 10 entrepreneurial teams are going to meet another 10 mentors. It's mentally exhausting for the teams, and, massively stimulating for the mentors. Today there are mentors who have run and built businesses that come from all over the world. Why are they here? Because, they have a need to want to put something back. The mentors are not paid; they are not allowed to invest or take equity in those companies as they mentor them.

But what is released in the café of the Hauser Forum that morning is an amount of intellectual capital which those teams would never have access to – the mentors' knowledge is practical not theoretical, it's hard won. Every mentor has their own way of engaging in the teams based upon their life experience. I find myself challenging sales channels, offering marketing advice, asking about revenue and where it is coming from, and connecting teams with a colleague who has a wealth of knowledge about micro-payments on mobile devices in gaming. There are no tick box interviews, every mentor has their own expertise and way of interviewing the entrepreneurial companies, and so by default the process is highly creative – you can tell that by the noise level in the room.

I go back for a second round two weeks later. I sit down with one team who have radically rethought what they are doing, and how they are going to do it – I am seriously impressed. And then reflect on my own journey and wished something like this had existed for me. Over a period of three months these 10 teams will benefit from the combined intellectual capital collectively created out of the hundreds of years of commercial and entrepreneurial experience represented by the network of mentors that Jon Bradford has curated so well. At the end of their journey, the entrepreneurial teams will have a honed vision of their business, with the probability of investment success significantly enhanced. They will be presenting then to a peer group and potential investors. Their chances of success have been increased significantly. So what's built over time is a powerful learning community that continuously improves through ongoing dialogue. Economic innovation and knowledge creation can now be harnessed through loosely connected and distributed communities, the shorthand for that is 'peer to peer' entrepreneurial learning. The method of mentoring recognises that there's too much knowledge in too many places, and the useful knowledge in fact lies in the minds of the many. So my last question is this: we know designing around human knowledge sharing works, we know that it is people which make a difference, so why is it so hard for our UK government which is busy with the fiscal axe and scalpel at present to realise the huge economic potential of the Springboard programme?

Wicked problems in healthcare

Let's start by asking a question: how could participatory culture and participatory tools be transformational for healthcare? Having already looked at the built environment with the Downe Hospital, and explored how mobile communications could be transformational, Dr David Lester states[303] that participatory health is breaking the traditional mould of the doctor–patient relationship, which relies upon patient passivity. In this traditional relationship, patients have been deliberately kept out of their own care. In participatory health, by contrast, patients actively engage in their own healthcare in a genuine partnership with trusted experts. Participation is enabled and enhanced by that little big word – trust.

Patients know best

To best illustrate participatory healthcare, let's take the story of Mohammad Al-Ubaydli a researcher at UCL Medical School in London. Mohammad has a rare medical condition, and, as he says, 'the only person that went to all the

---

303. *Participatory Health: Online and Mobile Tools Help Chronically Ill Manage Their Care*, California Healthcare Foundation, September 2009.

appointments was him' – so he became in fact the authority on his condition, as well as how it affected his health personally, to the point where doctors would ask him how he might treat his condition. This insight was not lost on Mohammad – deep knowledge translates into meaningful action. Patients know a great deal, they are curators of their personal histories, and all to a lesser or greater degree possess uncommon combinations of common conditions in unique personal circumstances.

For a period of time, Mohammad worked for a consulting firm in the US where he built from open source software a knowledge sharing platform, to great and lasting effect. This inspired him to consider the relationship between doctors and their patients, and that patients and patient histories were not a liability but an asset, were they to be curated in the right way and made available with the right type of access and context.

There was something else that Mohammad did as a stepping stone to Patients Know Best. Mohammad had run a trial at Cambridge University's medical school with his student peers. He wrote a piece of software and uploaded it to £100 Palm Pilots. His idea was to enable his colleagues to note down nuggets of information as they travelled the country. Whilst on various wards listening and observing frontline clinical practice, they would then share this information once a week by pointing their palm pilots at the clinical studies building where a server would pick up the information and publish it to the group. Initially there was reluctance, but this blossomed into active participation and a community of practice, once the student doctors realised the value of sharing knowledge in a dynamic learning environment. The service evolved to become the digital handover of patients at the first hospital he worked in as a junior doctor, much to the consternation of the resident CIO, as this innovation was bottom-up not top-down, and permission was not sought, and it hardly cost a penny.

Patients Know Best was created from all these insights, and welcomed into the world in July 2008. The best doctors with specialist knowledge – normally older and wiser, possessing a lifetime of knowledge, and who were comfortable in that knowledge – became the first recruits, rather than the patients themselves. This was for several reasons. Mohammad knew that by recruiting patients first but giving them a poor experience, the project would fail' bringing on young doctors would also present problems. Young Doctors, he explained, are more fearful of knowledgeable patients, as they worry their knowledge gaps would be exposed.

A great deal of time and thought has gone into what language is used at Patients Know Best. The use of language is seen as important in breaking down the barriers between those from the medical profession and those with medical conditions. In this way, a collaborative learning community is formed as there is no division; for example the word consultation is never used but discussion is –

it is teams that engage in those discussions rather than clinicians and patients. In this way, an equitable sense of mutuality and trust is fostered. Today Patients Know Best works with Great Ormond Street hospital for children, University College London, Imperial College London, the National Heart and Lung Institute, Torbay Hospital, plus all Thalidomide patients are engaged, encouraged by their charity, and many rare conditions are directed to the platform by leading charities. In the case of Parkinson's disease, they have realised that the dynamic flows of information formulated by case histories and discussion becomes the most effective way to conduct ongoing research in the best and most ethical way, as patients are empowered to freely provide their data. In fact Mohammad says it is cheaper and a greater degree of comprehensive accuracy is achieved in one to two orders of magnitude, which is why pharmaceutical companies are starting to use the platform their clinical trials. Patient control not only provides an ethical framework for the research, it also reduces the costs of recruitment and consent, while raising the quantity and quality of data.

All of this has been built on open source software, not only because it is cheaper but because it works; enterprise tools bought at great cost cannot be plugged into a network or networks easily, integration is costly and often fails. The growth of Patients Know Best has evolved from what Mohammad calls 'a noble conspiracy', by which he means seeking no permission, and going around internal bureaucracy to ensure that something good and useful can be brought into this world. Once it has demonstrated its usefulness the conspiracy will be recognised as good and useful. But because in this instance Patients Know Best is so unorthodox to conventional medical wisdom, it requires a conspiracy of noble proportions to bring it into the world – to declare its existence before then would ultimately mean its stillbirth. The prize is transformational for those that use Patients Know Best. The social capital invested equally by both patients and clinicians is the engine room of its success. At a time when we increasingly realise we cannot afford business as usual, what Patients Know Best demonstrates is that by understanding and designing from end user need, by being literate in open source participatory cultures and masterful with participatory tools, by building for lightness, adaptability and speed, proves there are realistically viable and sustainable alternatives to helping patients get better or manage their long-term health conditions in a better way.

Participatory healthcare lays the groundwork to build sustainable relationships. Relationships based on the development of mutual trust through time remain the vital essence which makes for a sustainable and enduring service.

Chart showing the relationship between Doctor, Patient and Data

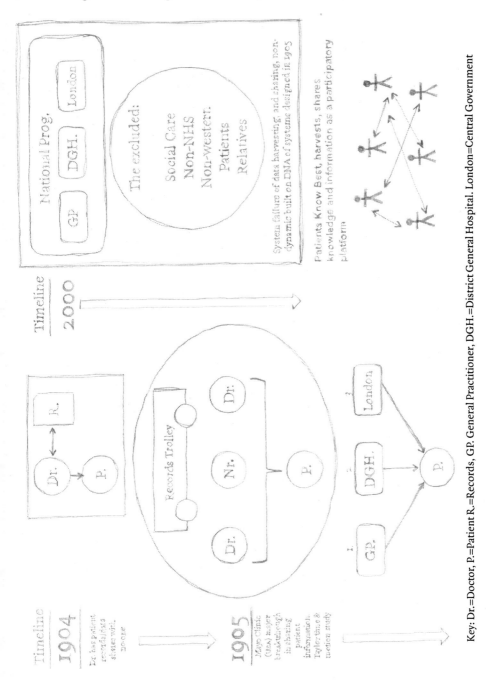

Key: Dr.=Doctor, P.=Patient R.=Records, GP. General Practitioner, DGH.=District General Hospital. London=Central Government

Transforming the public health system of Nova Scotia

Mohammad's People Know Best solution still might not convince some that by designing around what makes us as people we can create transformational actions – so let's look at a large scale wicked problem.

The region of Nova Scotia was facing significant challenges in how it was going to evolve its healthcare system. In 2006 the Government received a report that contained 21 recommendations, the first asking Nova Scotia's public health practitioners, to 'articulate and be guided by a collective vision for the public health system.' This is a complex challenge, and how does one go about articulating a collective vision?

In December 2008, a group of practitioners and partners in public health from across the province took on this challenge. They initiated a search to find a process that would bring people together to seek new solutions for the common good. They also knew the process would have to take into account the complexity of public health. And they also felt that any attempt to address the current challenges of public health demands the collective intelligence of all stakeholders. They sought a process that would launch Nova Scotia into a new beginning, an approach that would foster leadership and innovation.

The real insight was that the answer to such a complex problem lay in participatory leadership, that the way forward was held collectively in all the stakeholders that worked in the current system – not in the PowerPoint charts of a highly paid management consultant. The question was how to release that knowledge and turn it into action?

Tim Merry, who specialises in participatory leadership and hosting took an appointed leadership team which was representative of the health system on a retreat through exploring their purpose, and understanding the scale of what they had to achieve the realisation was they could not exclusively lead that change – they understood they had to empower a much wider group of people. From the 60 people identified as the core group, 25 committed to becoming practitioners of participatory leadership. These 25 people were then designing their engagement with larger stakeholder groups, notably an event with 250 people in a room and 650 people online. By using a variety of social technologies, the group was enabled to release its knowledge and move towards a consensus on particular issues. These social technologies are inspired by Otto Scharmer, a social scientist at MIT, who published a book in 2007 in which he outlined Theory U, an innovative yet common sense process for collectively creating solutions to complex problems. Scharmer writes, 'When the members of a group see together with depth and clarity, they become aware of their own collective potential. The group can see the emerging opportunities and the key systematic forces at work.'[304]

Scharmer has three key criteria on which he bases is U theory: sensing, presencing and realising. Sensing is about understanding the behaviours of the system, the challenges and opportunities that are really being faced. Presencing is the internalisation of those insights, and a process to discover the highest possible potential of their insights. Realising is the action that is to be taken.

It was these core processes that enabled a diverse team to dive deep into the Nova Scotia's health system, both with the people that run it and the people that use it, and realise solutions that previously would have been overlooked or misunderstood. And of course because the process has meaningfully engaged entire communities, by working constantly in dialogue, listening and developing action, Nova Scotia has been able to work sensibly through its wicked problems by surfacing the collective wisdom of large groups of diverse people, and being able to act upon this wisdom.

Tim Merry tells me that throughout this learning and discovery process, the team applied participatory leadership methodologies, a way of effectively working with others. Participatory leadership is built on the understanding that seeking change for the common good calls for involvement, collective intelligence and co-creation to discover and illuminate new solutions and wise actions. Tim tells me that through this process there was a significant shift in the consciousness, a collective awareness and worldview shift of understanding how to create a healthy society. Consequently, there was shared ownership both of the problem and the ways and means that problem could be addressed. This, to my mind, is a wonderful example of what I describe as a 'human operating system'. What might have been the cost for the state of Ontario had it gone down the 'orthodox route'? Look at the vitriol, and violent arguments which are defining the UK governments attempts at reforming the NHS. What we see here is the waste of time, effort, energy and resources.

More of the same is not good enough

It is worth pointing out that the logic for most healthcare systems in the developed world is that general hospitals are the flagships where general medicine is practised. However, it is clear that there are other viable alternatives that can significantly reduce costs, and dramatically increase efficiency. Which means for example, lives are saved, more babies are brought into this world safely and more people have the gift of sight restored to them. For example, the Narayana Hrudayalaya Hospital in Bangalore by specialising in heart surgery, and designing everything around that

---

304. C. Otto Scharmer, *Theory U: Leading from the Future as it Emerges*, 1st edn, Berrett-Koehler, 2009.

specialisation has reduced the cost of surgery to $2,000 this is 60% cheaper than most Indian hospitals. And the 42 surgeons perform 3,000 operations every year. LifeSpring specialises in the delivery of babies and has reduced the cost of delivery to $40 per child by intensely studying not birthing but manufacturing, and the Aravind eye clinic performs 70% of the total number of NHS operations for 1% of the budget. These are the types of transformational capabilities we must seek. And why should we ignore them because they come from India? In the US, there are attempts at running better healthcare systems by using remote monitoring of patients via mobile communications and data feeds, hospital admissions have been reduced by 30% at the Montefiore Centre in New York. One of the lessons of wicked problems is that more of the same doesn't really work – we have to learn to let go of perspectives that fix us to the same point on the horizon line.

Being adaptive and the wicked challenges of an uncertain world

Increasingly, the demand is placed upon all organisations to possess the ability to be adaptive. It requires a lightweight approach to how we touch the world around us, what we build and the culture we create, as largely the inability to adapt is cultural. Tom Kelly, a founder of IDEO, and I met when we were both speaking at a conference in Brazil. In his keynote address, he told a story about the terminal decline of his home town in Ohio, which was triggered by the collapse of the sole main employer in the town, a company that at one time made tyres for all the trucks and cars in America. Tom described how hubris and the thought that there could never be an outside force so disruptive that it could possibly threaten their dominant position led the company to put off the need to innovate, to the point that it was too late to do anything when the moment to respond to an economic threat, Michelin Radial tyres, arrived. The opportunity to adapt passed them by and they became obsolete.

When confronted with significant and disruptive forces, the ability to be prepared to think the unthinkable becomes all important. In *The Life and Death of Democracy* John Keane takes us through the story of how representative democracy was born. Contrary to some old-fashioned, devoutly British accounts, he says Parliaments were in fact an invention of what today is northern Spain. Keane tells us that Parliaments were born out of sheer and utter despair. Christianity believed that the tide of Islam was overwhelming it and encroaching upon its bastion strongholds in Syria, Palestine, Egypt, the North African coast, Constantinople, Spain, and southern France, Rome and Sicily – and overthrowing them. Tens of thousands of Christians felt squeezed by the combined forces of what they saw as unfair taxation and the contemptuous toleration by Islamic rulers.

Enter King Alfonso IX of Iberia. His kingdom, says Keane, was under intense military pressure, not only from neighbouring fiefdoms but also from the Moorish army. In facing up to this bleak situation Alfonso decided to fight his way to freedom. But to do this, he had to innovate to bring disparate parties to a table to agree collectively to a plan of sustained action.

> Both Alfonso IX and the local nobility agreed that the re-conquest required political deals to be struck, minimally by waging war in tandem. But that meant winning over the bishops of the Church, the estate that saw itself as the guardian of souls and the spiritual protector of God's lands. Launching war also meant costs. Permanent warfare against the Moors had to somehow be paid for. With the whole region now permanently under siege, and strategically vital towns like León now resembling a walled fortress, Alfonso decide to appeal for their solidarity.[305]

He achieved this by reaching out to those influential men in the town who were recognised by the community as being respected as 'good men'. These men could deliver trained soldiers, and could also provide the necessary cash to wage the war. But Alfonso IX also recognised that the 'principal of mutual compromise' had to apply, so he sought the backing of the warrior nobility and the church. He did this by offering protection to the besieged towns in return for fighting men and money. Alfonso IX understood that he must deeply engage with all affected parties, and make them accountable to each other. It meant he was no longer supreme ruler, but that was better in his opinion than having his subjects living as second-class citizens under the Moors and being coerced into adopting a Moorish way of life. And so it was within this triumvirate formed by the nobles, bishops and urban citizens that the modern practice of parliamentary representation was brought to life. In 1188 in León, Alfonso convened the first ever cortes.

Keane summarises:

> Although committed to open discussion, the first ever cortes was not an assembly of citizens of the Syrian-Mesopotamian, Phoenician, Greek, or Islamic kind. It was also not a western version of the Meshawara that developed during the Ottoman Empire. It was instead the brainchild of a self-interested Christian monarch bent on building up his realm, the creation of a political animal who saw that effective government required the creation of a new mechanism for resolving disputes and striking bargains among interested parties who felt they had a common interest in reaching compromise, so avoiding internecine violence.[306]

---

305. Keane, *The Life and Death of Democracy*, p. 172.
306. Keane, *The Life and Death of Democracy*, p. 176.

There is nothing like a good crisis to be the mother of invention

Kenya provides a recent and inspiring example of getting stuff done when you have no money and no resources, by being able to describe a real problem and then being literate and knowledgeable enough to conceive the possibility of creating an entirely new means to meet the needs of the problem. That problem at hand was not a small matter, it was the escalating violence ensuing from a bitterly contested election. In 2008, Kenyan citizen journalists and activists were actively using Web 2.0 tools and applications such as wikis, blogs, Facebook, Flickr, Twitter and SMS messages to organise and share news and information about the recent post-election crisis, chronicling violence, sharing crisis photos and raising funds to help the needy. However, the information was not being harnessed and aggregated as a singular source of information, making effective on-the-ground coordination difficult.

Kenyan blogger Ory Okolloh posted on her blog asking for volunteers to create a new service that would be able to document post-election violence and destruction. Her premise was that gathering crisis information from people on the ground would provide invaluable knowledge and information into events happening in near real-time. That would aid rapid reaction to events, and also could be used for a possible future reconciliation process. The service was designed and built by a group of volunteer developers and designers, hailing primarily from Africa; however, it also attracted people from other parts of the world including the Netherlands and the US. Rapidly, a tool was developed by combining (mashing up) open source software, mobile geo location data, Google maps, text messaging and information gathered from other data sources. It was called 'Ushahidi'. In Swahili it means testimony, and became the tool for people who, witnessing acts of violence in Kenya, could report the incidents. This information would then be displayed via a platform using Google maps in which all the information could be viewed.

Ushahidi have made their platform freely available for anyone to use. To collect and visualise information in crisis scenarios or when the gathering of information in real-time can play a crucial role in the outcome of fast-moving events. Ushahidi has been deployed in Haiti, Chile, Japan and is used now as an election monitoring system as well. That is their gift to the world, as Lewis Hyde might observe. The open source platform is adaptable, allowing for plug-ins and extensions; it is therefore flexible enough to accommodate different needs. Ushahidi has been used extensively since then, but again if we look under the hood of Ushahidi and reflect on its capability and its success, what can we learn?

The *New York Times* writes:

Ushahidi also represents a new frontier of innovation. Silicon Valley has been the reigning paradigm of innovation, with its universities, financiers, mentors, immigrants and robust patents. Ushahidi comes from another world, in which entrepreneurship is born of hardship and innovators focus on doing more with less, rather than on selling you new and improved stuff.

Because Ushahidi originated in crisis, no one tried to patent and monopolize it. Because Kenya is poor, with computers out of reach for many, Ushahidi made its system work on cell phones. Because Ushahidi had no venture-capital backing, it used open-source software and was thus free to let others remix its tool for new projects.

Ushahidi remixes have been used in India to monitor elections; in Africa to report medicine shortages; in the Middle East to collect reports of wartime violence; and in Washington, D.C., where the *Washington Post* partnered to build a site to map road blockages and the location of available snowplows and blowers.[307]

Ushahidi asks us to rethink how we view the process of innovation and organisation. Theirs was a non-linear response in every sense of the word where high levels of motivation and a blend of skill sets realised Ushahidi as a platform that circumvented all obstacles to its success. From an organisational perspective, we can see that participatory cultures, open source and collaborative tools, combined with communication networks, enable a coalition of the willing to form and work together.

Whole systems thinking in facing the wicked problem of the volatility of an oil-based economy

Tim Mead is the owner of the organic diary products company Yeo Valley Organic, based just outside of Bristol in the UK. Recently I spent an afternoon with Tim and his team walking through the Yeo Valley farm around Blagdon. I asked Tim why an organic approach to farming inspired him; he responded by pointing out that to get the best out of nature, you need to respect nature. To do that one must understand it's a fine balancing act to deliver yield performance of his diary herd and that of the land that supplies the nutrients to the cows to deliver that yield. 'Push nature too hard', says Tim, 'and she will bite you back', an observation that is so ingrained and implicit in Tim's worldview, to him, that it's blindingly obvious. In Tim's description of how they farm it's clear he sees the process of being a whole systems design problem. We start with the challenges of farming in the UK over the last 100 years; many small holders were locked into an economic model and way of life that, from a UK perspective referenced against the industrial-scale farming in countries

---

307. 'Africa's gift to Silicon Valley: how to track a crisis', *New York Times*, 14 March 2010. http://www.nytimes.com/2010/03/14/weekinreview/14giridharadas.html?scp=10&sq=Humanitarianism%202.0&st=cse.

such as Canada, meant that shortly after the Second World War the UK was importing 60%+ of its grain, diary, meat and vegetables. Fuelled bizarrely by the left-over nitrogen stockpiled during the war for munitions, and re-created as a miracle grow fertiliser to exponentially increase agricultural output, but with a deadly endgame of extracting more of natures goodness than we could put back. Ultimately leaving the earth unable to give back what we currently take for granted. We then get onto the economics of farming in the 21st century, the scale and volatility of the milk market (exacerbated by the financial meltdown of hikes in crude oil) and how one deals with such volatility without being beholden to the power and whimsy of the supermarkets. So part of the design challenge is independence, to be master and commander, as best as one can, of one's own destiny. And in amongst all of that are the cows that are key to Yeo Valley's success. Tim believes cows perform best, producing greater quantities of, and better-quality milk, under certain conditions. The cows need great product, a wide variety of rich nutrients to eat, to do that requires some nurture and networked thinking about what the cows eat, how to give it to them, and how to keep that raw material coming at the highest-quality level all year round. It's a complex operation, but when it's explained it makes, to me at least, common sense. The farm and the business cannot run without people so people count too, as a working community. In contrast, Tim believes that those agricultural companies completely dependent on an oil-based economy are in fact unsustainable, and vulnerable to a volatile global economy. He believes that his overall operation although organic, which does present its own unique challenges, is more enduring and economically viable. Nothing is wasted. It is also a fine balancing act between now, tomorrow and ten years time, but this constant headache means Yeo Valley Organic constantly invests in its future by investing in the whole ecosystem. It constantly invests in the quality of its soil, its herd, its manufacturing capability and its people. One simply cannot separate one from the other.

Community speaks truth to power in the Amazon

If Africa seems an unlikely place to be innovating with networked communications technology, then the Amazon rainforest seems perhaps an even more unlikely destination. Gregor MacLennan works for an organisation that campaigns for the rights and lives of indigenous tribes living in the Amazon rainforest in Peru.

MacLennan explains that huge tracts of the Amazon have been sold to international companies for mineral extraction. Those companies come and extract the minerals but they leave a lot behind: pollution on an unprecedented scale, deforestation, the undoable disruption of the communities that live there.

The mining companies literally tear up and destroy the habitat in which the indigenous people live. Rather than wishing to protect the indigenous people of the Amazon, MacLennan says the government in Lima perceives them more as an annoying irritant, so is quite content to let the murder of its own people continue, as long as the world doesn't know. A few years back, the indigenous tribes, after extensively trying to get the Lima government to engage in dialogue about deforestation and the threat to their way of life, and without success, came together to protest at a logging station and refused to move. This went on for several months. But at some point the authorities' patience snapped and they sent in the troops. Many people were brutally beaten, and killed. The government claimed it was putting down a terrorist attack: why would anybody believe differently? There was no evidence, no film crews, right? Wrong, two Dutch travellers filmed the event. They got to a local town with an internet connection and the murder and beatings of unarmed people now lives on YouTube.

This story demonstrates how powerful networked communications can be. MacLennan's objective is to enable the indigenous tribes to speak their truth to the power in Lima, and also to the power that sits in the boardrooms of the companies that come and rape the land of the Amazon. This is how he does it.

First, he gathers the entire village in the main house, and asks them to collectively pool their knowledge by drawing on a large sheet of paper the rivers where they fish, the land they hunt, the areas where they may grow crops or harvest the forest for its bounty – all the things that enable that tribe to flourish in the jungle. MacLennan and his team then teach the group to use GPS positioning equipment to turn the hand-drawn map that the entire village has contributed to creating into hard data. That information is then fed into survey maps of the area, which will not contain such detailed information. And so a new map is created. These maps are then presented to the government in Lima, to board directors and shareholders of mining companies, forcing them to accept that their actions can have tragic consequences to human life. The Achuar have also been trained to use video-recording technology, so evidence of the environmental damage that these extraction companies leave behind is also presented as prima facie evidence. The mashup of data that combines the historical collective intelligence of the village, created initially with pens and crayons and perhaps the odd spot of paint, and is then translated into millimetre perfect maps is transformational. These maps are causing companies to think harder about how and where they are going to mine in the forests of the Amazon. It certainly has changed the power relationships between the 'savage' people of the rainforest and the 'cultured' people of Lima, or should that be the other way around?

The hacker ethic, ambiguity and innovation

So what connects Springboard, Patients Know Best, the Nova Scotia health system, King Alfonso IX of Iberia, Ushahidi, Yeo Valley Organic and the Achuar in the Amazon? They have all been born out of various crisis situations that are so volatile they present a deadly endgame. The ability of the entrepreneurs or groups of dispersed individuals or situated communities to apply innovative thinking and action has enabled them to adapt to ambiguous, challenging and dangerous situations, consequently they have transformed healthcare, economies, communities and political outcomes. There is an artfulness, an underlying creativity that is able to operate because the creators have all allowed themselves to imagine what others thought to be impossible. Not because they think it's a nice thing to do, but because there is a very pressing need – in essence all obstacles must be overcome. Compare that approach to the institutionalisation and the accompanying waste to innovation in many organisations and industries, populated by a culture that simply would not allow 'heretical' thinking, constrained by conventional orthodoxies, siloed budgets, misaligned needs and wants all wrapped up with a struggle for power.

Thinking the unthinkable

In 2006 IBM produced a report called 'The enterprise of the future'. Their survey of CEOs revealed that 8 out of 10 CEOs saw significant change ahead and yet the gap between expected levels of change plus the ability to manage it had tripled. Why? Because, I would argue in part, these leaders did not have the means to understand, nor articulate the emergence of a new world defined by new organisational structures, legal frameworks, systems thinking, new production and design processes, ways to attract highly motivated individuals, that brought into this world better capabilities and new skills. Which all add up to a new philosophy and defined by a new language. And, of course, the reality is that it is not only business which is feeling the impact of a new way of living unfolding and decoupling from the dying system of our industrial age.

In this non-linear world, companies and organisations premised upon the old orthodoxies, linear, industrial-scale models must think and embrace the unthinkable and work out how they innovate to survive. Whether we survey the political, media, engineering, NGO, educational or healthcare landscape we can identity an increasing sophistication in how we are responding to the challenges of living in a more complex world. At the same time, there is the ever-increasing acceleration of the collapse of the old ways of command and control. Every work of art, said Wassily Kandinsky, is a child of its time.

So it's time to think the unthinkable, whether the challenges we face are commercial or let's say are civic in nature, small or large scale, the ability to resolve those challenges by a framework that is more holistic and open, more focused on service-orientated solutions does provide us with the means to imagine an alternative approach that is more humane, more sustainable and potentially a lot less costly. Technology is important, digital low-cost communication tools can be powerful enablers, legal frameworks and networked thinking are of equal importance, but it is critical to remember that although the world is increasingly brought together by digital communication tools, the lessons of non-linearity, for example, demonstrate it is the intelligent and creative blending of all these things together where true long-term success lies. Humanity is in a constant state of evolution, and now we have the means to progress, where we can tread more lightly, and provide a more sustainable future both for the sake of this planet but also for humanity, which has over the last 150 years paid a heavy price for our fast-paced industrialised world. As I pointed out earlier, throughout large swathes of our world we have become more machine like than perhaps we understand, and I make the case that as a species we are rebelling against living our lives as constructs of the machine age that can no longer support us.

Chapter Nine

Designing the world for Me We: six principles to guide our journey in creating a better world

A story about maps, or getting from here to there

We started this journey at the beginning of this book with a navigational guide, because maps have been with us since 2300 BC, illustrating topography to guide us safely to our final destination. Maps help us work out where we have come from and where we are going. That was their purpose in 2300 BC and is still their purpose today. What differentiates us from the Babylonians who first used them was their need to know how to reach the closest source of water or food, whereas today we want to know how to get to the other side of the world. The ability to look upon the world, and know it, enables us to traverse the unknown and maps have played a key role in that journey.

In 1569 the cartographer Gerardus Mercator, who conveniently shares my birthday, produced a revolutionary nautical map, called the Mercator Projection. It enabled for the first time the ability to represent lines of constant course by preserving the angles and shapes of small objects. Why was this important? Because, without being able to plot a constant course, ships could find themselves far from their destination, perhaps with tragic consequences. Mercator called it Nova et Aucta Orbis Terrae Descriptio ad Usum Navigatium Emendate: 'new and augmented description of Earth corrected for the use of navigation'. I like the idea of augmented reality being discovered in the 16th century.

Map-makers today still base their map projections on Mercator's methodology. I have a six-point map that will help you navigate this non-linear world. They are your latitude and longitude, become familiar with them, understand them, as the better you do the more you will be able navigate a safer course.

What I see is the possibility to co-create a world we can make more humane, made fairer when we design around what makes us and sustains us as human beings. We must ask what sustains humanity? Many institutions of government, education, commerce and the legal frameworks that currently shape and define our world are no longer fit for purpose, and to carry on business as usual, I would argue, is simply negligent. We need a new set of competencies that are born from a new set of literacies, which is how we create new ways of doing things. Now is the time to look up and see beyond what we think we know to defy the logic of the linear world. 'The way we see things is affected by what we know, and what we believe', wrote John Berger in *Ways of Seeing*; he added: 'The relation between what we see and what we know is never settled', so what might someone who has a high competency in no straight lines thinking look like? How do they anticipate what comes next? Here are the six principles which I believe can help guide us on whatever journey we are on, and how to get to arrive at our destination safe from harm.

Principle One: The cultures the non-linear society seeks to nurture and the tools it uses to do so must be participatory

If we start to think about how our world is being redefined and the socialness of our world today, we should begin a critical enquiry into participatory cultures. Not only is there is a body of scholarship that suggests potential benefits of participatory culture, including opportunities for peer-to-peer learning, a changed attitude towards intellectual property, the diversification of cultural expression, the development of skills valued in the modern workplace and a more empowered conception of citizenship,[308] there is also enough real life practical evidence to supporting that scholarship. The way people are getting what they want and need from each other demonstrates new organisational capabilities, and economic models all built around collaborative effort. Our literacy must start with being able to properly discuss and understand human motivation in participatory cultures, and the tools that they use, and then how these can be used to make organisations more lightweight, more effective and deliver accelerated innovation, plus greater social cohesion at a variety of societal levels. From politicians to CEOs, leadership must be properly understood within the context of the Gestalt switch of participatory culture.

Highly successful participatory systems are also by default social, and much of what drives the communications revolution as we have identified is the need for meaningful connection. I would argue therefore from a designer's perspective we need to embed sociability into everything, from the buildings we design to the software code we write, the processes we create, the business and organisational models we conceive, the governmental institutions we create and the means by which those institutions operate. The multidimensionality of humanity needs to be

---

308. Jenkins, *Confronting the Challenges.*

coded into the fabric of all those things. Embedded sociability must be something that we all sign up to and be conscious of. It is far more important than the much misunderstood term social media. We need to migrate the silos in organisations, where people feel they are just component parts in a machine, and provide them with opportunities to express themselves and feel they're part of a bigger whole. We need to provide a sense of an open learning environment, where people can learn the things that are important to them, to enable people to find joy in what they do. We need to evolve how we work, and in so doing evolve the institutions and organisations that we commit to every day of our lives.

Carl Jung made the observation that 'I' needs 'We' to truly be 'I', by which he meant that it is through our connectedness, and the meaning that we make through each other, that we find a sustainable model for humanity. Another way of explaining this truth is being a 12-year-old boy watching the celebrated UK chat show host Michael Parkinson interviewing the great Muhammad Ali. In the interview, Parkinson observed that he understood Ali wrote poems. Ali said yes, Parkinson asked Ali for his shortest poem and without hesitation or pause for breath, Ali uttered two magnificent words, 'Me, We', and they hung somehow heavy in the air without explanation. It did not occur to me at the time that some 35 years later I would make a connection between Jung and Ali, but I believe they both meant the same thing. Human identity is created through co-created narrative, the bonds created through deep connections we make when we act collectively as meaningful members of a wider group. This mechanism is a vital component part for the construction of identity and healthy societies. Without it we become like dead leaves falling from autumnal trees. This is our DNA, the fundamental needs of our nature; our bodies, minds and souls are designed to work collectively and where we all experience collective joy. Nobel prize winner and economist Amartya Sen argues:

> happiness as it is can hardly be the only thing that we have reason to value, not the only metric for measuring other things that we value. But when being happy is not given such an imperialist role, it can, with good reason, be seen as a very important human function among others. The capability to be happy is, similarly a major aspect of the freedom that we have good reason to value. The perspective of happiness illuminates a critically important part of human life.'[309]

And, as Christopher McCandless wrote before he died alone, 'happiness is only real when it is shared'.

If that right is taken from humanity, we find no happiness, and all else is valueless, we have no will to live. But if we have the means to identify ourselves as

---

individuals, finding at the same time a sense of collective belonging, then all is, or could be, better with the world that we inhabit. It comes back to the fundamental question I asked in the beginning of this book, I + We = Why? For too long our world has operated on a high level of 'I' and not of 'We' – cohesion is lost both within the commercial and civic spaces we inhabit as a consequence. Understanding participation means understanding that economic and commercial life can be and must be richer than a series of purely financial transactions, where we are all co-actors and co-creators in knowledge and information exchange, commercial exchange. A moral economy is defined largely in part by our social connections and our broader humanity. We seek joyful communities, why can't we, you and I get up on a Monday morning to do the work we 'want to do' as opposed to the work we must?

Participatory cultures are built upon trust; cultures, networks and organisations built on trust are more resilient. Trust also demands transparency. One of the defining features of a world defined by participatory cultures is its demand for transparency; without transparency there can be no trust. In this world we must acknowledge and accommodate communities of practice, interest and passion in a variety of ways. Therefore, we must ask ourselves how do we attract and engage people into communities and create positive outcomes for all?

Understanding participatory cultures requires us to think about creative leadership: bottom-up or top-down? Can a leader inspire people to give their creative best, cooperatively? The question then arises how do we become realistic leaders of people who are; able to take responsibility and authorship to lead people into the future, as it emerges; capable of designing conversations and situations that foster effective stewardship of teams and organisations; able to prepare people and environments to absorb the dynamics of non-routinely changing situations; use an appreciative focus on lessons learned from unexpected drawbacks, while focusing on opportunities to make a difference, rather than targets? And that creative leadership is defined by creating narrative leadership rather than operating in broadcast mode – one could equally ask the same question of any part of an organisation, commercial or otherwise.

Participatory cultures enable us to get stuff done faster, in understanding how high levels of participation inspired by the high motivation of many people, sometimes dispersed, but also connected to each other, can rapidly foreshorten the time in delivering desired goals. We have an alternate process available to us which can additionally significantly reduce costs. Harnessing the power of participatory cultures can do some wonderful things. And participatory culture can unleash the collective wisdom, and from large bodies of people; as the old adage goes, sharing information is power. A better world is shaped by what I + We share.

Principle Two: The almost forgotten art of craftsmanship is what will build this new participatory culture

Richard Sennett in *The Craftsman* reminds us of a number of things to reflect upon. First the craftsman represents the special human condition of being 'engaged'. Secondly, Hephaestus was the Greek god presiding over the craftsman, the bringer of peace and the maker of civilisation. 'More than a technician, the civilizing craftsman has used his tools for a collective good', he writes.[310] And it was through the spirit of the Enlightenment that the craftsman brought forward a huge surge of social and creative innovation that made the lot of ordinary humans better. So the craftsman questions why he makes things; he must evaluate the energy, effort and time that will consume him in his craft and the final act of creation – is he doing good, is he solving a real problem and offering up something better, is he using all his skills as a civilizing force? These questions must weigh constantly in his mind. The craftsman is always in beta. His mind must be open to new ideas, techniques, tools and processes; to close his mind to the new, or new ways of doing things, is the greatest risk he will take. The ability to bring two unlikes together in close adjacency and recognise a pattern or a new possibility is the true act of creation; Lennon and McCartney or the fusion of medical knowledge and computing are but two real life examples of what I mean. The craftsman must combine technique and expression so that he is also able to act intuitively. This can only happen when he possesses deep or what is called implicit knowledge. Rather than acting only upon empirical information, the craftsman's ultimate act is one of unique expression which can only be delivered through the mastery of these skills.

Play is another aspect of the self-confident craftsman; the ability to remain curious and explore is a part of play and playfulness and in that exploration some things just won't work out. In modern management culture, failure is all too often seemed as absolute, a moralistic perspective which ultimately rewards mediocrity, and punishes those that yearn for something better, but which carries perceived risk. Allowing the opportunity to constantly explore, play and fail and then learn, move on and improve is how the craftsman constantly evolves his knowledge, his skills and technique; it is what some describe as the hacker ethic. Google allows all of its staff 20% of their working time to develop projects that inspire them, that could be used as Google projects. Rather designing the firm around 100% efficiency, it has designed in 20% inefficiency to seek the altogether more interesting possibility – effectiveness.

We are all designed to be risk averse, yet there are ways to mitigate risk, and that is through pattern recognition. Where people see no connection, no pattern, no new

---

310. Sennett, *The Craftsman*, p. 21.

pathways, only chaos, the craftsman see patterns, which he can then deconstruct into steps that will lead him successfully to achieving his goal. 'What do you see?' and 'What do I see?' are questions we need to ask as we seek. For example, if I use Creative Commons legal frameworks in the design and manufacture of cars what might that mean to accelerate innovation? If I use a highly motivated community open source software connected up to Google APIs and mobile GPS technology, what might that mean? If I use revenue sharing, how will that make my business more attractive yet more disruptive at the same time? Pattern recognition comes from insight – it doesn't come from an inflexible linear process. This is also a form of systems thinking – the craftsman thinks about the whole system, as Gabriel Branby described it, 'The Total'. This pattern recognition allows new innovative forms to be created that can dramatically reduce start-up costs, running costs and wastage, and dramatically improve the lives of those that those forms, products or services touch. So the craftsman has a creative mind, creating fresh, conceptual blends, novel ideas, and artefacts, all stemming from an original and autonomous position, showing awareness of the cultural meaning of events, expressing playful and passionate dedication to think and act beyond the familiar. The craftsman is able to inspire and release the potential of others, by expressing ideas and joyfully sharing. The craftsman also knows how to deliver quality without it necessarily costing the earth.

This then leads on to the idea of whether creativity is a resource or a competence. Organisations from a linear world are designed to function at 100% efficiency, which largely means there is no way in which they can also be creative organisations, as this requires room for reflection, deliberation, conversation, trying stuff out; that's the practical stuff, but also industrial organisations ideologically fear creativity – anything deemed 'creative' is outsourced – but for the craftsman, and the crafted organisation, creativity, to be creative, to think and act creatively is something that is a fundamental part of what makes them who they are.

So it is with his head, heart and hand that our world craves the innovative capability and the civilising force of the craftsman.

Principle Three: Adaptiveness is the key quality needed to craft the new non-linear society

We must always be prepared to adapt, to upgrade constantly and understand that to be agile is a key survival principle. We must of course recognise that we have asked the craftsman to always be in beta, so he can be open, but the organisation too must always be in beta. This ability to upgrade constantly in its hardware, software, organisational structures, business models is required at least for the time being. The crafted organisation is therefore constantly creating, collaborating, critiquing, communicating. Altogether this is a cognitive action at a group and social level; it is a learning culture, where the default setting is open rather than closed, CompanyCommand being one very good example. Like the craftsman, it means knowledge is absorbed and becomes implicit, enabling creativity to be a true and natural expression of that knowledge. It means there is a culture of emergence: for example, to see beyond cutting edge technology, capable of identifying the key drivers of emerging technology, as well as the pace at which they continue to develop, and capable of evaluating the relevance of a particular technology in order to design a resolution for the challenge at hand. Think beyond pre-inventive integrations of different emerging technologies on a conceptual and functional level, leading to the design of new combinations, while explicitly spelling out the expected consequences.

Adaptiveness is also an art of understanding the distinction between achieving a work of quality and becoming obsessed by perfection, which leads often to complete failure. As a CTO friend once said to me, if you want to get something right, get it wrong as quickly as you can so you can start fixing it. You could say we need to design for adaptation. This is one of the profound problems that many companies predicated in 150 years of industrial, and latterly free market, ideology could never have legislated for. But today, we have tools and technologies, software and hardware, computing capability and organisational processes that mean we can now design for adaptation.

Principle Four: Accept the uncertainties of an ambiguous world and become master of them

In many ways ambiguity is the output of our current trilemma, but for that very reason it must also be a defining principle. When we individually and collectively live in an age of uncertainty, we must all become masters of managing uncertainty. As individuals or organisations we need to demonstrate the ability to face the future openly; we have to replace fear of the unknown with curiosity. We need to become aware of what is around us. To do that requires a step change in learning and self-improvement – this is achieved through continuous contemplation and self-reflection which ultimately enables the mastery of an aware self/organisation, with the motivation to pursue truly motivated goals.

There is a need to accept a lack of control, and of uncertainty, not only being prepared to accept being taken outside of one's comfort zone but deliberately seeking it out – the consequence of which is a more disciplined mind or organisational culture, that is now capable of strong creative and conceptual thinking.

This strong creative mind or culture will now possess the strength of working and thinking in a number of disciplines, enabling multiple perspectives to be drawn which will enable deeper insight with it consequent clarity. Consequently it is possible to detect and identify underlying patterns and hidden relationships where previously there was only chaos. Pattern recognition enables us to move from a position of perceiving potential alternatives of organising, creating, designing and building as risky and unrealistic to recognising new common sense opportunities. So when others see disorder, someone who has developed a mastery of ambiguity can explain assumptions and logically lead others through their critical analysis.

A good example of mastery of an uncertain world is how Tim Mead and his team at Yeo Valley Organic have utilised systems thinking, creativity and knowledge to design, build and maintain a viable, resilient and sustainable ecosystem by confronting the sources of volatility and ambiguity. This company looks far more likely to avoid and survive the soaring costs of running a farm on an oil-based economy and the vagaries and whims of the big chain supermarkets who are super-sensitive to consumer mood, than many others.

Principle Five: Openness is resilience

The concept of being open facilitates a new organisational, social and commercial capability. And it plays a key role in helping participatory cultures to function properly, as part of a new operating system where mutuality and the sharing of knowledge, information, data and resources can accelerate innovation and redistribute wealth and provide for a better world. It is inclusive by design, and its by-product is organisational and social cohesion. In designing for a more sustainable world, we must seek mutual gain and mutual benefit. Mutuality recognises a sustainable world which can only be achieved through, as Elinor Ostrom described, the sharing of common pool resources. I think that those companies and organisations that go the furthest in exploring and seeking mutual benefit will be the most resilient, whether tending the land, a people or an organisation. This requires organisations therefore to be open and collaborative. Leadership must then be divested from a few to the many, bottom-up not top-down, narrative led rather than in broadcast mode. And organisations need to learn how different designs in open innovation and collaboration can significantly enhance their performance.

For example the GrowVC funding platform and platforms like it democratise the funding of entrepreneurial companies. Ushahidi's crisis management platform could only have been built using open innovation, and open source tools, and it now makes its platform free for others to use. Local Motors has used Creative Commons and an open approach to its business to reinvent an entire industry. Openness releases untapped potential such as the London Data Store or the Ordnance Survey; both organisations now make available their data released under a Creative Commons licence for others to access, identify and create new and valuable uses of that data for the benefit of the wider society. Until recently, such an idea would have been considered an affront to conceived wisdom. Even within large business we see the diseconomy of conventional notions of scale and the wider benefits of the economy of scope, with Google's Android operating system being built by an army of developers, or the Health Service in Nova Scotia working in an open and collaborative process to realise transformational change. Openness helps people to come together, to share, compete, discuss, vote, deliberate and create for a whole variety of rich and complex human needs and motivations which takes us far beyond how an industrial world thinks about markets, motivation and commercial exchange.

Both philosophically and practically we must always be open to new knowledge, and open platforms, open legal frameworks stimulate collaboration and innovation, whereas closed knowledge systems have a finite shelf life. Therefore, we need to challenge whether we are working in closed silos or in open ecosystems. This open ecosystem is also supported by the human ethos of sharing, and that sharing in fact opens up and stimulates our world in many wonderful ways. We need to become literate in really understanding how open as a concept and reality can help us deliver better in today's world.

Principle Six: In crafting an epic solution seek epic wins

Faced with the trilemma of our current age and the wicked problems that have presented themselves, individuals, groups, commercial or non-commercial tribes or communities have demonstrated an approach coined from the language of gaming – they seek epic wins. They seek a transformational answer to intractable problems; they are not satisfied with traditional orthodoxies and the limitations they put upon us. I argue that this is not about grandiose posturing but seeking real answers to those inherently wicked problems.

We must therefore seek effectiveness, to be effective and not be seduced into believing efficiency as a form of management control is our salvation. Nature is highly inefficient but she is powerful and effective. So in the same way the craftsman asks himself, is what I seek to bring into this world a good thing? He must also ask himself do I seek an epic win? Is it possible to imagine and create something that delivers true transformation? Ushahidi has been used as a crisis management tool throughout the world; Patients Know Best is a powerful new tool for which many with long-term chronic illness are better able to manage their condition. And I believe that is brought about by vision combined with being literate and the ability to communicate and inspire that vision to a wider group and community.

Being Epic is about having the vision, the courage and the conviction to seek and implement lasting change, like Patients Know Best, or how Jamie Lerner transformed the ailing city that was Curatiba in Brazil. Being Epic requires individuals and companies to seek an entrepreneurial spirit; that entrepreneurial spirit demonstrates the ability to recognise opportunities for value creation and then be able to design innovative ways to capture that value. Being able to mobilise the necessary resources in a responsible and sustainable way, accepting the inherent risks and upfront personal investment involved and favouring speed in implementation. Being Epic means showing persistence and tenacity to convert great ideas into tangible results and the ability to implement them. Being Epic means acting proactively, enabling innovation with practical intelligence, and seeking collaboration to get things done.

Be realistic, imagine the impossible then create it

In turning full circle in this story, our collective challenge requires better thinking for a better world in designing transformationally and sustainably for humanity, and in so doing, accommodating humanity's richness and complexity, which means striving for sustainable economic success, better government, education and healthcare. It demands innovation and the transformation of all the existing organisations, legal systems, economic or otherwise, that currently frame and define our world. It is an epic goal. But like all the stories told in this book, all very doable. Because ultimately like a craftsman we are defined by what we do as opposed to what we think or what we say. Of course not everyone will welcome such a point of view as this is a defining story about power and control. To make for a more sustainable and equitable world, organisations whatever and whoever they are, currently holding positions of power, with monopolistic intent, are going to have to relinquish their white-knuckle grip. But as we have seen from the streets of Cairo, to the behemoths of the corporate world and everything in between, no one will be left untouched by the desire of humanity to find a better way of existing and happily going about their daily work and their daily lives.

Bibliography

Ahonen, Tomi and Alan Moore, *Communities Dominate Brands: Business and Marketing Challenges for the 21st Century*, Futuretext, 2005.

Alavi, Nasrin, *We Are Iran: The Persian Blogs*, Soft Skull Press, 2005.

Alperovitz, Gar, *America Beyond Capitalism: Reclaiming Our Wealth, Our Liberty, and Our Democracy*, John Wiley & Sons, 2004.

Ballard, J. G., *Kingdom Come*, Fourth Estate, 2006.

Barber, Benjamin R., *Consumed: How Markets Corrupt Children, Infantalize Adults and Swallow Citizens Whole*, W. W. Norton & Company, 2007.

Bauman, Zygmunt, *Consuming Life*, Polity Press, 2007.

Beinhocker, Eric D., *The Origin of Wealth: Evolution, Complexity, and the Radical Remaking of Economics*, Harvard Business School Press, 2006.

Benkler, Yochai, *The Wealth of Networks*, Yale University Press, 2006.

Bennett, W. Lance (ed.), *Civic Life Online: Learning How Digital Media Can Engage Youth*, John D. and Catherine MacArthur Foundation Series on Digital Media and Learning, 2007.

Birdsall, Derek and Carlo M. Cipolla, *The Technology of Man: A Visual History*, Wildwood House, 1980.

Borsodi, Ralph, *This Ugly Civilization*, Porcupine Press, 1929.

Boyle, David, *Authenticity: Brands, Fakes, Spin and the Lust for Real Life*, Harper Perennial, 2004.

Boyle, James, *The Public Domain: Enclosing the Commons of the Mind*, Yale University Press, 2008.

Boyle, David, and Michael Harris, *The Challenge of Co-Production*, NEF and NESTA, 2009.

Briggs, Asa and Peter Burke, *A Social History of the Media: From Gutenberg to the Internet*, Polity Press, 2005.

Brown, John Seely and Paul Duguid, *The Social Life of Information*, Harvard Business School Press, 2000.

Burgess, Jean and Joshua Green, *YouTube*, Polity Press, 2009.

Burleigh, Michael, *Blood and Rage: A Cultural History of Terrorism*, Harper Press, 2008.

Cacioppo, John T. and William Patrick, *Loneliness: Human Nature and the Need for Social Connection*, Norton, 2008.

Carson, Kevin A., *Organization Theory: A Libertarian Perspective*, Booksurge, 2008.

Carr, Nicholas, *The Big Switch: Rewiring the World from Edison to Google*, Norton, 2008.

Castells, Manuel, *Communication Power*, Oxford University Press, 2009.

Castells, Manuel (ed.), *The Network Society: A Cross-Cultural Perspective*, Edward Elgar Publications, 2005.

Chydenius, Anders, *The National Gain*, trans. from the Swedish original of 1765, Prime Minister's Office, Helsinki, 1994.

Cohen, Lizabeth, *A Consumer's Republic: The Politics of Mass Consumption in Postwar America*, Vintage, 2003.

Coles, Robert (ed.), *The Erik Erikson Reader*, 1st edn, W. W. Norton, 2000.

Crossley, Michele L., *Introducing Narrative Psychology: Self, Trauma and the Construction of Meaning*, Open University Press, 2000.

Darwin, Charles, *The Origin of the Species*, Penguin, 1985.

Davies, Nick, *Flat Earth News*, Chatto & Windus, 2008.

De Pree, Max, *Called to Serve: Creating and Nurturing the Effective Volunteer Board*, Wm B. Eerdmans Publishing Company, 2001.

Deiser, Roland, *Designing the Smart Organisation: How Breakthrough Corporate Learning Initiatives Drive Strategic Change*, Jossey-Bass, 2009.

Diamond, Jared M., *Collapse: How Societies Choose to Fail or Survive*, Penguin, 2006.

Dijk, Jan van, *The Network Society*, 2nd edn, Sage, 2006.

Dunne, Stephen, Stefano Harvey and Martin Parker, *Speaking Out: The Responsibilities of Management Intellectuals: A Survey*, Sage Publications, 2008.

Eggers, Dave, *Zeitoun*, McSweeny, 2009.

Ehrlich, Paul R. and Richard W. Holm, *The Process of Evolution*, McGraw-Hill, 1963.

Ehrenreich, Barbara, *Dancing in the Streets: A History of Collective Joy*, Granta, 2007.

Erikson, Erik, *Identity: Youth and Crisis*, Norton, 1968.

Frank, Thomas, *One Market under God: Extreme Capitalism, Market Populism and the End of Economic Democracy*, Secker & Warburg, 2001.

Goldsmith, Stephen, *The Power of Social Innovation: How Civic Entrepreneurs Ignite Community Networks for Good*, Jossey-Bass, 2010.

Gould, Stephen Jay, *The Richness of Life*, Vintage, 2007.

Gray, John, *Straw Dogs: Thoughts on Humans and Other Animals*, Farrar, Straus and Giroux, 2007.

Hamel, Gary, with Bill Breen, *The Future of Management*, Harvard Business School Press, 2007.

Handy, Charles, *Gods of Management: The Changing Work of Organisations*, new edn of 3rd revised edn, Arrow Books, 1995.

Handy, Charles, *The Hungry Spirit*, Arrow, 1997.

Hawken, Paul, *The Ecology of Commerce: A Declaration of Sustainability*, Collins, 1993.

Hawken, Paul, Amory Lovins and L. Hunter Lovins, *Natural Capitalism: Creating the Next Industrial Revolution*, Little Brown, 1999.

Herriot, Peter, *Religious Fundamentalism and Social Identity*, 1st edn, Routledge, 2007.

Himanen, Pekka, *The Hacker Ethic: A Radical Approach to the Philosophy of Business*, Random House, 2001.

Holland, John, *Adaptation in Natural and Artificial Systems*, University of Michigan Press, 1975.

Hyde, Lewis, *The Gift: Creativity and the Artist in the Modern World*, 25th anniversary edn, Vintage, 2007.

Hoover, Kenneth (ed.), *The Future of Identity: Centennial Reflections on the Legacy of Erik Erikson*, Lexington Books, 2004.

Howe, Jeff, *Crowdsourcing: How the Power of the Crowd Is Driving the Future of Business*, Random House, 2008.

Howley, Kevin, *Community Media: People, Places and Communication Technologies*, Cambridge University Press, 2005.

Illich, Ivan, *Deschooling Society*, Calder and Boyers, 1971.

Inglehart, Ronald and Christian Welzel, *Modernization, Cultural Change and Democracy: The Human Development Sequence*, Cambridge University Press, 2006.

Jaokar, Ajit, et al., *Social Media Marketing: How Data Analytics Helps to Monetize the User Base in Telecoms, Social Networks, Media and Advertising in a Converged Ecosystem*, Futuretext, 2009.

Jacobs, Jane, *The Death and Life of Great American Cities*, 1961; Modern Library edn 1993.

Jenkins, Henry, *Confronting the Challenges of a Participatory Culture: Media Education for the 21st Century*, John D. and Catherine MacArthur Foundation, 2006.

Jenkins, Henry, *Convergence Culture: Where Old and New Media Collide*, New York University Press, 2006.

Judt, Tony, *Ill Fares the Land*, Allen Lane, 2010.

Kay, John, *The Truth about Markets: Their Genius, Their Limits, Their Follies*, Penguin, Allen Lane, 2003.

Keane, John, *The Life and Death of Democracy*, Simon and Schuster, 2009.

Kelly, Kevin, *Out of Control: The New Biology of Machines*, Fourth Estate, 1994.

Klein, Naomi, *The Shock Doctrine: The Rise of Disaster Capitalism*, Penguin/Allen Lane, 2007.

Kluger, Jeffrey, *Simplexity: Why Simple Things Become Complex (and How Complex Things Can Be Made Simple)*, Hyperion, 2008.

Lasica, J. D., *Darknet: Hollywood's War against the Digital Generation*, Wiley, 2005.

Lenhart, Amanda and Mary Madden, *Teen Content Creators and Consumers*, Pew Internet & American Life Project, 2 November 2005.

Lessig, Lawrence, *Free Culture: The Nature and Future of Creativity*, Penguin, 2005.

Lessig, Lawrence, *The Future of Ideas: The Fate of the Commons in a Connected World*, Vintage, 2002.

Lessig, Lawrence, *Remix: Making Art and Commerce Thrive in the Hybrid Economy*, Bloomsbury, 2008.

Levy, Stephen, *Hackers: Heroes of the Computer Revolution*, Anchor Press, Doubleday, 1984.

Logan, Robert K., *The Alphabet Effect: A Media Ecology Understanding of the Making of Western Civilization*, Hampton Press, 2004.

McChesney, Robert W., *The Problem of the Media: U.S. Communication Politics in the 21st Century*, Monthly Review Press, 2004.

McLuhan, Marshall, *The Gutenberg Galaxy: The Making of Typographic Man*, University of Toronto Press, 1962.

McLuhan, Marshall, *Understanding Media: The Extension of Man*, Ginko Press, 2003.

Merleau-Ponty, Maurice, *Phenomenology of Perception*, trans. Colin Smith, Humanities Press and Routledge & Kegan Paul, 1962; trans. revised by Forrest Williams, 1981; reprinted, 2002.

Mills, C. Wright, *White Collar: The American Middle Classes*, Oxford University Press, 1951.

Moore, Geoffrey, *Crossing the Chasm: Marketing and Selling Technology Products to Mainstream Customers*, revised edn, Capstone, 1998.

Naughton, John, A Brief History of the Future: The Origins of the Internet, Phoenix, 2000.

Papanek, Victor, Design for the Real World: Human Ecology and Social Change, Pantheon Books, 1971.

Perez, Carlota, Technological Revolutions and Financial Capital: The Dynamics of Bubbles and Golden Ages, Edward Elgar, 2002.

Postman, Neil, The End of Education: Redefining the Value of School, Alfred A. Knopf, 1995.

Proust, Marcel, In Search of Lost Time, 1913–27, vol. V: The Captive, 1923.

Putman, Robert D., Making Democracy Work: Civic Traditions in Modern Italy, Princeton University Press, 1993.

Ramo, Joshua Cooper, The Age of the Unthinkable: Why the New World Disorder Constantly Surprises Us and What We Can Do about It, Little Brown, 2009.

Raymond, Eric, The Cathedral and the Bazaar, O'Reilly, 1999.

Reich, Robert B., Supercapitalism: The Transformation of Business, Democracy and Everyday Life, Alfred A. Knopf, 2007.

Rheingold, Howard, Smartmobs: The Next Social Revolution, Basic Books, 2002.

Rheingold, Howard, Technologies of Cooperation, Institute for the Future, January 2005, SR-897.

Robertson, Geoffrey, The Levellers: The Putney Debates (Revolutions Series), Verso, 2007.

Robertson, Geoffrey QC and Andrew Nicol QC, Media Law, 4th edn, Penguin, 2002.

Robbins, Lionel, 'Interpersonal Comparisons of Utility: A Comment', Economic Journal (1938).

Romer, Paul, Economic Growth in the Fortune Encyclopaedia of Economics, ed. David R. Henderson, New York Time Warner Books, 1993.

Ross, Richard, The Architecture of Authority, 1st edn, Aperture, 2007.

Ryan, M. J., The Power of Patience: How to Slow the Rush and Enjoy More Happiness, Success, and Peace of Mind Every Day, 1st edn, Crown Archetype, 2003.

Sachs, Jeffrey, Common Wealth: Economics for a Crowded Planet, Allen Lane, 2008.

Sachs, Jeffrey, The End of Poverty: Economic Possibilities for Our Time, Penguin, 2005.

Sacks, Oliver, The Man Who Mistook His Wife For A Hat, and Other Clinical Tales, Summit Books, 1985.

Scharmer, C. Otto, Theory U: Leading from the Future as it Emerges, 1st edn, Berrett-Koehler, 2009.

Scitovsky, Tibor, The Joyless Economy: The Psychology of Human Satisfaction, Oxford University Press, 1992.

Seddon, John, Systems Thinking in the Public Sector: The Failure of the Reform Regime and a Manifesto for a Better Way, Triarchy Press, 2008.

Seigel, Jerrold, The Idea of the Self: Thought and Experience in Western Europe since the Seventeenth Century, Cambridge University Press, 2005.

Sen, Amartya, The Idea of Justice, Allen Lane, 2009.

Sennett, Richard, The Corrosion of Character: The Personal Consequences of Work in the New Capitalism, new edn, W. W. Norton & Co., 1999.

Sennett, Richard, The Craftsman, Allen Lane, 2008.

Sennett, Richard, The Fall of Public Man, Cambridge University Press, 1977; Penguin 2002.

Sennett, Richard, Respect: The Formation of Character in an Age of Inequality, Penguin, 2003.

Shlain, Leonard, The Alphabet Versus the Goddess: The Conflict between Word and Image, Viking, 1998.

Sifry, Micah, '"You can be the eyes and ears" – Barack Obama and the wisdom of the crowds', in Daniel Lathrop and Laurel Ruma (eds.), Open Government, Transparency, Collaboration, and Participation in Practice, O'Reilly, 2010.

Stiglitz, Joseph, *Globalization and its Discontents*, Penguin, Allen Lane, 2002.

Stiglitz, Joseph, *Making Globalization Work*, W. W. Norton, 2006.

Suchman, Lucy, *Plans and Situated Actions: The Problem of Human–Machine Communication*, Cambridge University Press, 1987.

Sugai, Philip, Marco Koeder and Luovico Ciferri, *The Six Immutable Laws of Mobile Business*, Wiley-Interscience, 2010.

Taylor, Charles, *Sources of the Self: The Making of the Modern Identity*, Cambridge University Press, 1989.

Thackara, John, *In the Bubble: Designing in a Complex World*, MIT Press, 2006.

Tönnies, Ferdinand, *Community and Society: Gemeinschaft und Gesellschaft*, 1st edn, 1887; Dover, 2002.

Toynbee, Polly, and David Walker, *Unjust Rewards: Exposing Greed and Inequality in Britain Today*, Granta, 2008.

Turner, Fred, *From Counterculture to Cyberculture: Stewart Brand, the Whole Earth Network and the Rise of Digital Utopianism*, University of Chicago Press, 2006.

Wade, Nicholas, *The Faith Instinct: How Religion Evolves and Why It Endures*, Penguin, 2009.

Warren, Robert Penn, *All the King's Men*, Harcourt, 1946.

Weiner, Norbert, *The Human Use of Human Beings: Cybernetics and Society*, Da Capo Press, 1988.

Wells, Spencer, *Pandora's Seed: The Unforeseen Cost of Civilization*, Random House, 2010.

Williams, Raymond, *The Country and the City*, Hogarth Press, 1973.

Williams, Raymond, *Culture*, Fontana, 1981.

Williams, Raymond, *Culture and Materialism: Selected Essays*, Verso, 2005.

Williams, Raymond, *Television: Technology and Cultural Form*, Fontana, 1974; Routledge Classics, 2003.

Wilson, Edward O., *Consilience: The Unity of Knowledge*, Vintage, 1999.

Yunus, Muhammad, *Creating a World without Poverty: Social Business and the Future of Capitalism*, Public Affairs, 2008.

Zeldin, Theodore, *Conversation: How Talk Can Change Our Lives*, Hidden Spring, 2000.

Zuboff, Shoshana, *The Support Economy: Why Corporations Are Failing Individuals and the Next Episode Of Capitalism*, Viking Adult, 2002.

Index

About Alan Moore:

In his working life, Alan has designed everything from books to businesses, and has been described as a charismatic visionary who studies the disruptive trends in the world of innovation and makes them explicitly tangible to his audience.

Alan is recognised as a great distiller of complex arguments into their most salient points, who can take concepts from many sources and detect the previously hidden relationship between them. He has a firm grasp of the changes which are reshaping our world. With his insight on these interlocking trends, Alan enables companies to develop true insight, and winning ways for how businesses and organisations can succeed in the early 21st Century.

As well as the founder of the business and communications innovation company SMLXL Alan acts as Head of Vision to the worlds first venture fund, funded by a global community GrowVC. He sits on the advisory boards of a number of other companies.

Alan is a mentor on the Springboard startup accelerator programme based in Cambridge, he sits on the board of inspiration at the Dutch Think Tank Freedom Lab. He is a visiting lecturer at the Cambridge University Judge Business School, and at the Oxford University Saïd Business School including Exec Ed programs. Alan is a Fellow of the Royal Society of Arts.

Alan is an author of several books including, *Communities Dominate Brands: Business and Marketing Challenges for the 21st Century*. Amongst other plaudits Communities Dominate Brands has been described as prescient.

More information:
For more information on media formats for *No Straight Lines*, plus products services, workshops and induction days related to the *No Straight Lines* project.
Go to: www.no–straight–lines.com

Living Bibliography:
If you are interested in a personal learning journey we have created a *Living Bibliography* which contains information about all the authors cited in *No Straight Lines*. Here you can read about and watch videos of those authors and their work.

Discussion:
If you want to join in a discussion about *No Straight Lines* with a wider community, then we invite you to take part in the discussion via the e-browser format which enables you to comment on the work with others within a variety of social network media.
You can find a link to that at: www.no–straight–lines.com

Speaking:
To book a speaking engagement with Alan
contact: info@smlxtralarge.com
or
Sandra Nolan @ The Connect Speakers Bureau
Tel: + 353 1 284 1111
or go to: http://ht.ly/6rALj

CPSIA information can be obtained at www.ICGtesting.com
Printed in the USA
BVOW02s1811270813

329682BV00002B/19/P